CAL-STATE UNIVERSITY, HAYWARD
LIBRARY

THE SWINGBACK-MOTION OFFENSE FOR WINNING FOOTBALL

THE SWINGBACK-MOTION OFFENSE
FOR WINNING FOOTBALL

BRUCE EVANS

Parker Publishing Company ● West Nyack, New York

© 1978, by

PARKER PUBLISHING COMPANY, INC.

West Nyack, New York

All rights reserved. No part of this
book may be reproduced in any form or
by any means, without permission in
writing from the publisher.

Library of Congress Cataloging in Publication Data

Evans, Bruce,
    The swingback-motion offense for winning football.

   Includes index.
   1. Football--Offense. 2. Back field play
(Football) 3. Football coaching. I. Title.
GV951.8.E93   796.33'22   78-9309
ISBN 0-13-879825-7

Printed in the United States of America

To Bobby Lee, Tara and Mitzi

Three wonderful reasons for living and coaching who were there when I needed them most. It was I who wasn't there when they needed me.

The Author Acknowledges . . .

John Petercuskie, my high school coach who I love as a father for all that he has done for me. If it weren't for Coach "Cuskie," I wouldn't be in football today.

Bill Sherman, my good friend and a great coach who gave me my first coaching job at St. Genevieve High School in Panorama City, California, and who has contributed immensely to the input of this offense.

John Becker, a great coach and football mind who tried much of this offense at the college level while he was offensive coordinator at New Mexico State University.

Bob "Gump" May, a Christian man and coach who grew to understand me and who allowed me to install the Swingback-Motion Offense in his first head coaching job at Bishop McDevitt.

Father Joseph Gotwalt, my principal and a great man and priest who had faith in me and our program when things weren't going well.

Marino DeFilippo, my athletic director and good friend whose only wish was that I throw the ball 45 times a game.

Dick Dougherty, Sports Editor of the Bucks County, Pennsylvania Times and a true friend who is always there when the going gets tough to make sure I get going.

Mike Allsup, Mark Bergdale, Joe Bressi, Harry "Zip" DeFrank, Mike Fry, George Kolarac, Tom Lapkowicz, Joe Makosky, Marty Pavelic, John Rados and John Ziegler, a super group of hard-working coaches who over a three-year period helped the Swingback-Motion Offense to grow by continually testing and questioning the system's foundation.

Dolores Malesic, Cindy Ribic, Patti Connelly and John Ziegler, who proofread, typed and diagrammed much of this manuscript.

The 1977 Senior Football Players at Bishop McDevitt High School, who through their leadership and enthusiasm helped this offense to grow. I love those guys and everything they did for me.

WHAT THIS OFFENSE WILL DO FOR YOU

The strength of the Swingback-Motion Offense is its ability to take advantage of what the defense has been forced to yield. By employing the swingback in a variety of offensive sets that force predetermined defensive adjustments, the offense can methodically run and pass at the weakened areas.

Although seven basic offensive sets are used, the learning process is kept at a minimum and hence simplicity is achieved through the use of a limited number of plays that are camouflaged through this variety of sets.

By employing a swingback, motion, and shifting, the offense effectively neutralizes the defense's use of a rover, monster, or any type of defensive overshift. Motion forces your opponents to adjust on the move while still enabling you to run the base plays of your Swingback-Motion Offense.

Tactical positioning of the swingback enables your offense to gain a numerical advantage when running to the shortside of the field versus teams that try to force you to run into the boundary.

The Swingback-Motion Offense uses the same plays coming out of its own territory as it does going in to score. The position of the swingback reinforces, but is not essential to, the success of each play in the offense.

In conjunction with the inherent simplicity of the Swingback-Motion Offense is the concept of mirrored plays and flip-flopping offensive linemen. Teams that employ a wideside/boundary-type defense in most instances will position their best defenders to cover the boundary side of the field, compensating for possible wideside weaknesses through the positioning of a rover or monster to that side.

Through flipping linemen you are able to gain the Big Three—your BEST ball carrier behind your BEST blockers at your opponent's WORST defenders.

Another very important advantage of the Swingback-Motion Offense is its capability to run the inside and outside veer or triple option, as shown in Chapter 3.

Positioning your swingback normally forces defensive compensation in the secondary. It then becomes a simple matter of attacking the defense with the veer/option away from the swingback. Teams that play their defense balanced or "straight across the board" will be attacked with the veer/option or complimentary I-back plays directed toward the swingback, gaining that vital numerical mismatch.

Utilization of the veer/option in the basic Swingback-Motion offensive game plan helps to decrease your opponent's ability to play adequate pass defense, for every defender must first be conscious of his veer/option responsibilities before they can actively participate in the pass defense scheme. A delay on the part of one defender of only one second is all that is needed to have your quarterback find the open receiver.

Versus eight-man fronts (Chapter 4) you can "load" the veer/option or gain a lead blocker on the play through the strategical positioning of your swingback. Your swingback blocks the quarterback key (load), blocks the defender supporting the pitch (lead), or becomes the pitchman when the veer/option is run away from his initial alignment (Z Veer).

The I-back set is used in the basic Swingback-Motion Offense, allowing for a quick and balanced attack to either side of the center with basic I-back plays to the tailback or fullback.

Coaches who are having trouble gaining yardage on the ground against multiple defensive schemes will find the blocking calls concept of line blocking at the point of attack extremely useful (Chapter 6).

Your offensive tackles make the blocking calls on the line of scrimmage that will enable the playside blockers to optimally block the point of attack.

Although blockers and execution, not blocking calls, make holes for your backs, blocking angles are considered and the tackles on your front line work to create the optimal blocking situation. These calls create an explosive running game based on simplicity and execution.

The Swingback-Motion passing game is an effective means of moving the ball against opponents who gear their defense to stop the Veer-I running attack.

The entire passing game can be run from any position that your swingback assumes. However, some positions are better than others, as discussed in Chapters 7 and 8, and motion is used to have the swingback in the desired position at the snap of the ball.

We have drawn on our past experiences, as well as from other coaches, and have arrived at the exciting Swingback-Motion Offense that is capable of moving the ball from goal line to end zone; an offense that is imaginative but fundamental, unique but systematic; an offense that your players will enjoy practicing and playing.

However, the Swingback-Motion Offense, with its shifting and motion and wide-open passing attack, is not just a nice offense to watch. It moves the ball and gains those all-important first downs.

The fundamental simplicity of this offense couples nicely with our philosophy of doing the little things—the details, getting the first down. The bigger things—the touchdowns, the victories—will follow the intelligent application of the Swingback-Motion Offense.

Bruce Evans

TABLE OF CONTENTS

WHAT THIS OFFENSE WILL DO FOR YOU **9**

1. SELECTING YOUR SWINGBACK-MOTION PERSONNEL **17**

Swingback (18) . . . Quarterback (19) . . . Fullback (21) . . . Tailback (22) . . . Tight End (23) . . . Split End (24) . . . Center (26) . . . Strongside Linemen (27) . . . *Strong Guard (27)* . . . *Strong Tackle (28)* . . . Quickside Linemen (28) . . . *Quick Guard (28)* . . . *Quick Tackle (29)*

2. INSTALLING SWINGBACK-MOTION OFFENSIVE MECHANICS **31**

Changing Offensive Sets with the Swingback (31) . . . Set Descriptions (34) . . . Huddle Mechanics (37) . . . Quarterback Responsibilities in the Huddle (38) . . . Pre-Set Position at the Line of Scrimmage (40) . . . Set Position at the Line of Scrimmage (40) . . . Cadence Mechanics (41) . . . "Line of Scrimmage" (41) . . . Hole Numbering and Line Splits (43) . . . Numbering and Lettering of Backs and Receivers (46) . . . Alignment of the Backs (47) . . . Motion (49) . . . Motion Mechanics (50) . . . *Fly Motion (50)* . . . *Peel Motion (52)* . . . Motion Considerations (55)

3. COACHING THE VEER/OPTION FROM THE SWINGBACK-MOTION OFFENSE **57**

Quarterback Mechanics of the Veer/Option (58) . . . Mesh Phase (59) . . . Give Phase (61) . . . Disconnect Phase (62) . . . Keep Phase (64) . . . Pitch Phase (65) . . . Counting Defenses (66) . . . Reading the Veer/Option (68) . . .

Phase One of the Veer/Option (69) . . . Mechanics of the Read (71) . . . 37/38 Veer (75) . . . Blocking Calls for the Inside Veer/Option (76) . . . "Fred" Call (77) . . . "Willie" Call (78) . . . "Ted" Call (80) . . . "Tom" Call (80) . . . "George" Call (80) . . . "Mike" Call (81) . . . Outside Receiver (82) . . . Inside Receiver Techniques (85) . . . Offside Receiver(s) in the Veer/Option Play (88) . . . Tailback/ Swingback Techniques as Pitchmen (89) . . . Outside Veer/ Option (91) . . . Mechanics of the Outside Veer Quarterback (93) . . . Fullback (94) . . . Tailback (95) . . . Receivers (95) . . . Quarterback Reads for the Outside Veer (96)

4. RUNNING THE VEER VERSUS EIGHT-MAN FRONTS WITH THE SWINGBACK-MOTION OFFENSE 100

Quarterback Mechanics (104) . . . Fullback Mechanics (106) . . . Swingback Mechanics (109) . . . Junction Play Versus Eight-Man Fronts (111) . . . Give Play Versus Eight-Man Fronts (113) . . . Read Play Versus Eight-Man Fronts (113)

5. USING I-BACK PLAYS TO AUGMENT THE SWINGBACK-MOTION OFFENSE 116

Technique Numbering System (121) . . . 57/58 Blast (121) . . . *Specific Blast Assignments (122)* . . . 37/38 Give (123) . . . *Specific Give Assignments (124)* . . . 37/38 Keep (124) . . . *Specific Keep Assignments (124)* . . . 55/56 Power (126) . . . Specific Power Assignments (127) . . . 11/12 Option (129) . . . *Specific Option Assignments (129)* . . . 11/12 Counter Option (130) . . . *Special Counter Option Assignments (132)* . . . 21/22 Option (133) . . . *Special 21/22 Option Assignments (133)* . . . *Blocking Calls (134)* . . . *Offensive Sets (135)* . . . Traps (135) . . . *Specific Trap Rule for Linemen (136)* . . . *Special Influence Trap Rule (136)* . . . Specific Trap Assignments (138) . . . 20/29 Scissors (139) . . . *Specific Scissors Assignments (140)* . . . 51/52 Toss (141) . . . *Special Toss Assignments (142)* . . . 51/52 Flip (143) . . . *Special Flip Assignments (143)* . . . Coaching Philosophy of the Running Game (144)

Table of Contents

6. BLOCKING TECHNIQUES THAT ENABLE THE SWINGBACK-MOTION OFFENSE TO SCORE 146

Blocking Theory (151) . . . Basic Blocking Position (151) . . . Individual Blocking Techniques (152) . . . Reach Block (153) . . . Double-Team Block (154) . . . Criss Block (155) . . . Turnout Block (156) . . . Tony Block (157) . . . Seal Block (157) . . . "Railroad" or Wedge Block (158) . . . Pulling Techniques (159) . . . Influence Blocking (162) . . . Downfield Blocking (163) . . . Separation Block (163) . . . Pass Blocking (164) . . . *1. Aggressive "Mike" Blocking (164)* . . . *2. Digit Protection (164)* . . . *3. Gap Hinge Block (168)* . . . *4. Screen Blocking (169)* . . . Receiver Blocking Techniques (170) . . . *1. Stalk Block (X,Y, SB) (170)* . . . *2. Crack/Stalk Block (X, SB) (170)* . . . *3. Near Safety/Corner Block (X, SB, Y) (171)* . . . *4. Jam On/Out Block (SB, Y) (172)* . . . Backfield Blocking Techniques (173) . . . *Blast Block (173)* . . . Kickout Block (173) . . . Log (Pin) Block (174) . . . Fill Block (174) . . . *Chop and Roll Block (175)* . . . Influence/Turnout Block (175) . . . *Lead Block (176)* . . . Backfield Pass Blocking Techniques (176) . . . *1. Aggressive "Mike" Block (176)* . . . *2. Digit Protection Blocking (177)* . . . *3. Sprint/Jet Protection Blocking (178)* . . . Pass 37/38 Tailback Blocking Techniques (179)

7. INCORPORATING A SIMPLIFIED PASS OFFENSE INTO THE SWINGBACK MOTION SYSTEM 181

Receiver Legs (181) . . . Quarterback Drops (182) . . . Introduction to the 90/70 Series (182) . . . *90/70 Series Mechanics (183)* . . . *90/70 Series Passing Tree (183)* . . . *Route Descriptions of the 90/70 Series (184)* . . . *Tight End/ Hot Curl Middle (186)* . . . *Quarterback Actions in the 90 Series (187)* . . . *Quarterback Actions in the 70 Series (187)* . . . *90 Series Protection (187)* . . . *90 Series Protection Rules (187)* . . . *70 Series Protection (188)* . . . *70 Series Protection Rules (188)* . . . Quarterback Reads in the 90/70 Series (189) . . . Introduction of the 60 Series (190) . . . *Flare Control Numbering (191)* . . . *Tailback/ Fullback Routes (191)* . . . *Pass Routes in the 60 Series*

(192) . . . 60 Series Quickside Routes (193) . . . 60 Series Strongside Routes (194) . . . 60 Series Passing Tree (195) . . . 60 Series Protection (196) . . . Quarterback Reads in the 60 Series (196) . . . Introduction of the 80 Series (197) . . . 80 Series Mechanics (197) . . . 80 Series Huddle Calls (198) . . . 80 Series Routes (199) . . . Quarterback Thought Processes in the 80 Series (199) . . . 80 Series Sprint Protection (200) . . . 80 Series Jet Protection (201) . . . Flare Control in the 80 Series (201)

8. PLAY ACTION PASSES, SCREENS, DRAWS AND SPECIAL PLAYS OF THE SWINGBACK-MOTION OFFENSE 203

Play Action Passes (203) . . . *Mechanics of the Play Action Passes (204)* . . . Pass 11/12 (205) . . . *Pass 37/38 (206)* . . . *Pass 55/56 (210)* . . . *Pass 57/58 (211)* . . . Boot 11/12 (212) . . . Boot 57/58 (214) . . . Screen Passes (215) . . . *Tailback Quick Screen (215)* . . . 58 X Screen (218) . . . *58 Z Screen (220)* . . . *37 Y Screen (221)* . . . Draw Plays (223) . . . *Tailback Lead Draw (224)* . . . *Fullback Lead Draw (225)* . . . Special Plays of the Swingback-Motion Offense (228) . . . 37 (Quarterback) Counter (228) . . . *37 X Reverse (229)* . . . *37 Veer Pass (Z) (231)*

Index 235

1

SELECTING YOUR
SWINGBACK-MOTION PERSONNEL

The Swingback-Motion Offense requires personnel that can adapt to and execute the basic concept of changing offensive sets through the use of a swingback while employing the same basic plays. Certain positions require specific physical and mental attributes in order to accomplish this objective.

As is the case for most high school teams, you cannot always come up with the ideal player for each position. Many players lacking in some of the measurable qualities—size, speed, agility—find a way to break into the lineup by possessing those certain intangibles—an intense desire to compete, hustle, leadership, and the absence of the word "can't" from their vocabulary—that make this offense or any offense win.

Player qualities will not be listed in any specific order of importance. This priority list can only be determined by each coach as his emphasis on particular phases of the Swingback-Motion Offense emerges.

The following are the Swingback-Motion offensive positions and some of the major considerations and qualities that are sought when attempting to fit each player into a position that best suits his capabilities and potential. All things considered, we would select our personnel based on the following criteria:

SWINGBACK

1. *Speed/Quickness/Acceleration:* These three qualities are essential. Ideally, the player will possess enough speed to be considered a deep pass threat as well as a potentially dangerous ball carrier. Quickness and the ability to accelerate once he gets the ball are also needed.

2. *Size:* Durability is more important than size. The player must be sturdy enough to withstand the rigors of his position, which include blocking at the point of attack, as well as running and catching the football. Our first swingback was 6'2" tall and weighed 165 pounds, while our second was 5'9" tall and weighed 170 pounds. The more you ask your swingback to block and run the football, the more durable he must be.

3. *Body control/Balance:* These are extremely important qualities because of his dual role as a pass receiver/running back. He must have control so that he can adjust to and catch the badly thrown ball. In addition, during motion he must be able to transfer his lateral, east-west momentum into vertical, north-south speed on the snap of the ball.

4. *Discipline:* Your swingback must be one of the most self-disciplined individuals you have. His ability to shift into the proper set and to align himself the same way every time, along with running his motion course sharply and quickly, are as important to the offense as his potential to run a 4.7 40-yard dash. This discipline must be apparent in the passing legs he runs. Your swingback must run disciplined patterns not only when he is the primary receiver, but also when he is clearing a zone if the passing game is to be successful. Last, his discipline must be evident when he runs pass legs from the various positions he assumes. His curl, for example, must be run differently from a power set than it is from a pro set.

5. *Blocking ability:* He must be able to stalk block on the veer/option as well as double-team with either tackle. He also acts as a lead blocker on the isolation or blast play and as a single blocker on the toss and flip plays to his side. Your swingback must possess the ability and desire to knock people down.

Selecting Your Swingback-Motion Personnel   19

6. *Running ability:* Your swingback has run inside on the trap and scissors plays if the offense is to be effective, providing much needed misdirection. If the speed factor is there, he will also act as the pitch man on certain veer and option plays to the outside.

7. *Catching ability:* Since most zone defenses will rotate toward him (two-receiver side), the swingback must be able to catch the ball in traffic as well as in the open. The pro set, where he is used as a wide flanker, is of little use to you if your swingback cannot catch the football.

8. *Toughness:* He must be a tough kid who doesn't mind blocking hard and decoying a good deal of the time, running hard, and making the difficult catch. In the backfield, he ranks second to your fullback in this very important attribute.

9. *Mental alertness/Intelligence:* Your swingback must be able to think quickly and clearly. He must know the basic mechanics of the offense and his role in each play from each set. Much of the flexibility of the entire offense lies in his ability to know what to do when he declares the formation. He must know when he is to block at the point of attack and when he is to influence the point of attack and block elsewhere. You have no offense if your swingback doesn't know the offense.

QUARTERBACK

1. *Speed/Quickness/Acceleration:* He must accelerate along the line of scrimmage with the veer/option play, pitching quickly or accelerating up-field. Quick feet and hands, and the ability to see things quickly and react accordingly, are vital to his position. Quickness of hands gives the play a chance for success by insuring the safety of the ball.

2. *Ability to run the veer/option:* Your quarterback must be able to think and react on the move, both essential attributes required to read the play. It is very seldom that the veer/option will be predetermined, and therefore his mind must function as quickly as his hands and feet.

3. *Passing ability:* This attribute is vital to the success of the

Swingback-Motion Offense. He must be able to throw the curl, wide and quick post patterns off of play action or the dropback (sprint/half sprint) positions. We have utilized the dropback attack because we feel that it forces the defense to defend the entire field with a maximum number of defenders.

4. *Mental alertness/Intelligence:* The Swingback-Motion quarterback must understand the offense and the role that the swingback assumes in it. He must have a basic knowledge of defenses (recognition of, strengths, weaknesses, counting of for the veer/option, and basic pass defense zone reads). He should know how each play is going to attack and defeat each defense.

5. *Toughness:* The quarterback is going to get hit. He must be a fighter who is willing to remain poised and accept the hitting as part of his role in the offense.

6. *Poise/Attention to the details:* With the swingback shifting positions, motion, linemen flexing, the intricacies of the veer, etc., it is vital that your quarterback remain poised. He must also do the little things that are necessary for the offense to succeed while not becoming awed by his position. Every play begins with him and, unfortunately, every play can end with him if he fumbles the snap from center. His stance, the position of his hands and the pressure he exerts on the center, his reverse pivot and handoffs must mean as much to him as scoring touchdowns do. His attention to the little things will have a very direct effect on the success of the offense.

7. *Leadership qualities:* He must be willing to be the first player on the practice field and the last man off it. He must never let his teammates think that he is not willing to put in the time necessary to become the best possible athlete that he is capable of becoming. His leadership, therefore, comes from a positive example of hard work and self-sacrifice.

8. *Ability to move the offense:* No one is more aware of this capability than the team itself. This is without a doubt the single most important factor in the selection of your quarterback in the Swingback-Motion Offense. Regardless of all other talents, he must be able to move the team.

9. *Running ability:* Your quarterback must be respected as a runner so as to force the defense to defend all phases of the veer/option while taking some of the pressure off your other backs. This ability will also affect the pass rush that he receives.

10. *Ability to get along with teammates:* It is only because of the position of the player changing the offensive sets that the name Swingback-Motion Offense was derived. In fact, it is a non-selfish offense in which a systematic, precise unit moves the ball by taking advantage of what the defense yields. Friendships, or the desire for personal glory, must not interfere with the important decisions that your quarterback must make in regard to the offense. He must be respected, not necessarily liked, by all of his teammates. He can have no favorites among pass receivers nor can he choose which back to pitch to. Your quarterback has to be abrasive when necessary, in order to get the job done.

FULLBACK

1. *Toughness:* Your fullback must be the toughest player you can find. He must be a hitter because he is going to get hit on every play in the offense. He must understand that he is a blocker first and a runner second, and that he and the team will be rewarded as a result of his toughness. You must make him feel proud to be the toughest player on the team.

2. *Respected running ability:* The veer/option starts with his going over the ball. He has to be a good enough runner so that the defense must assign defenders to cancel him. His running may be respected because of his speed, toughness, agility or balance, but it must be respected nevertheless. His ability will determine how many predetermined gives and quick traps are used.

3. *Competitor:* Like your quarterback, the fullback in the Swingback-Motion Offense must be willing to do whatever it takes to win—make the key block, carry the ball for a crucial first down, ram the ball into the end zone.

4. *Durability/Size:* He must be sturdy enough to withstand the hitting and being hit on every play. Your fullback has to last through a season of continual pounding. In selecting a fullback, size (at least 5′10″ tall and weighing 180 pounds) is often a prerequisite for durability. Although not necessarily true, size in many instances will dictate that the defense cancel him with more than one defender.

5. *Speed/Quickness/Acceleration:* Speed is not essential, although it is highly desirable, in your Swingback-Motion fullback. He must, however, be able to start quickly and accelerate once he gets the ball. On the toss and regular option plays, he has to be able to get out in front of the play.

6. *Blocking ability:* The Swingback-Motion Offense is designed to be a veer/option, tailback-oriented offense. The fullback must be able to lead block, roll block and pass block. His blocking ability supersedes all other qualities. If your fullback can't or won't block, the Swingback-Motion Offense is severely handicapped.

7. *Catching ability:* Your fullback must be able to come out of the backfield and catch the ball. Being a tailback-oriented offense, the defense many times tends to forget the fullback once the ball is moved toward the tailback. This ability is imperative to flare control and misdirection passes in that he releases and helps influence the underneath coverage as well as in providing the offense with an oftentimes disregarded pass receiver.

TAILBACK

1. *Speed/Quickness/Acceleration:* The faster the tailback, the more dimensions the Swingback-Motion Offense has to exploit. He must utilize his speed on plays to the inside as well as to the outside. Regardless of speed, the tailback must be able to accelerate.

2. *Running ability:* Depending on the defense's adjustment to the veer/option, motion, and the Swingback-Motion offensive sets, the tailback is going to carry the ball 20-25 times per game. He must be able to break the long run to the outside as

well as to gain the tough yards inside and off-tackle if the offense is to produce.

3. *Durability/Toughness:* A different type of toughness is required of the tailback than of the fullback. Since he carries the ball 20-25 times a game, he must be sturdy enough to take the hitting and last through the game as well as through the season.

4. *Blocking ability:* Your tailback must possess some ability to lead block on the veer/option when the pitchman is the swingback. He must also be an average pass blocker on dropback passes, blocking the weakside end or linebacker who in many instances will drop off. Your tailback also has an important block on the veer/option play action passes, attacking the playside defensive end.

5. *Body balance/Agility:* Like all good ball carriers, the tailback in the Swingback-Motion Offense must have good body balance and agility. Diving arm tackles cannot or should not bring him down.

6. *Catching ability:* Your tailback should possess a good, sure set of hands in order to safely handle the pitch in the veer/option or to receive a forward pass. He will be called upon to release and get into the vital underneath areas as an integral part of the Swingback-Motion Offense.

TIGHT END

1. *Blocking ability:* Select the tight end first on his ability to block. He must be able to double-team, reach block, stalk block, and eliminate the first linebacker to the inside. This is probably his most important contribution to the offense.

2. *Speed/Quickness/Acceleration:* Speed, although desirable, is not a primary consideration. Your tight end must be quick and agile within the 5-10 yard area around the line of scrimmage. Explosion and acceleration off the line are his key qualities in regard to speed.

3. *Toughness/Durability:* He must be a tough kid who can block hard and get defensive movement at the point of attack, and

should be a difficult man to bring down when the ball is thrown to him. Your tight end quite possibly could be a tackle with the best speed and hands.

4. *Catching ability:* Your tight end must be able to catch the football with people hanging onto him because many of his routes are run into the short, middle zones. In this regard he should have the third best set of hands on the team.

5. *Size:* Ideally, the tight end in the Swingback-Motion Offense should be at least 6' tall and weigh 180-190 pounds. Size becomes important in that he provides your quarterback with a relatively big target in the middle while also insuring maximum blocking at the off-tackle hole.

6. *Mental alertness/Intelligence:* Because of the swingback's mobility, the tight end has to be aware of the swingback's position so that he can make the commensurate adjustment to the blocking scheme, especially on the inside veer/option. He must understand the complete passing game and his vital role in it, recognizing a "hot" situation and the principle behind it (anti-sack principle). With defenses changing their perimeter defenders and their assignments, your tight end must be able to recognize and block the most dangerous defender to the success of the play.

7. *Running ability:* Ideally, your tight end would be the kind of player who could be an adequate running back. When the ball is thrown to him, he should be a tough man to bring down. Balance and agility are essential to his success.

8. *Ability to run disciplined legs:* He must understand the coordination that is inherent in the passing game because of his running disciplined pass routes (legs). Timing is the key to the Swingback-Motion passing game, and good legs are the means of achieving success. The tight end may not have the ball thrown his way very often, but he must be selfless in his determination to run his legs to the proper area on the field and occupy the defenders in that area.

SPLIT END

1. *Ability to run disciplined legs:* The split end in the

Swingback-Motion Offense is primarily a pass receiver, and therefore must run the pass legs as they are designed. Proper speed, angle of release, and the length of each leg must be emphasized in coaching him. By declaring the swingback to the tight end side, you are able to predetermine that your split end is most likely to be the receiver who will receive single coverage. Most four-deep teams will rotate their zone pass defense toward the two-receiver side, leaving the split end with basic man-to-man coverage.

2. *Speed/Quickness/Acceleration:* Your split end must possess enough speed and quickness to get deep quickly, and possess the acceleration necessary to explode off the line of scrimmage. His ability to move rapidly downfield forces the secondary to show its coverage immediately, which aids the quarterback in reading the defense. Quickness in getting his head and shoulders around to focus on the ball that is thrown many times before he makes his break is essential to his position.

3. *Catching ability:* The split end in the Swingback-Motion Offense must possess the best pair of hands on the team. They must be quick, sure hands, catching every ball that they touch. He must also have the body balance and control necessary to catch the badly thrown ball.

4. *Size:* Your split end does not need to be big.

5. *Blocking ability and attitude toward blocking:* Your split end must possess the desire to be the best blocker that he can be. He must be able to stalk block on the veer/option as well as to block the near safety or corner on all plays run away from him. The latter is a hustle block and he must realize that his block could spring one of your backs for the big play. The stalk block, or shielding action, is within their capability. They are not asked to knock any one down. Getting position on the defender and making him come through them to the ball carrier is the technique used.

6. *Running ability:* He must be able to "make something happen" once he catches the ball. He should possess the ability to cut quickly and accelerate into the open field once he has the ball.

CENTER

1. *Mental alertness/Intelligence:* The center in the Swingback-Motion Offense must know the playside for every play. He must have an overall concept of the offense as well as knowing his role in the blocking scheme that is called. He should be mature enough to realize the need for intelligent action instead of fanatical chaos in snapping the ball. All plays begin with his snap and, unfortunately, all plays can end with him through a poor snap.

2. *Size:* Ideally, the center should be at least 6' tall and weighing 190 pounds. Sturdiness and a good control over his center of gravity are possibly more important than actual physical size.

3. *Balance/Agility/Mobility:* After snapping the ball, he must be agile and mobile enough to block an active noseman or to attack an offside linebacker. In pass blocking, he must be able to block where he is needed if his assignment doesn't rush or if his linebacker in an even front stunts. You cannot play with a center who snaps the ball and then stands up and watches the play.

4. *Poise:* In tight situations, your center must maintain his composure and make sure that the ball is snapped safely to the quarterback. This is essential when you are playing with a young quarterback; he must become oblivious to defenders jumping around and to the threat of a stunt.

5. *Long snapping ability:* It is imperative to a sound kicking game that your center be able to snap deep for the punt and PAT. Inherent pressure during most of these situations adds to the difficulty of his task. Poise is vital in conjunction with his long snapping ability.

6. *Speed/Quickness:* Your center should possess good speed because he must be one of the first men downfield to align or center the punt coverage unit and to force the returner to change direction if he cannot make the tackle.

STRONGSIDE LINEMEN

In the Swingback-Motion Offense, the strongside linemen are normally your bigger and stronger blockers. Although the offense is based on mirrored plays, certain plays are executed best to the tight end or strong side of the formation. When the tough yards are needed and the Big Three must be created, these are the people who should block the point of attack.

The types of blocks required on such plays as the blast and power, require explosive strength and size more than mobility and finesse. Therefore, size and strength are of primary importance in selecting your strongside linemen.

STRONG GUARD

1. *Size:* Your strong guard ideally should be 5'11"-6' tall and weigh 185-195 pounds.
2. *Explosiveness:* He must be able to explode off the line of scrimmage on the snap count and get defensive movement away from the line. This quality is essential when your strong guard may be lacking in size. His explosive power will enable the offensive line to capture and control the neutral zone.
3. *Toughness:* Your strong guard must be a tough kid who thrives on the contact of blocking defenders "in the pit" who, in many instances, will be bigger than he is.
4. *Speed/Quickness:* The optimal strong guard has size and speed. He has to be able to pull quickly and get out in front of the wide plays and bootlegs. Along with his quickness, he must possess agility and body control so that he can sustain the block once he strikes the initial blow, as well as avoid fallen bodies as he pulls to the point of attack.
5. *Pass blocking ability:* On all dropback passes, your strong guard blocks the defensive tackle to his side. He will never block a stunting linebacker, and therefore must be a strong pass blocker against a tackle who is coming hard on the pass rush.

STRONG TACKLE

1. *Size:* Size is vital to this position. The player must have a body frame that allows for the addition of weight through a sound weight program. In theory he should be your biggest, strongest offensive lineman. Speed and quickness can be sacrificed for the player who can get the job done in a five-yard area around the line of scrimmage.
2. *Mental alertness/Intelligence:* Since he makes the blocking calls for the strongside plays, your strong tackle must possess an overall knowledge of the offense, of basic defensive fronts, and of how to successfully block each strongside point of attack in the Swingback-Motion Offense. This knowledge and alertness carries over to the defense's stunting, slanting or angling capability once the ball is snapped. He must play heads up football, constantly looking for keys that will indicate a defensive change.
3. *Toughness:* Your strong tackle must like to play football and be willing to get off on the ball and own the neutral zone. In our situation this was especially important because of an obvious lack of size in our strong tackles.
4. *Pass blocking ability:* In most defensive schemes, your strong tackle will block the strongside defensive end. He must be mobile enough and possess good body balance to handle quick, aggressive defensive ends.

QUICKSIDE LINEMEN

In the Swingback-Motion Offense these are your quicker, faster linemen who lack the size and strength to be employed on the strongside. Certain plays in this mirrored offense lend themselves to quick blockers. These players are your trap, veer/option and toss/flip specialists of the offense.

QUICK GUARD

1. *Size:* Although it is not absolutely essential, your quick guard should be around 5'10"-5'11" tall and weigh 170-180 pounds.

He must utilize his quickness when blocking man on man, but his blocking mainly involves angle blocking and double-teaming.
2. *Speed/Quickness:* These are the number one prerequisites of a good quick guard in the Swingback-Motion Offense. He must be able to pull and trap as well as to pull and lead through the point of attack. Your quick guard must be a tough kid who thrives on contact, and he should be your fastest offensive lineman.
3. *Pass blocking:* He has to be mobile enough to block the number one defender on or off the line of scrimmage to his side. In certain defenses, this is a linebacker who will drop off or stunt. This mobility allows him to help the center with a noseman, or to look outside and help your quick tackle with his block.

QUICK TACKLE

1. *Size:* Your quick tackle is basically a player who does not have the size or strength to be a strong tackle.
2. *Speed/Quickness:* He should be the quickest offensive tackle you have. He has to be able to pull and execute the long trap on the scissors play, and also must be quick enough to seal to the inside when the quick guard pulls.
3. *Toughness:* Occasionally, your quick tackle is going to have to block big defenders one on one. His toughness and quickness must compensate for any lack of size. He must be a strong competitor who gets the job done one way or the other.
4. *Mental altertness/Intelligence:* He makes the quickside blocking calls by possessing a sound knowledge of the Swingback Motion Offense and of basic defensive fronts. Realizing the size differential of our quickside linemen, he must be able to make the call that will insure the offense of at least a standoff at the point of attack. He must constantly be alert for keys that might tip a defensive change on the snap of the ball.
5. *Pass blocking:* Your quick tackle is assigned to block the number two defender on or off the line of scrimmage on all

dropback passes. He must be able to set up quickly and not allow the rusher to the inside. Body control and balance, along with his quickness, enable him to perform his task of protecting the quarterback.

2

INSTALLING SWINGBACK-MOTION OFFENSIVE MECHANICS

Simplicity is the keynote of the basic mechanics of the Swingback-Motion Offense. Everything that is incorporated into the offense was chosen for its capacity to lend simplicity to the offense. By keeping the mechanics simple, execution can be stressed and attention to details emphasized.

CHANGING OFFENSIVE SETS WITH THE SWINGBACK

The Swingback changes the Swingback-Motion offensive sets. He lines up in the full I, or base set, and then shifts or swings into the set called in the huddle. As your swingback gains better control of the offense, he can line up in any offensive set that he chooses, and then swing to the desired set.

Whenever the pro or twin sets are used, the swingback has the option to go immediately to his position or to swing to it. Lateral field position of the ball will most often determine which option he uses.

Your swingback can align himself in any one of the following seven positions. Words are used to describe the alignment that he is to assume. (See Diagram 2-1.)

With a strong left or right formation capability, your Swingback-Motion Offense is able to utilize 14 different sets. (See Diagram 2-2.)

32   *Installing Swingback-Motion Offensive Mechanics*

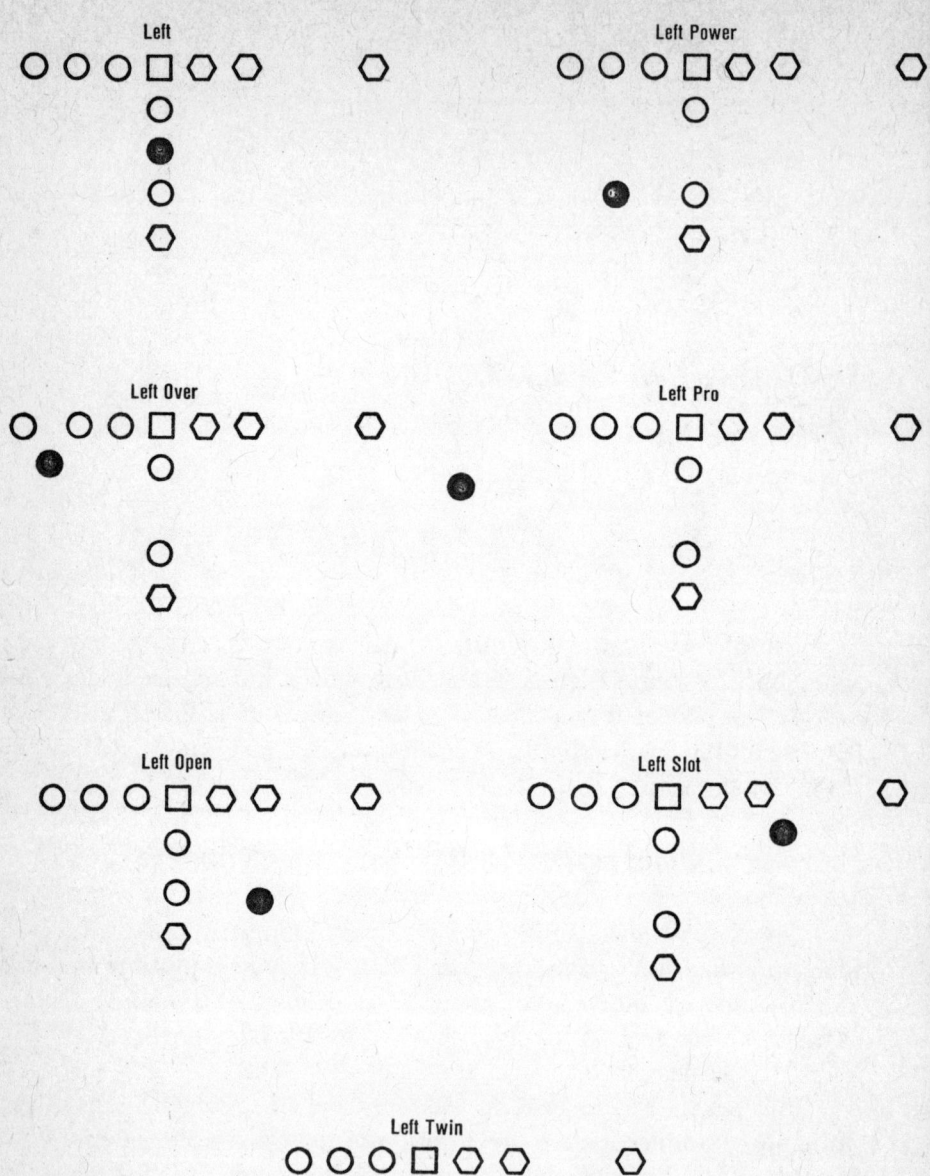

Diagram 2-1

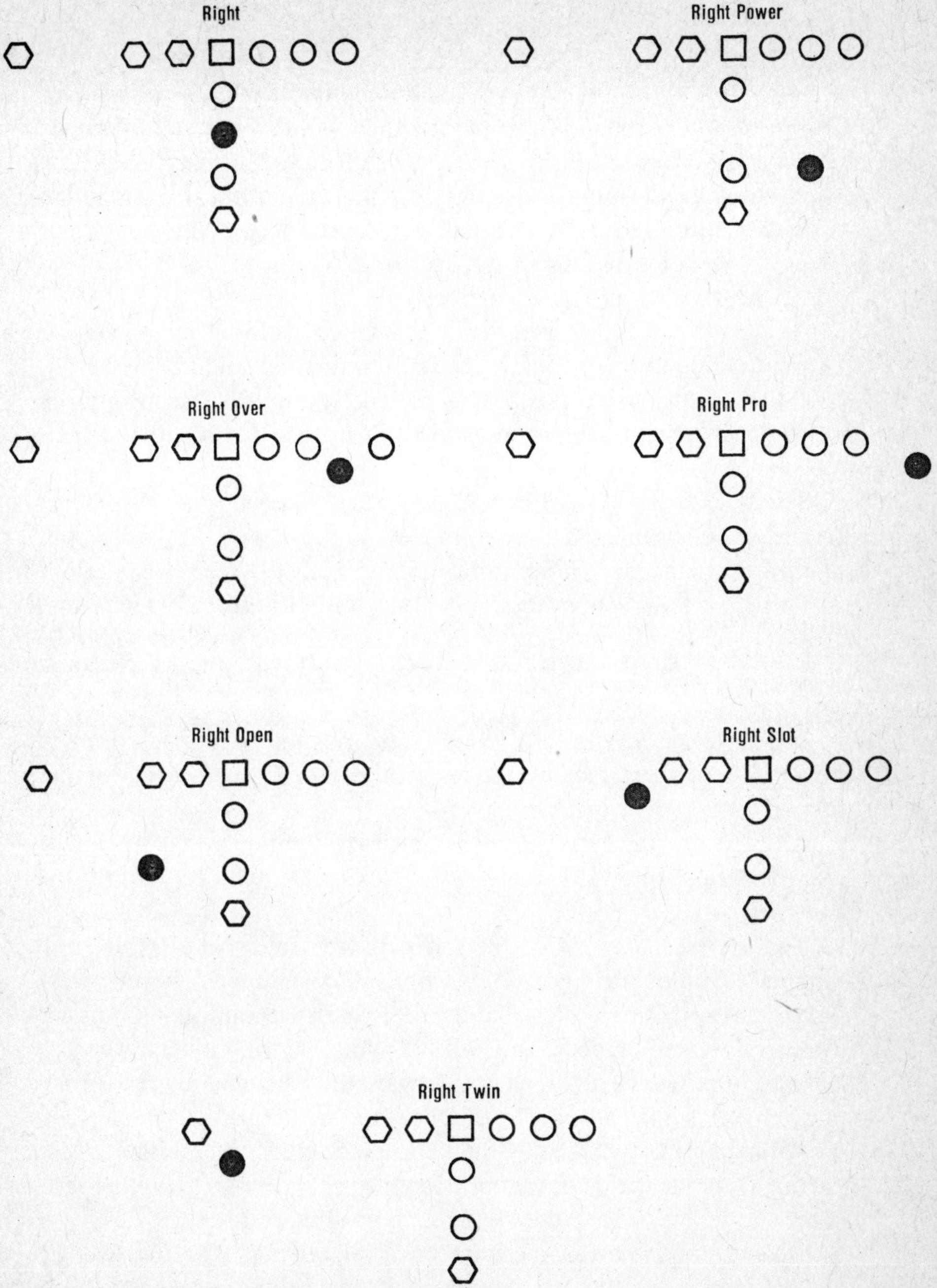

Installing Swingback-Motion Offensive Mechanics

Diagram 2-2

Formations shown: Right, Right Power, Right Over, Right Pro, Right Open, Right Slot, Right Twin

SET DESCRIPTIONS

In the full I (Left or Right call), the swingback lines up between the quarterback and fullback in a balanced four-point stance. His distance from the quarterback is approximately three feet, fitting snugly between the quarterback and fullback. He must not push the fullback deeper than his standard four to four and one-half yard position from the front tip of the ball, while not crowding the quarterback. This is the set from which most of the shifting of the swingback originates.

Along with his full I alignment, the swingback has three strongside (tight end side) and three quickside (split end side) alignments.

His first strongside position is called "power." The swingback lines up directly behind the strong tackle and even in depth with the heels of the fullback.

Second, he positions himself between the strong tackle and the tight end, who has taken a three-yard flex, in the "over" set. His depth is one yard off the line of scrimmage.

Third, as a flanker in the "pro" set, the swingback widens to a position 12-15 yards outside the tight end and one yard off the ball. When the ball is on the hash mark, his maximum split is approximately seven yards.

From the quickside, the "open" set finds the swingback directly behind the quickside tackle and even in depth with the heels of the fullback.

As a "slot," the swingback assumes an alignment to the quickside of the formation, one yard outside the quick tackle and one yard off the line of scrimmage.

The last set, or "twin" set, which we feel is one of the best Swingback-Motion offensive sets, finds the swingback three yards inside of the split end and one yard off the ball. Depending on how the perimeter defenders react to the twin set, you may find it necessary, on occasion, to move the swingback in toward the ball, making the formation a wide slot instead of a true twin set.

Adjusting the twin forces the perimeter defenders to either widen someone from the inside or to rotate a safety or corner up to help protect against the quick pass to the swingback or split end.

Because of the offensive linemen flipping sides with the strength call, it is imperative that your swingbacks learn their positions as they are described above in order to avoid confusion.

As he matures and begins to grasp the offense and his role in it, your swingback can line up in one set and, on the quarterback's command, shift to the position called in the huddle. (See Diagram 2-3.) This tactic is of value against opponents who declare their rover/monster after the swingback takes his position.

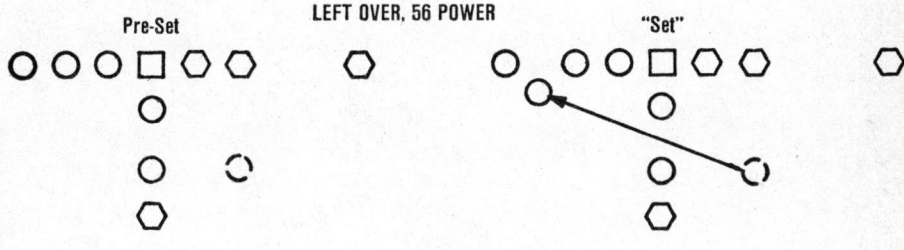

Diagram 2-3

Another tactic that can be used to confuse the defense is to line the swingback up in his declared position. On the quarterback's command of "set," he realigns himself away from the playside, remains set for one full second, then starts in motion toward his original position. This tactic can also be used versus a rover/monster defense. (See Diagram 2-4.)

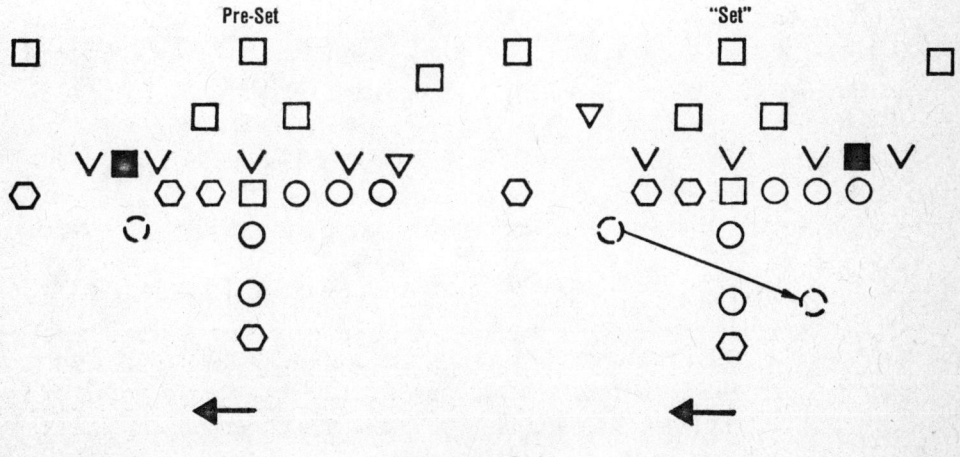

Diagram 2-4

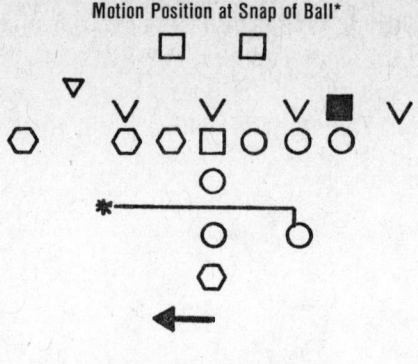

Diagram 2-4 (cont'd)

One final technique regarding changing offensive sets, is to begin the game with two tight ends. One is designated as the left end, the other as the right end. This can be effectively used in the Swingback-Motion Offense versus an opponent who flip-flops its perimeter defenders according to the strength of the formation.

The quarterback calls the set and play and the offense breaks the huddle. The end to the strongside splits out and the end to the quickside remains tight. On the quarterback's command of "Set," the end that was split closes down while the end that was tight splits out. (See Diagram 2-5.)

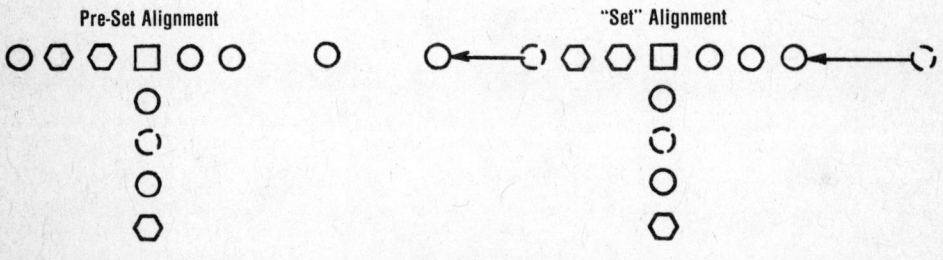

Diagram 2-5

What has been created is a situation in which the defense's strongside defenders are aligned to the quickside (because the left end was tight during the pre-set alignment). The normal quickside defenders are to the strongside (because the right end was split during the pre-set alignment). You have now achieved your goal of gaining your strongside players against defenders who normally play to the quickside of the formation, and vice versa.

The swinging or shifting of your swingback, coupled with motion and some minor adjustments of your ends, leads to the maturing of your Swingback-Motion Offense into a strong unit that is capable of moving the ball against any defensive team.

HUDDLE MECHANICS

Probably one of the most important facets of any football system, in terms of psychology and motivation, is the huddle. It is here that plays are relayed from the coach to the players on the field via messengers or hand signals. The tempo for the next play starts when your center organizes the huddle. Sloppiness and disorganization in the huddle often become primary traits of the play being executed. For this reason, the huddle in the Swingback-Motion Offense is given special attention.

The Swingback-Motion Offense utilizes a choir-type huddle in order to gain an advantage of a few seconds over the defense whenever possible. In most cases, the defense will break its huddle first. New defenders coming into the game might indicate an alignment change (a down lineman in and a linebacker out) and can be spotted by the offensive team that is facing the line of scrimmage. Therefore, everyone in the huddle except the quarterback is facing the line of scrimmage. (See Diagram 2-6.)

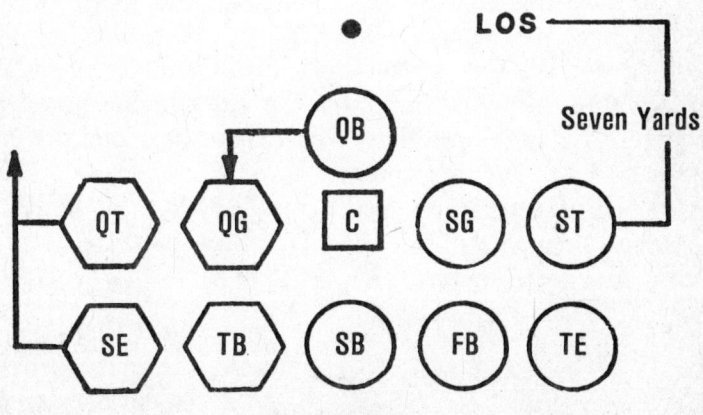

Diagram 2-6

Your center has the responsibility to quickly form the huddle seven yards and centered from the ball. It is set up in a basic right formation. The linemen are in a pre-set position—bent over at the waist, heads up, back straight and their hands on their knees. The second row (backs and receivers) stands erect with their hands on their hips.

Huddle discipline is emphasized. There is no talking except for the quarterback. All eyes are on the quarterback's mouth and no one is leaning on anyone else. This is the start of a new play and the proper tempo and attitude for the successful completion of that play starts here.

QUARTERBACK RESPONSIBILITIES IN THE HUDDLE

In the Swingback-Motion huddle the quarterback will call:

1. Offensive set
2. Play
3. Motion (if used)
4. Snap count

A typical running play would be: "Left, 58 Blast, Peel, on 1."

Running plays are two-digit numbers with the first number indicating either the back to carry the ball or the back who will begin the play with the ball. The second digit designates the point of attack. A word is also added to give everyone a verbal cue as to what the play should look like as well as to how the defense is being attacked. (The pass offense will be discussed in Chapters 7 and 8.)

The quarterback stands off to the side of the huddle, closest to his bench, awaiting the messenger from the sideline coaches. Once he receives the play, he centers himself on the huddle and directs his first call of the play to the strongside.

After his initial call, the center leaves the huddle and the swingback steps forward and replaces him. The quarterback now repeats the call to the quickside. (See Diagram 2-7.)

After the second call, the quarterback breaks the huddle by saying, "Ready, Break." If the offensive set was a right call, the offense sprints to the line of scrimmage. (See Diagram 2-8.)

A left call necessitates coordinating the players who must cross.

Installing Swingback-Motion Offensive Mechanics

The strongside player passes first, followed by his quickside counterpart—strong guard, then quick guard, etc. The tight end and split

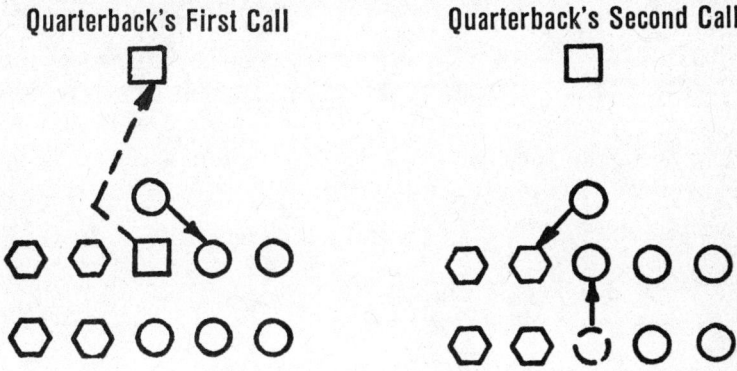

Diagram 2-7

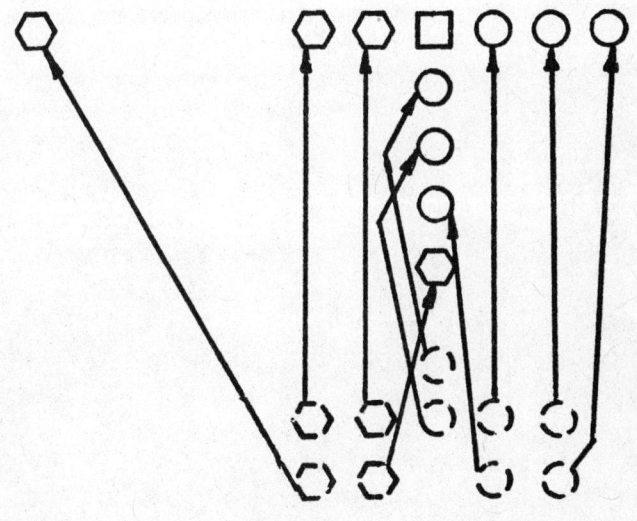

Diagram 2-8

end cross behind the huddle to alleviate some of the congestion in front of the huddle. (See Diagram 2-9.)

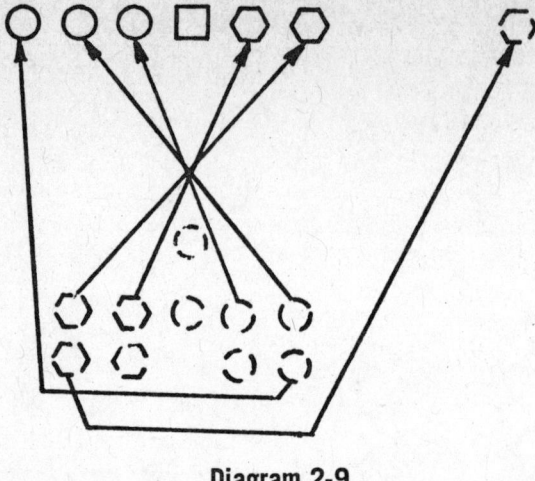

Diagram 2-9

PRE-SET POSITION AT THE LINE OF SCRIMMAGE

On the quarterback's command of, "Ready, Break," the linemen sprint to the line of scrimmage and assume their pre-set position. This position is the same one that is used in the huddle. It is a balanced two-point stance, head up, back straight with their hands resting comfortably on their knees.

Along with the linemen, the swingback and fullback also assume the pre-set position. The tailback's pre-set position is the same stance that he will start the play with. It will be discussed in detail in Chapter 3.

Although it is considered a pre-set, or pre-snap position, the ball can be snapped on "set," and therefore the linemen and backs must be able to transform their pre-set stance into an attack position.

The pre-set position is used to adjust line splits that will be dictated by the play and by the defensive alignment. It also helps to delay the defense's recognition of the swingback's declaration. The fullback uses the pre-set position so that once the swingback declares his position, he can adjust his depth according to the job that he has to do.

SET POSITION AT THE LINE OF SCRIMMAGE

On the quarterback's command of "Set," the linemen flex, the fullback assumes his stance, and the swingback shifts to his designated alignment. The flex is a straightening of the back and legs by the linemen and a lateral shuffling to the inside or outside as they adjust their splits. They then go down into their stance. Flexing is employed for the dual purpose of first enabling the linemen (backs) to adjust their splits (depth) and second, to delay the defense's recognition of the swingback's alignment.

In the set position, the linemen and fullback will be in a functional four-point stance while the tailback assumes a balanced two-point stance. The swingback's stance is a semi-sprinter's three-point stance unless he remains in the full I. In the full I, he will employ the same four-point stance as the fullback.

CADENCE MECHANICS

The cadence used in the Swingback-Motion Offense, with minor adjustments, was originated at the University of Maryland. It is a non-rhythmic cadence composed of the following words:

"Set": Linemen flex and adjust their splits from their pre-set position while the swingback declares his position. (If a Right or Left set is being used, the three backs assume their full I alignment.)

"Hit": The ball can be snapped on any number of "hits." "Right Open, 37 Veer, on 2 (3, 4)" would indicate that the ball is going to be snapped on the second (third, fourth) "Hit."

The ball can be snapped on any word in the cadence. If it is to be snapped on "Set," everyone must know that they will be firing out from their pre-set position. With the ball being snapped on "Set," the swingback must declare his position immediately. To eliminate any possible defensive keys from the swingback's early declaration, your swingback periodically must declare his position without shifting.

"LINE OF SCRIMMAGE"

"Line of Scrimmage" is a call made in the huddle that alerts the offense that the play will be called on the line. The quarterback calls the set in the huddle and then adds, "Line of Scrimmage."

This audible device can parlay an intelligent quarterback's taking advantage of the defensive alignment (especially the rover/monster) into an offensive advantage. It can be effectively used with any play in the offense, but its real value lies in its use with the veer/option and other option plays that are striving to gain a numerical advantage at the point of attack.

Minor adjustments must be made to the cadence. The first word that the quarterback uses is "Ready." He then calls the play twice, leaving out the word description of the play. He directs his first call to the right side and his second call to the left side of the offensive set. It is extremely important that he establishes this pattern of play calling and defensive scanning at the line of scrimmage because good scouts can detect a quarterback's penchant to look to the playside first when calling his cadence.

This is also the procedure that is used when a regular play is called in the huddle. The quarterback looks at the defensive left first, then scans the field to the defensive right (from right to left from the quarterback's viewpoint).

From year to year, as you evaluate your quarterbacks' mental and physical capabilities, it becomes a simple matter to employ the appropriate cadence. Dummy calls, as well as the live call, must be made on every play when using the "line of scrimmage" system.

After the play is called twice, the quarterback sets the offense and continues on with his cadence. To help alleviate problems, all "line of scrimmage" plays will be triggered on the second "hit."

This offensive weapon is essential when the defense does not establish a definite pattern in its rover/monster declaration (i.e., wideside, swingback side, tight end side, etc.), but rather plays a guessing, "cat and mouse" game with the offense. It also helps eliminate the bad play by enabling the offense to run the play that has the most chance of success at the defensive area.

Obviously, the quarterback is the key to the "line of scrimmage" system. He must understand the game plan thoroughly and must be aware of what plays can be run successfully from each set, and when it is vital to have the swingback positioned to the point-of-attack side of the formation. A sound knowledge of basic defensive fronts is also a prerequisite for employing this tactic.

An example of a "line of scrimmage" play is Diagram 2-10.

Installing Swingback-Motion Offensive Mechanics

"Left Power, Line of Scrimmage (on 2)"

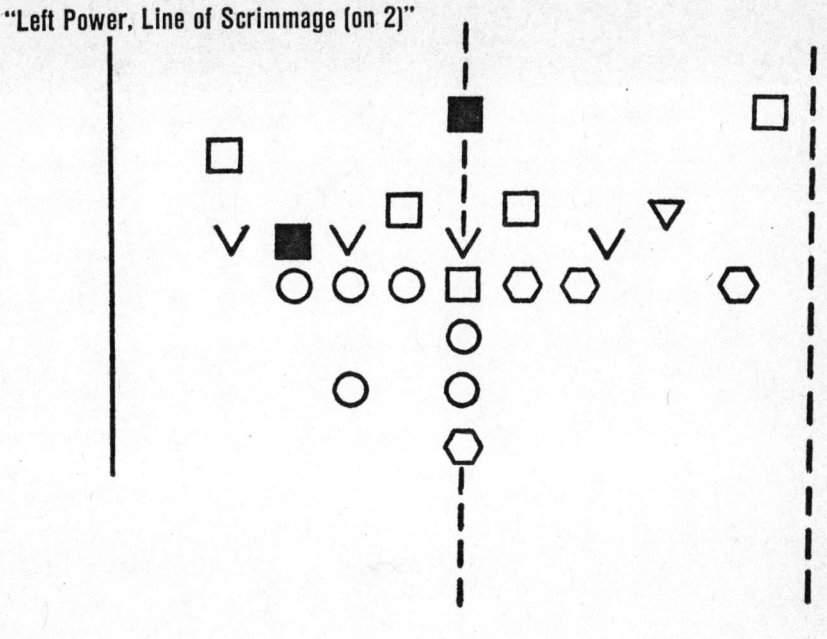

Diagram 2-10

In Diagram 2-10, as the quarterback scans the defensive alignment, he notices that the rover has declared to the swingback side and that the safety has moved to the hash mark to the short side of the field. His decision would be to call 37 Veer with the play being run to the quickside away from the rover and rotated safety. (See Diagram 2-11.)

HOLE NUMBERING AND LINE SPLITS

The strongside (in all diagrams designated by the circle) holes will always be even numbered while the quickside (designated by the hexagon) will always be odd numbered. (See Diagram 2-12.)

The holes are numbered from the inside out, with the larger numbers inside and the smaller numbers outside. There is no four hole to the strongside. The number six is used to designate the off-tackle or power hole.

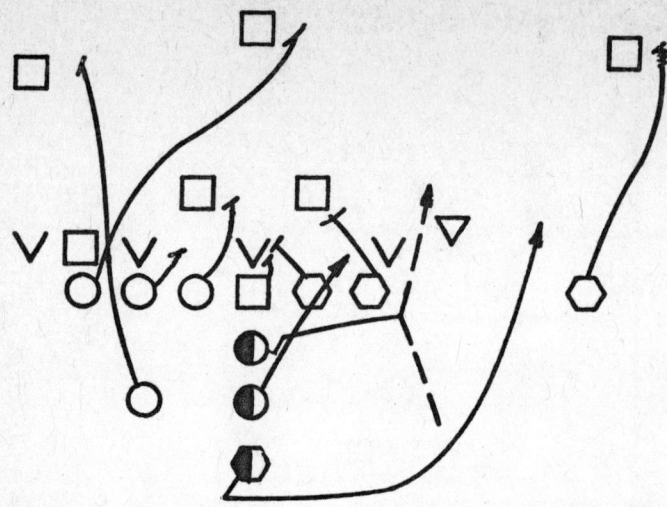

Diagram 2-11

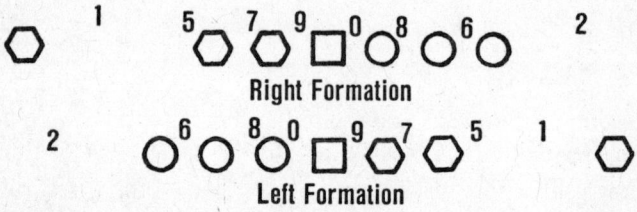

Diagram 2-12

From tackle to tackle, the maximum splits are three to three and one-half feet, while the minimum split is two feet. (See Diagram 2-13.) Line splits are vital to the option-style running of the tailback in the Swingback-Motion Offense. During the course of the game, as your linemen tire, the tendency is for them to narrow their splits. Your coaches in the pressbox, or someone on the field, must constantly remind the linemen to take their proper splits.

The general rule of thumb for your linemen is to take an intelligent,

Installing Swingback-Motion Offensive Mechanics 45

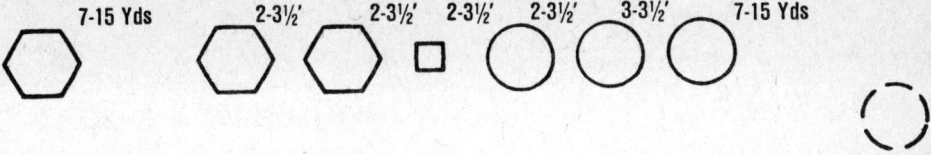

Diagram 2-13

working split that will enable them to perform their tasks while insuring their inside gap.

There are two specific rules that your interior linemen must follow. On the inside veer/option play to their side, your guards must take a constant two-foot split. On the outside veer/option, your playside tackle must use a split of two feet. Both of these constant splits facilitate a sound mesh of the quarterback and fullback on these plays.

The tight end's basic split is three to three and one-half feet. The only time he is encouraged to reduce his split is on the goal line. Versus certain defenses, he will flex, or split out three to four yards from the strong tackle, in order to gain an anticipated advantage.

The split end and the swingback, in a pro set, will vary their splits according to the play called and the vertical position of the ball on the field. Consideration will also be given, at times, to the defensive scheme that your opponent is using.

Your wideout's minimum split is seven yards from the next player to the inside. Both the split end and swingback will also use a seven-yard rule. This rule alerts them never to line up within seven yards of the sideline.

Considering the seven-yard rule, the ball on the hash mark to their side, the split end or swingback can only split approximately seven yards from the quick tackle or tight end. (See Diagram 2-14.)

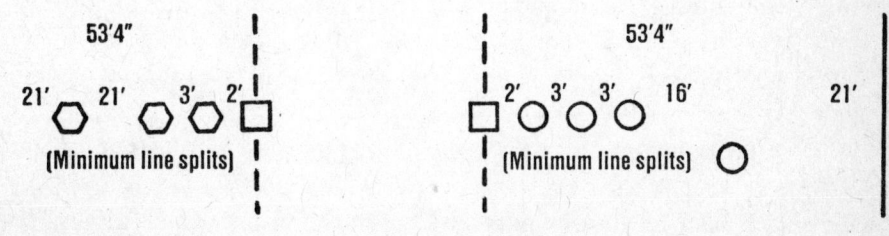

Diagram 2-14

The seven-yard rule is designed to keep the secondary defender concerned about the inside and outside pass route capability of the wideout. Lining up too close to the sideline indicates to the defender that the only areas he has to worry about are deep and to the inside. He has the sideline as an extra defender to help him if the wideout tries to run an out pattern. (See Diagram 2-15.)

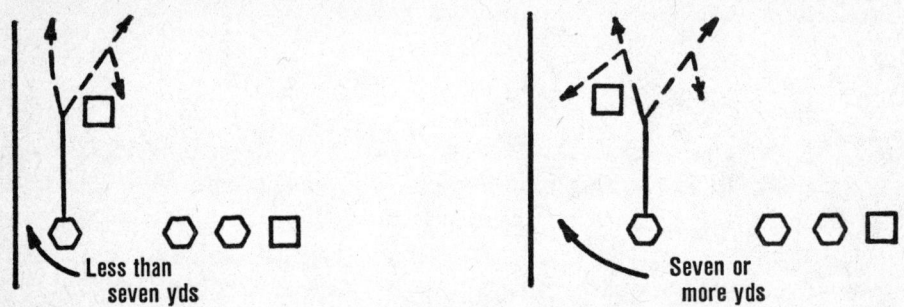

Diagram 2-15

Furthermore, a seven-yard split from either the quick tackle (split end) or tight end (swingback) requires some type of defensive adjustment by the perimeter defenders because of the potential crackback block.

Another variable that will aid in determining the maximum split of the wideouts is the strength of your quarterback's arm. If he doesn't have the strength needed to throw the 10 to 12 yard wide pattern to a receiver split 12 to 15 yards, your receivers must make the appropriate compensation. The basic rule, however, is to keep the split within the 7 to 15 yard range.

Maximum splits by the wideouts are encouraged versus a three-deep defense, in order to help open up the quick post or goal route.

Disciplined, winning football teams take the time to do the seemingly little things. Taking proper line splits is one of the little things that must be worked on if your Swingback-Motion Offense is going to be productive.

NUMBERING AND LETTERING OF BACKS AND RECEIVERS

Each back in the Swingback-Motion Offense is given a number designation while each receiver is designated by a letter. The

Installing Swingback-Motion Offensive Mechanics 47

swingback, who has a dual role in the offense, is given a number and a letter designation. (See Diagram 2-16.)

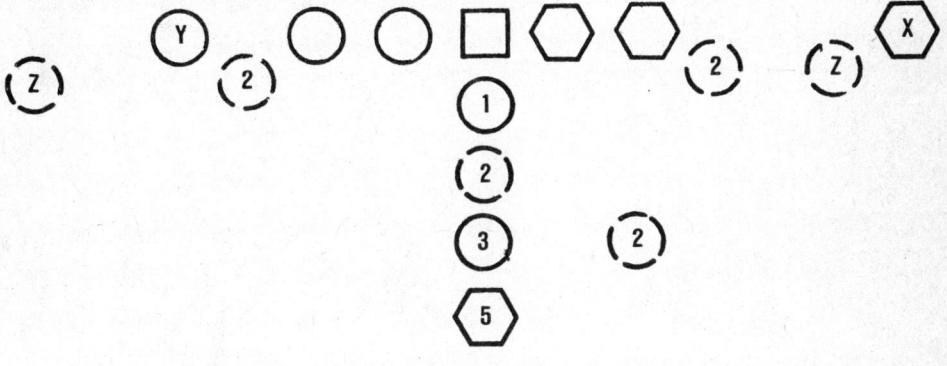

Diagram 2-16

In those offensive sets in which he is used primarily as a runner or lead blocker, your swingback is designated as "two." He carries the ball on 20/29 traps and 20/29 scissors. As a potential ball carrier on the veer/option and option plays, and on all pass plays, he assumes the letter "Z."

ALIGNMENT OF THE BACKS

The alignment of the backs (see Diagram 2-17) in the Swingback-Motion Offense plays an important role in the operation of the offense. As with offensive line splits, coaches must make sure that their backs are lining up properly on every play and set that is called.

Along with the concept of option running, which is of paramount importance to the success of the offense, is an accurate evaluation of the speed and acceleration of your tailback. His depth should be at least five and one-half yards and not more than six to six and one-half yards. His two-point alignment directly behind the fullback is one of the major factors of a successful running game in the Swingback-Motion Offense. If he is not an exceptionally quick starter, you must employ him closer to the line of scrimmage.

However, if you move him closer than five yards, you limit his ability to run to the open area because he will receive the ball too close to the line of scrimmage to veer to the inside or cut outside as the open area appears along the line of scrimmage.

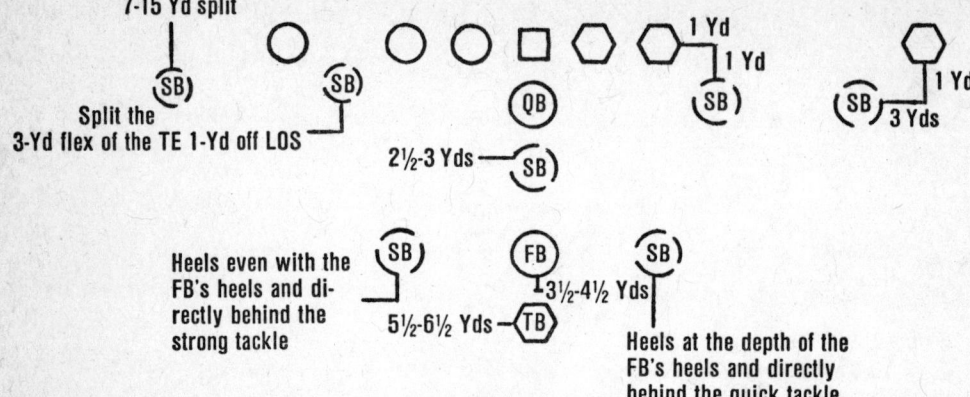

Diagram 2-17

Your fullback assumes a four-point stance (preferred) with his heels three and one-half to four and one-half yards from the front tip of the ball. His depth will depend upon his ability to accelerate on the snap count. A slower fullback may have to line up even closer, but ideally he will be at four and one-half yards. This depth leads to a smooth mesh during the veer/option while affording the quarterback adequate time to read his give key. It is also an optimal depth for his trap plays.

The swingback's alignment will change as the offensive set changes. In the base set, or full I, he lines up between the quarterback and fullback, which makes his depth approximately two and one-half to three yards from the ball. It is important that he doesn't crowd the quarterback so as to impede his ability to open up or reverse pivot. And yet, he cannot be too deep so as to push the fullback deeper than his optimal depth.

In the power and open sets, he lines up directly behind the tackle with his heels at the depth of the fullback's heels. It is important that the swingback does not cheat inside or outside. He must be able to equally support the isolation and off-tackle plays as well as to get out as a pass receiver in the passing game. Cheating of the swingback's position in any direction can lead to defensive keys that can aid them in predetermining the play.

Installing Swingback-Motion Offensive Mechanics 49

As a slot, the swingback is in a one and one-yard relationship with the quick tackle. On the off-tackle play to the quickside he assumes the tight end's block, which, versus most seven-man fronts, is a double-team with the quick tackle. He must not vary his depth or width so that he is capable of functioning as a lead blocker in the post-lead double team. He must insure his inside gap.

The swingback uses his game plan intelligence when assuming the role of a twin. His basic alignment is three yards inside of and one yard off the line of scrimmage from the split end. The latter is constant. The former variable can be adjusted according to the play called and the defense's adjustment to the twin.

Your swingback will never position himself closer to the split end, but he will move in occasionally toward the quick tackle. The crackback block or his inability to lead block the number two defender are the major reasons for his adjustments. He will also mix up his alignment when the play is going to the other side of the formation.

MOTION

Probably one of the most important factors in gaining a numerical advantage at the point of attack in the Swingback-Motion Offense, is the use of motion. This offensive capability, parlayed with a swingback who can run well and who occasionally can throw the ball, gives the offense the potential to score from anywhere on the field.

Besides disrupting pass coverages, and creating the need for some form of defensive adjustment, motion will often create an unnerving effect in the minds of many high school defenders. Why are they motioning? When will they cut it off? Is the player motioning toward the playside or away from it? These and other questions lead to an unstable mental condition surrounding your use of motion. It also serves to change the offensive set and balance of the formation.

Motion must be used intelligently. Using motion for the sake of adorning your offense, with no set design or plan, is futile. It should be used on the first few plays of the game so that your coaches upstairs can view the defensive adjustments that the defensive unit is making.

After analyzing the effect of motion on the defensive scheme of your opponent, motion can then be intelligently incorporated into your game plan. It may be vital in order to gain a numerical advantage over the defense or it may simply act as a decoy by removing defenders from the point of attack.

MOTION MECHANICS

On plays involving motion, the offense breaks the huddle and the swingback lines up in the predetermined offensive set. At a specified word in the quarterback's cadence, and after the offensive unit has been set for at least one full second, the motioning back begins his motion. In most cases it will be the swingback. His progress can be disrupted anywhere along his motion course, which is parallel if not slightly backwards from the line of scrimmage. (See Diagram 2-18.)

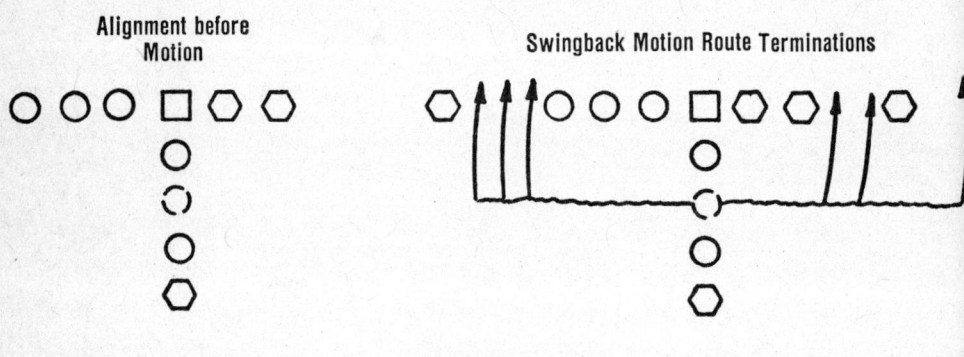

Diagram 2-18

Code words are used to designate which back is to motion and in which direction he is to go.

FLY MOTION

"Fly" is any motion away from the point of attack (run) or away from the pro set (pass). Fly motion is divided into "Fly" and "Hi-Fly." "Fly" is the swingback motioning while "Hi-Fly" designates the tailback as the motion-man.

Diagrams 2-19 and 2-20 represent the two types of Fly motion in the Swingback-Motion Offense.

In Diagram 2-19, Fly motion of the swingback to the quickside has

Installing Swingback-Motion Offensive Mechanics   51

brought the anticipated rotation of the defense, as indicated by the dotted lines. The fake of the fullback to the motion side helps to hold the linebackers, affording the offense the wide option capability away from the motion.

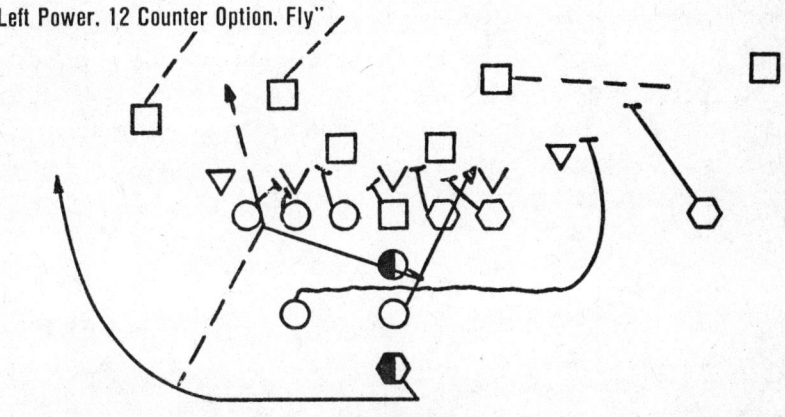

Diagram 2-19

Diagram 2-20 shows a quick trap to the swingback with the tailback going in motion toward the quickside. Anticipating that most defenses will be keying your tailback and will direct a good deal of their attention to him, you have used motion as a means of diverting the defense while you quick trap with the swingback.

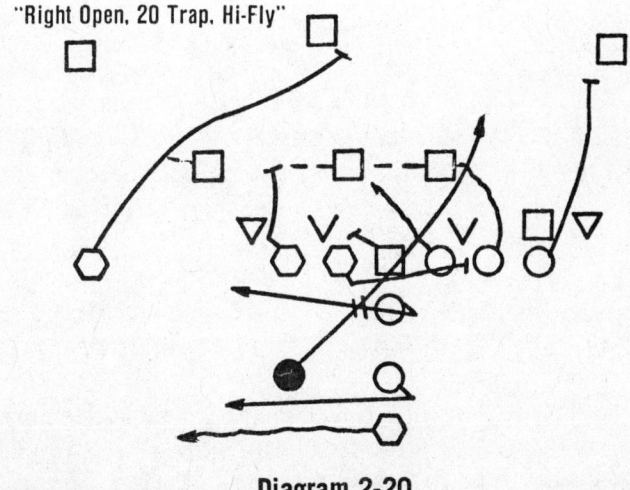

Diagram 2-20

It is important that your swingback, who will run 95 percent of your motion, understands the concept behind motion and the different types of motion. He must always know where the strong and quick sides of the formation are so that he can motion in the proper direction.

PEEL MOTION

"Peel" is any motion toward the point of attack (run) or toward the pro set (pass). It is also divided into two types. "Peel" is swingback motion and will be used approximately 50 percent of the time. (See Diagram 2-21.) The second type is "Hi-Peel," in which the tailback becomes the motion man. (See Diagram 2-22.)

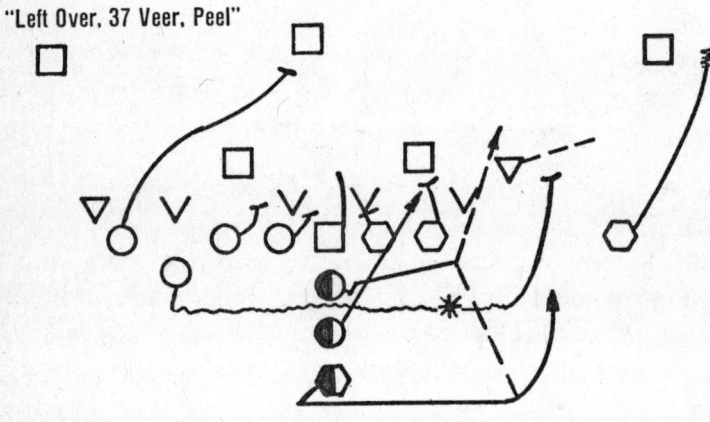

Diagram 2-21

In Diagram 2-21, you could expect the Wide Tackle or Maryland Six defensive end to walk away with the swingback's peel motion to the quick-side. This enables the swingback to achieve the lead block angle on him.

If there were no perimeter adjustment, the quarterback would have the ball snapped where the asterisk is on the swingback's motion path. This would still enable the swingback to make the block on the defensive end.

The other possibility, if there were no perimeter adjustment to your peel motion, would be to throw the ball to the split end or swingback on a quick wide or post. (See Diagram 2-23.)

Installing Swingback-Motion Offensive Mechanics

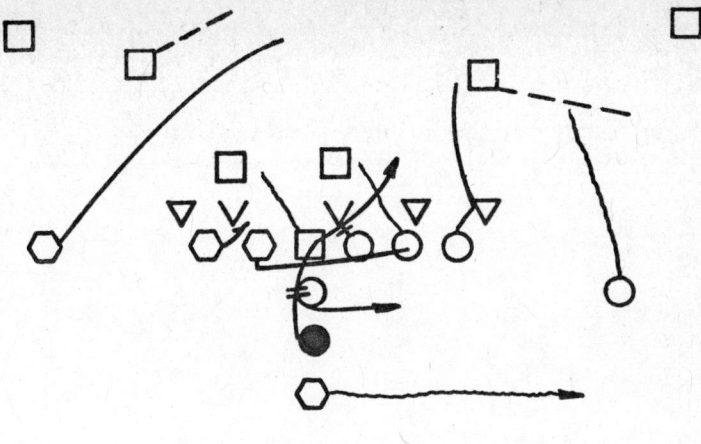

"Right Pro, 30 Trap, Hi-Peel"

Diagram 2-22

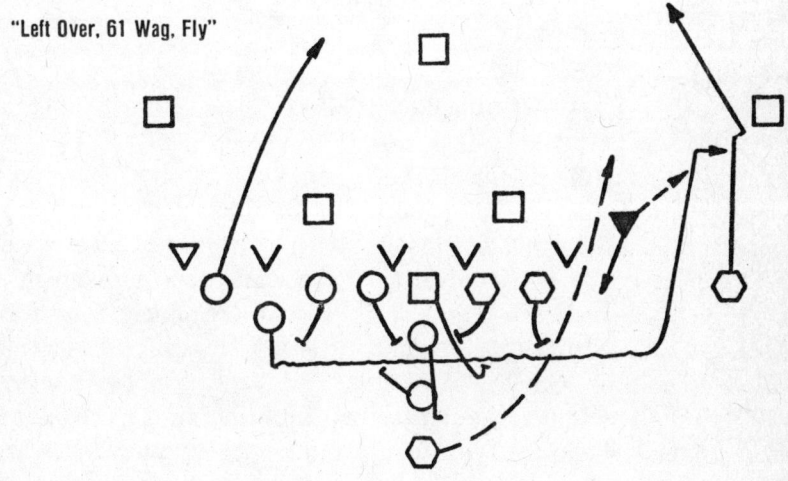

"Left Over, 61 Wag, Fly"

Diagram 2-23

Diagram 2-22 shows the fullback trap off of tailback motion to the strongside, which presents the defense with a three-receiver or trips set. You now have three immediate receivers to the strongside of the formation and the defense can no longer be tenable by playing a balanced secondary ("Four across the board"). If no adjustment were forthcoming, the ball would be thrown to the tailback as the swingback clears deep. (See Diagram 2-24.) The ball could also be thrown to the tight end if the defender playing the flat moved up to cover the tailback.

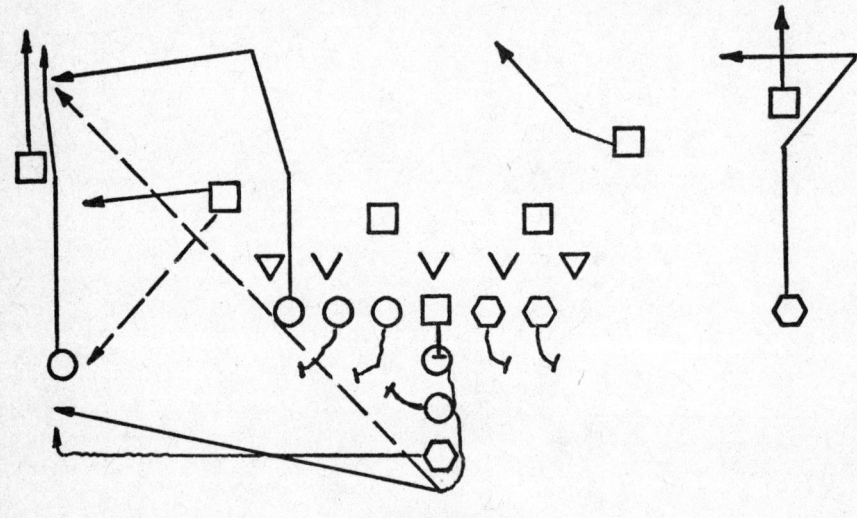

Diagram 2-24

Any rotation to the strongside (dotted lines in Diagram 2-22) would open up the quick post or goal pattern to the split end.

Peel motion allows the Swingback-Motion Offense to get an extra blocker to the playside, especially if the defense makes no adjustment to it. If the defense makes a radical shift such as complete four-deep rotation, or an overshift of the defense toward the motion, Fly motion would then be employed.

Motioning has forced the defense to eliminate someone from the point of attack. Therefore, you would run or throw away from the motion.

Fly or peel motion can be stopped at any time in order to achieve the optimal result. For example, one method of gaining the corner on 51 Toss is through the crack/stalk block of a wideout. In a twin set the swingback could go in peel motion. He knows that he is already aligned to the play side and that his motion course will not take him to the other side of the formation.

Installing Swingback-Motion Offensive Mechanics 55

Therefore, the swingback begins his motion and anticipates the quarterback's snap count as he nears the perimeter defender that he is to block. (See Diagram 2-25.)

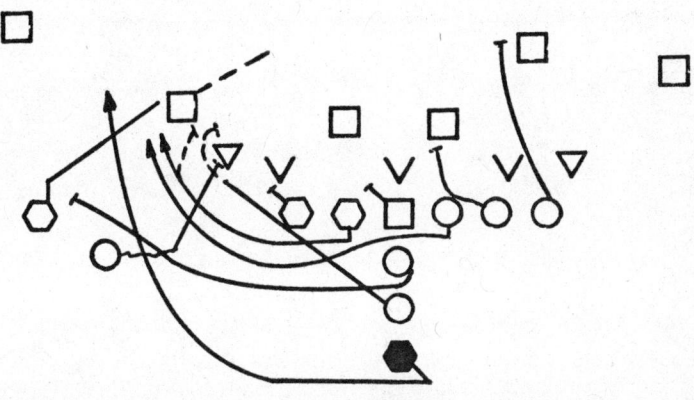

Diagram 2-25

MOTION CONSIDERATIONS

With the basic design of the Swingback-Motion Offense centered around a tailback-oriented running game, most of the motioning will be done by the swingback. Occasionally, hi-fly and hi-peel motion can be used when teams are definitely keying your tailback.

Regardless of which back is running the motion, or whatever type of motion is being used, the motion man must sprint. The main purpose of motion is to force the defense to adjust to it. This objective cannot be adequately met if the swingback (tailback) jogs along his motion course.

Although a full sprint is not required, the motion man must be running at a three-quarter sprint. Near the end of his course there is a gathering phase in which the back, in anticipation of the snap count, lowers his center of gravity in order to slow down. He then plants the foot furthest from the line of scrimmage and turns upfield.

This "gearing down" or gathering phase occurs only on the last three or four steps of the motion course. The rest of the course is a three-quarter sprint and must be run as such if the results are to be beneficial.

Your quarterback's cadence must be lengthened when motion is used. This enables the motioning back to reach his required position at the snap of the ball while also eliminating the rest of the offensive team from having to hold its stance after getting set. In order to alleviate this problem, it is best to go on two or three so that the team does not have to sit and wait for the first sound after "set" to fire out.

Any back, going in motion, must be set for one full second before starting his motion. After the command "set," the back hesitates for a full count to enable the rest of the offense to get set, and then begins his motion while the quarterback is calling the rest of the cadence.

The timing of the quarterback's cadence with the progress of the motion man is vital. Therefore, it may be necessary for the quarterback to visually follow the motioning back so that he can stop the motion at the desired position.

A method we employed initially was to have the swingback tap the quarterback as he crossed behind him. This enabled the quarterback to check the defensive reaction to the motion and, as the swingback tapped him, the quarterback then turned his attention to the swingback.

One final consideration that motion can afford your offense is in the elimination of rolled up corners or "bump and run" coverage. With the swingback's fly and peel capabilities, the defense cannot effectively roll its zone because motion can change the two-receiver side. In theory, therefore, motion can dictate which wideout can be freed up to get cleanly off the line of scrimmage.

3

COACHING THE VEER/OPTION FROM THE SWINGBACK-MOTION OFFENSE

The Swingback-Motion Offense employs the veer/option, or triple option, along with its basic I-back plays to form the nucleus of its strong running game. The veer/option and supplemental running plays are designed to create defensive problems that the offense can exploit. Defensive alignments capable of adequately covering the four aspects of the veer/option (give, keep, pitch, pass) are attacked in areas left vulnerable by its utilization of the option defense.

The veer/option is truly a team play, capable of being run against any defense. The key to its success lies in each player's unquestionable confidence in its design while performing his tasks thoroughly. The coaching staff can achieve this end through a repetitive learning situation. The play must be practiced over and over again from the part to the whole and then back to the part.

Scrimmaging is not necessary to perfect the veer/option, although contact work at times is beneficial to prove to your players that the play can be successful against live defenders. Repetitive mesh drills, designed to perfect the mental and physical skills of the backs, along with the coordinated stalk and lead blocks of the receivers, must be practiced daily for at least 20 minutes.

In order to capitalize on what the defense yields, the veer/option in the Swingback-Motion Offense is, for the most part, a read play. Each phase of the play is read by the quarterback, from the time he takes the snap from center and begins his mesh with the fullback, until he either keeps or pitches the ball. We will, however, predetermine the play to some extent versus eight-man front defenses.

Reading the play enables the offense to determine where the ball is going according to defensive reaction. The defense must have defenders in pass defense, the give, keep and pitch areas. Once the ball is committed to an area, defenders supporting the other areas are hindered in their pursuit.

Before proceeding, it is necessary at this time to discuss our numbering of defenders in regard to their defensive responsibilities versus the veer/option. Normally, in a straight defensive scheme, the number four defender is responsible for the give, the number three defender will cancel the keep, and the number two defender's role is to support the pitch. (See Diagram 3-6 for a more detailed account of numbering and counting various defenses.)

Regardless of his decision and the alternatives considered, your quarterback must insure that the ball reaches the original line of scrimmage. Inherent problems in this potentially high risk play must be minimized by intelligent coaching of your quarterback to gain the line of scrimmage as a minimum whenever the veer/option is run.

To facilitate your quarterback's reading ability, a logical, well organized teaching progression must be established. This educationally sound progression will allow your quarterback to gain the confidence needed to successfully execute the play. "A journey of a thousand miles begins with a single step" is a timeworn adage that your coaching methods must reflect when working with your quarterbacks on the veer/option play.

The first priority in this teaching progression centers around the quarterbacks being mechanically sound and confident that they possess the necessary skills required to run the veer/option.

QUARTERBACK MECHANICS OF THE VEER/OPTION

In the Swingback-Motion Offense, the physical skills that are required to execute a successful veer/option play must be practiced diligently until each quarterback has gained control over the mechanics of the play. Each one must be willing to work hard until he is able to perform the play flawlessly.

During the early season of double sessions, at least 20 minutes of practice must be allotted for quarterback skill development. There are no keys to read or reactions to make. Each quarterback has a fullback, tailback and swingback along with a center. The latter is needed to insure that the timing of the play is achieved and that the quarterback does not need to worry about getting the snap from center. The quarterback/center exchange must become automatic.

The play is run to the left and to the right until each phase of the play is executed properly. Areas in which the quarterback is experiencing difficulty are emphasized, and more time is allotted for those areas.

Considering that most of your quarterbacks will be right-handed, drills should be run to the left (which will accentuate left-handed skill development) at least three times as much as they are run to the right. This would be reversed for a left-handed quarterback.

To simplify the coaching progression of the veer/option, the play is dissected into the mesh, give, disconnect, acceleration, keep, pitch and delay pitch phases so that each quarterback can logically understand his role in the total play.

MESH PHASE

The term "mesh" is used to describe the first phase of the Swingback-Motion veer/option play. It is imperative that the mesh phase be practiced as much as, if not more than, any other phase of the play. Fumbles simply must not occur during the mesh.

It is the fullback's responsibility to properly mesh with the quarterback. This principle allows the quarterback to begin reading his keys as soon as the ball is snapped.

The fullback's course is directed at the outside hip of the playside guard. He aims his headgear at the guard's outside hip and doesn't leave this path. The only time he will leave this course is when the quarterback gives him the ball or when he disconnects.

Once he is certain that he is not going to receive the ball, your fullback becomes a blocker, attacking either the number four defender (give key) or any linebacker in the area who might be stunting to the outside to become the fourth defender whom the Swingback-Motion Offense cannot block. (See Diagram 3-1.)

The mesh begins with your quarterback receiving the snap and stepping back toward the playside at approximately a 45 degree angle to the line of scrimmage with his playside foot. This step ends with the foot nearly parallel to the line of scrimmage, and there must not be a false step with the remaining foot.

Diagram 3-1

Your quarterback grasps the ball by its "belly" (widest point) and it is carried parallel to the ground as he moves the ball back toward the mesh point.

His shoulders are turned almost perpendicular to the line of scrimmage, and his arms are extended straight from the shoulders as they move the ball away from the line toward the fullback. This position prevents the quarterback and fullback from colliding and thereby destroying the vital timing of the mesh.

It is important that your quarterback doesn't overstride during his first step. He must understand that it is his full shoulder turn and straight-arm movements that are responsible for getting the ball far enough in front of the fullback at the mesh point.

Overstriding causes problems with the quarterback's balance while also hindering his weight shift. This common error impedes his second step, causing him to be overextended which considerably hampers his ability to accelerate down the line.

The second step of your quarterback is referred to as his adjustment step. This step came from Pepper Rodgers of Georgia Tech, and its primary purpose is to keep the ball in front of the fullback until your quarterback has made his decision to give or keep the ball.

The adjustment step in most instances will be slightly into the line as your quarterback attempts to align his toes in a parallel plane with the path of the fullback.

There will be times, however, when your quarterback will receive a fast read to disconnect the ball. In this situation, he uses his adjustment step to "run through" the fullback as the fullback passes, exploding down the line toward his number three read (keep or pitch read).

The more distinct the adjustment step is into the line of scrimmage, the longer the ball stays in front of the fullback. This creates a more realistic fake but conversely increases the time it takes your quarterback to move outside with the ball.

Your quarterback's decision to give or disconnect must be made before the ball passes his inside hip (hip closest to the line). His adjustment step affects this distance. A shorter step will mean that the ball will get to his front hip sooner than if a longer one were taken. In most cases, the number four defender's reaction will greatly determine the fine line between the mesh phase and the give/disconnect phase.

The mesh and adjustment step cannot be too long or too short, for either instance will enable the defenders to determine where the ball is going.

This union, or meshing of your quarterback and fullback, must be smooth if the play is to have any chance for success. Your quarterback's steps and your fullback's course must be exactly the same every time if they are to achieve the confidence needed to run a successful veer/option play in the Swingback-Motion Offense.

GIVE PHASE

As your fullback drives on his course, beginning with a crossover step with his foot that is away from the playside, his inside elbow is up and the thumb of his inside hand is down. His outside hand is placed palm up on the lower part of his outer rib cage.

Your quarterback, holding the ball in its belly with his palms facing each other, places the ball in the pocket formed by the fullback's hands. Your fullback comes over the ball with his inside hand and slides his outside hand under the ball.

Hand control of the ball by the quarterback, coupled with a soft squeeze by the fullback are the keys to a good mesh. Your quarterbacks must warn the fullback if they are grabbing for the ball or are squeezing it too tight.

As your fullback comes over the ball, the back of your quarterback's playside wrist contacts the fullback's navel. During the give phase, your quarterback simply withdraws his playside hand and exerts pressure inward with his other hand. The give must be coached as nothing more than a safe, simple handoff.

Once your fullback doesn't feel the quarterback's wrist between his stomach and the ball, or as he feels the quarterback pulling his hand out, he firms up his grip on the ball and accelerates upfield. He should keep both arms over the ball for added protection until he clears the traffic around the line of scrimmage. Your fullback should also use his body as an additional blocker.

After the give, the quarterback and tailback accelerate down the line. It is our belief that acceleration, and not extraneous arm and hand movements, constitutes the faking of the Swingback-Motion veer/option play. Your quarterback sprinting down the line carrying his hands at the belt level, accompanied by a trailing tailback racing to maintain his pitch relationship, is all that is needed to keep the perimeter defenders from folding back to the inside to help with the fullback.

If the only time that your quarterback moves past the playside tackle is when he has the ball, he is providing a very reliable key to the defense. This common tendency must be avoided if you are to have any play at all.

DISCONNECT PHASE

The term "disconnect" is used to describe the quarterback's unhooking from the mesh and moving outside with the ball. The disconnect phase begins when the number four defender makes a definite move to the inside to cancel the fullback. Your quarterback must quickly recognize this visual cue and react by withdrawing the ball from his fullback.

The straight-arm position of the quarterback during the mesh facilitates the smooth unhooking of the ball. By having the ball as far away from his body as is physically possible, the quarterback allows the fullback to make a tighter mesh without their running into each other. His straight arms create a tolerance between himself and the fullback that acts as a buffer zone. This buffer zone is invaluable once the signal to disconnect is presented to the quarterback.

The quarterback withdraws the ball toward his stomach ("third

Coaching the Veer/Option from the Swingback-Motion Offense   63

hand'') as the fullback passes. He then sprints through the area previously occupied by the fullback. He must avoid running around the fullback and getting off the line of scrimmage as he disconnects. (See Diagram 3-2.)

Diagram 3-2

An important coaching point to continually make to a quarterback is that he must decide to give or disconnect before the ball passes his inside hip. If he waits any longer to decide, the security of the ball is jeopardized and the chance of a mesh fumble increases because the ball is leaving the middle of the fullback's pocket and is moving toward the fullback's inside hip. The fullback can no longer feel the quarterback's wrist between his stomach and the ball. This is his cue to squeeze the ball and run with it.

Another problem that arises if your quarterback delays, is that the ball is closer to the line of scrimmage and the defenders who are being blocked. From this position, it is difficult to return the ball to its proper position in front of the quarterback as he disconnects.

As your quarterback disconnects, he sprints down the line toward the inside hip of the number three defender. It is critical to the success of the play that he accelerate past the disconnect point as quickly as possible. This helps eliminate the number four defender from recognizing the quarterback's decision and playing off the fullback to the quarterback, forcing him into a premature pitch.

If the number four defender is allowed to make this reaction, the defense is able to get the extra defender to the outside that the base veer/option blocking scheme cannot handle. Only the number three defender, or whoever becomes the number three defender, must force the quarterback to pitch the ball.

KEEP PHASE

As the quarterback accelerates down the line of scrimmage toward the inside hip of the number three defender, he immediately establishes eye contact with him. This eye contact is designed to occupy the defender while allowing the quarterback to ascertain what the defender's responsibility is in the veer/option play.

If the number three defender does not establish eye contact with the quarterback, the quarterback turns quickly upfield, accelerating on a 45 degree Hero Lane away from the inside pursuit and toward the goal line. (See Diagram 3-3.)

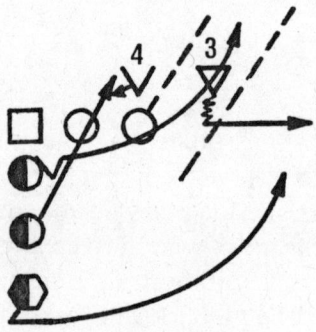

Diagram 3-3

Your quarterback should work to get his shoulders at a 45 degree angle to the goal line before breaking inside or outside. By doing this, his field of vision is expanded to cover a larger portion of the field. Numerous fumbles occur when ball carriers are tackled from their blindside. This technique helps to decrease the quarterback's blindside while enabling him to stay in the Hero Lane to the goal line. (See Diagram 3-4.)

Keeping the ball, and getting quickly upfield into the Hero Lane, opens up the possibility of the delayed pitch. The quarterback now options the first defender that shows from the outside. The tailback or swingback turns upfield when the quarterback does and sprints to maintain a pitch relationship alongside of, but slightly behind the quarterback. Last year, the delayed pitch was responsible for four touchdowns of over 30 yards, with two of them being over 55 yards. If the delayed pitch situation occurs, the quarterback must look the pitch into the pitchman's hands. (See Diagram 3-5.)

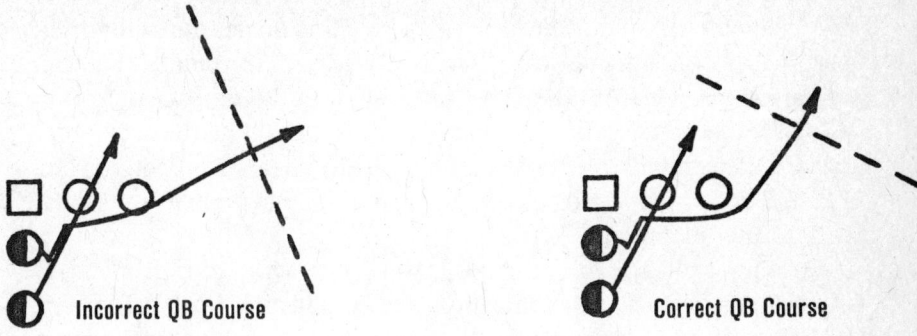

Incorrect QB Course   Correct QB Course

Diagram 3-4

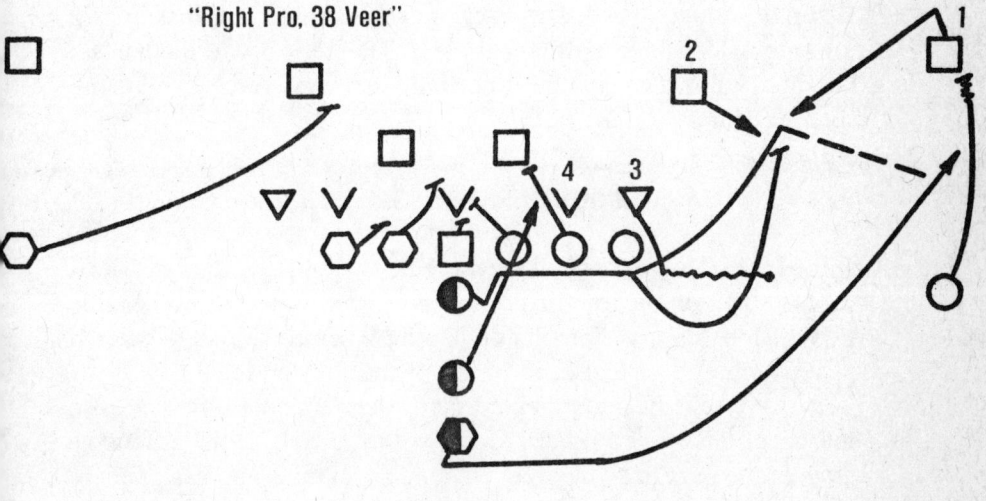

"Right Pro, 38 Veer"

Diagram 3-5

PITCH PHASE

As the quarterback nears the number three defender, he begins to shorten his stride while not sacrificing any momentum or speed. He must be able to pitch the ball off of either foot. Finally, the quarterback must be under control so as not to run into the defender, thereby allowing him to destroy the pitch.

The quarterback's pitch is a one-handed pitch that is similar to that of a basketball player's foul shot. As the pitch is made, the palm of the quarterback's pitch hand drops down and faces the ground. The pitch must always come from the hand furthest from the defender.

Once the decision is made to pitch the ball, the quarterback maintains eye contact with the defender so as to eliminate his playing off the quarterback and supporting the pitch. He uses a blind pitch to get the ball safely to the pitchman.

If a poor pitch is to be made, it should be low and in front of the tailback or swingback rather than high and behind him. With the former, the ball is still in a position to be fielded and advanced by the pitchman without having him sacrifice much momentum. The latter requires him to slow down and even stop in order to safely field the ball that is behind him.

After the pitch, the quarterback gathers himself and assumes a position from which he can protect himself. Theoretically, if no one hits him he should not have pitched the ball. He must force one of the perimeter defenders to take him.

COUNTING DEFENSES

Following the mechanical development, your quarterback next focuses his attention on counting defensive schemes which will enable him to broaden his concept of anticipating, before the snap, which defender is going to cancel each phase of the veer/option.

Defensive schemes are counted, and each defender numbered, so that the coach and quarterback, along with the rest of the offensive personnel, talk in terms of which defender (number) is assigned to cancel which phase of the play. Counting can also indicate possible number changes (number two becoming number three, etc.) that a stack or cheated alignment can lend itself.

Numbering begins with the defender closest to the sideline and continues from the outside to the inside. Any stack alignment dictates counting the down lineman first, while the safety in a three-deep secondary will not be numbered. (See Diagram 3-6.)

Coaching the Veer/Option from the Swingback-Motion Offense

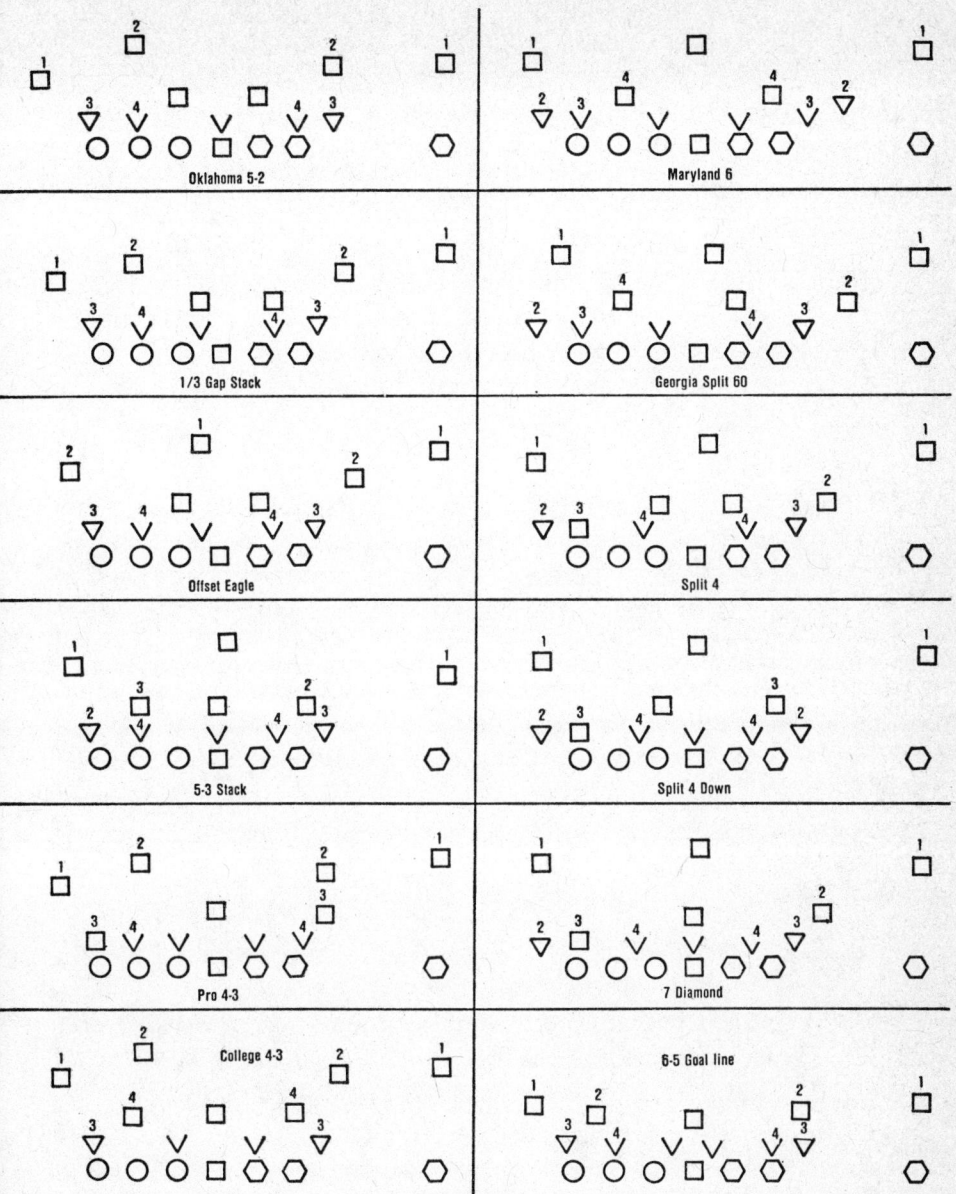

Diagram 3-6

READING THE VEER/OPTION

After your quarterback has learned to count the defensive alignments shown in Diagram 3-6, he can begin to logically program his thoughts and reactions for the various phases of the veer/option.

We begin schooling our quarterbacks in the early summer in what we feel are the two most important phases of the Swingback-Motion Offense. They are the veer/option (inside and outside) and the passing game. The latter will be discussed in detail in Chapter 8. Every summer, the same principles will be covered, so that a sophomore quarterback will receive the same information three years in a row.

Initially, the following ten basic veer/option principles are thoroughly discussed and each quarterback must understand them if you are going to read the veer/option successfully:

1. By the very nature of the play, and its capability of being run to either side of the offensive formation, the defense must align balanced across the field if they are to be tenable. That is, there must be five and one-half defenders to each side of the center.

2. The number four defender from the outside must be eliminated by either reading him or blocking him.

3. There can be no more than three defenders outside of the number four defender to cover the three remaining options (quarterback keep, pitch, pass defense) after the fullback goes over the ball.

4. Defenses will try to have one of their inside defenders move to the outside to become the fourth defender whom the offense cannot occupy or block.

5. Most defensive change-ups occur on the perimeter between those defenders assigned to play the quarterback, pitch and pass defense (outside receiver) phases of the play.

6. Seven-man fronts must absorb either the quarterback or the pitch with someone from the secondary.

7. As a quarterback, you must employ pre-snap reads that will help you gain insight into which defender is going to support which phase of the play.

8. As a quarterback, you must begin with a definite plan of action and must not alter that plan until your key dictates such a change. You are encouraged to begin with the premise of giving the ball to the fullback until the number four defender (give key) makes a definite move to cancel him.
9. You must expect a quicker number three defender read to the quickside because there is no tight end to occupy that defender.
10. Defensive adjustment to the swingback must be considered when determining whether the veer/option should be run toward him or away from him.

PHASE ONE OF THE VEER/OPTION

The first phase of the Swingback-Motion veer/option that is to be read is the mesh phase. While it is the fullback's responsibility to insure a sound mesh, it is the quarterback's job to find the number four defender who is known as the give key. In most seven-man fronts, he is the defender lined up on or outside of the offensive tackle.

The number four defender must be eliminated by either the reading or by an offensive player blocking him. If he is aligned on or outside of the offensive tackle, your quarterback will eliminate him by the reading technique.

In reading the number four defender, your quarterback keys his hat. Since most defenders tackle with their hats leading their bodies, this key is probably the most reliable. If the defender does not get his hat in front of the fullback, he should be able to run for adequate yardage (3.4 yards per play).

If the number four defender is positioned inside of the offensive tackle, which is the case in the Split Four and Maryland Six defenses, he will be eliminated by the block of the offensive tackle. (See Diagram 3-7.)

It is imperative to successful reading of the veer/option that your quarterback understand this principle of eliminating the number four defender before you, as a coach, can advance with the reading progression.

The second and third phases of the veer/option, in which your quarterback decides to keep the ball or pitch it, necessitate reading the number three defender, or the defender who, through a stunt, becomes the number three defender.

Most defensive change-ups occur on the perimeter between the defenders assigned to take the quarterback or pitch. Your quarterback must comprehend this concept if he is to remain poised when stunts and change-ups occur at the corners.

In conjunction with the keep/pitch decision is the basic principle that seven-man fronts must support the keep or pitch with someone from the secondary, while the basic design of an eight-man front enables the defense to absorb the keep or pitch phases with one or more defenders aligned on or near the line of scrimmage.

Diagram 3-7

If the number three defender commits himself to the quarterback, the decision is to pitch the ball. This decision becomes difficult to make when the number three defender, on the snap of the ball, moves upfield to support the pitch. Although his decision is the same, the quarterback must expand his vision in order to discover which defender is going to become number three. (See Diagram 3-8.)

Because the quarterback's first reading is perhaps his most important, and his most difficult due to the minimal amount of time allotted to make it, most of this section on reading will deal with his reading of the number four defender.

If your quarterback misreads the give key and hands the ball off to the fullback when he should have disconnected, there is still the chance that his fullback can overpower the number four defender and gain yardage. The worst that can happen is that he at least returns the ball to the original line of scrimmage.

Problems arise when the give to the fullback is open and the quarterback misreads the number four defender and disconnects. The defense now has the fourth defender to the outside that the offense cannot eliminate. Number four takes the quarterback and number three (who originally was to play the quarterback) is now free to support the pitch along with the number two defender.

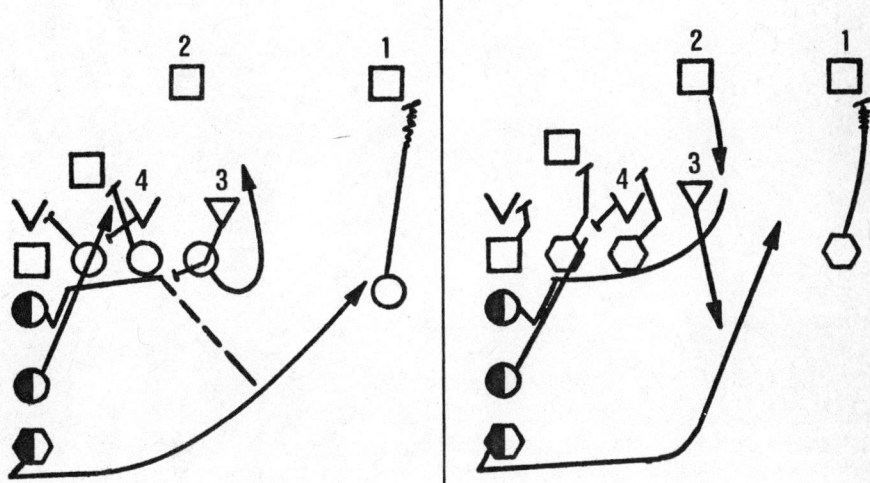

Diagram 3-8

MECHANICS OF THE READ

Your quarterback should begin every veer/option play by predetermining in his mind to give the ball to the fullback. Pepper Rodgers and Homer Smith, two renowned Wishbone football experts, advocate this approach to the quarterback's initial thought process.

With this preliminary plan in mind, the quarterback runs the play. His plan will be executed unless the number four defender's hat makes a definite move to the inside (which it must if the offensive tackle has taken a proper split). (See Diagram 3-9.)

Once the quarterback sees the number four defender close down to the inside to cancel the fullback, he aborts his preliminary plan and disconnects. (See Diagram 3-10.)

When defensive teams realize that you are reading the veer/option, they may use a false-keying scheme in an attempt to confuse your quarterback. The number four defender will give the quarterback a fast read by initially flattening out to cancel the fullback. Instead of going through with his maneuver, however, he will plant his inside foot and work upfield to take the quarterback. This enables the defense to get the extra defender to the outside that the play cannot handle. (See Diagram 3-11.)

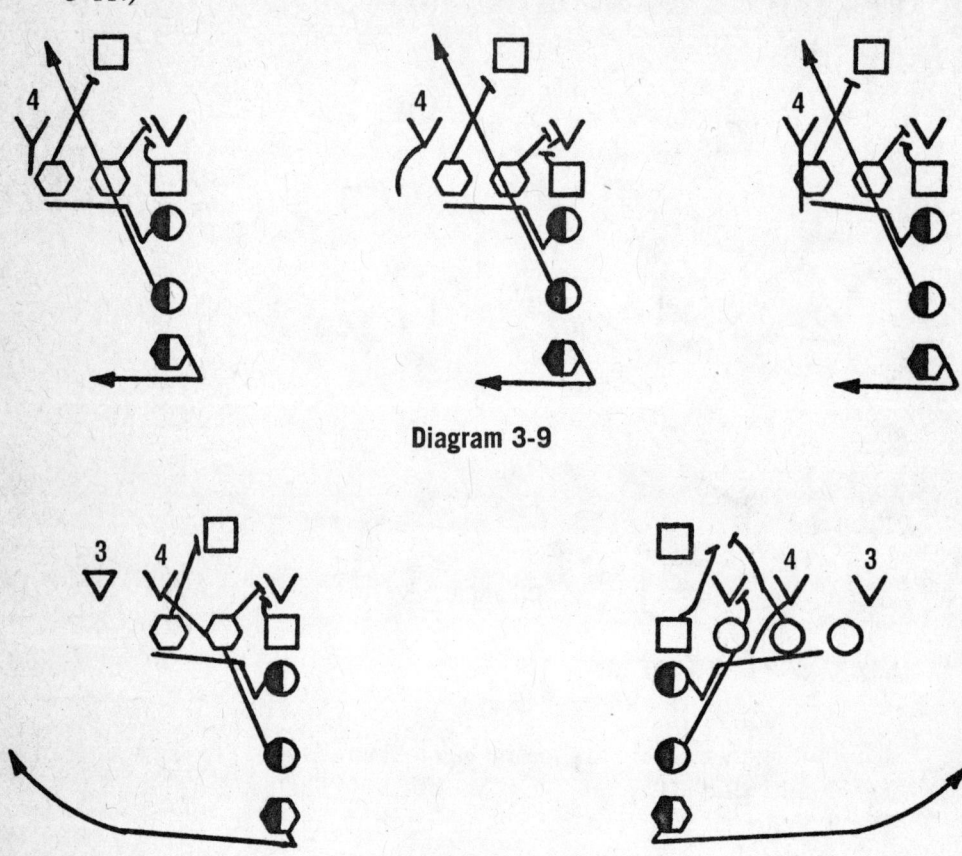

Diagram 3-9

Diagram 3-10

If defenses are false-keying their number four defender it is probably because they do not respect your fullback. To keep them concerned about the inside phase of the play have your linemen block either "Mike" (man blocking) or "Chuck" (inside) and give the ball to the fullback. You must establish the fullback and make them respect him if you are to have a sound offensive play. (See Diagram 3-12.)

Coaching the Veer/Option from the Swingback-Motion Offense 73

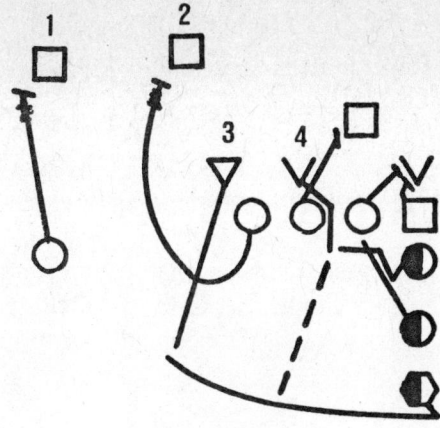

Diagram 3-11

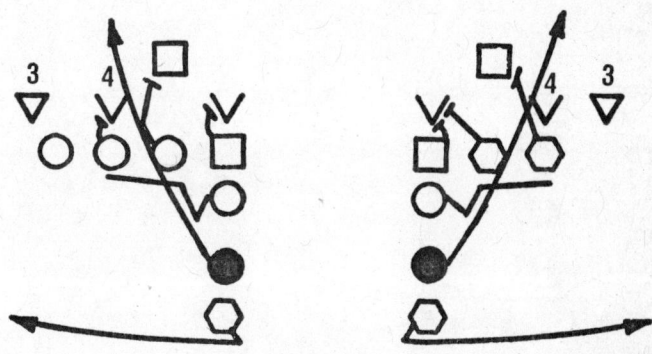

Diagram 3-12

In reading the number three defender (keep or pitch key), the quarterback immediately establishes eye contact with him while driving for his inside hip. He attacks the defender's inside hip in order to force him to commit himself completely to the quarterback. If he is going to take the quarterback, the number three defender must turn inside to do it. Once he turns inside, the quarterback pitches the ball. The number three defender has now eliminated himself from being able to adequately support the pitch.

Versus a slow-playing or deliberate number three defender, the quarterback must force him to commit himself to either the quarterback or the pitchman. It is imperative that he not allow the defender to string the play out laterally. A definite move upfield by the quarterback may be needed to force the defender's decision. After his fake keep, the quarterback pushes off his inside foot while stepping toward the pitchman as he pitches the ball.

The quarterback must make sure that he doesn't pitch the ball if the defender has gotten between himself and the pitchman. If the defender doesn't honor the feint, he keeps the ball and gets upfield. (See Diagram 3-13.)

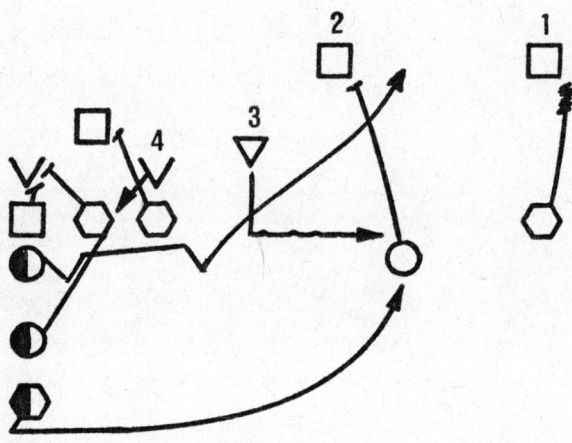

Diagram 3-13

If your quarterback is having difficulty with a slow-playing defender, coach him to keep the ball and get as many yards as he can upfield. This will tend to make the slow-playing defender respect him and will force him to commit himself earlier. The high risk aspect of the veer/option play can be reduced only through your quarterback making an intelligent, uninterrupted pitch.

The potential of a pitch fake, in order to force the number three defender to open up to the outside, is also there. This play can be effective versus a number three defender who is being heavily counted on to support the pitch.

The quarterback must be continually drilled on his reading and specific situations that he may encounter during the game. Nothing should occur that he has not worked on in practice. His execution when reacting may not be perfect, but at least he is aware of what reaction and technique he is to pursue.

He must understand the veer/option play so that he will be better able to cope with the play when it does not succeed. He can analyze and explain why the play failed. Your quarterback must accept this play as his personal play and must work and study diligently to master it.

37/38 VEER

The base inside veer/option plays are 37 Veer (quickside) and 38 Veer (strongside). When defenses play the Swingback-Motion Offense in a balanced posture, the inside veer/option will always be run toward the swingback. If there is a defensive adjustment that moves a defender toward the swingback, the play should be run away from him.

Depending on the defense's adjustment to motion, the play will be run either with peel motion (Diagram 3-14), or with fly motion (Diagram 3-15.) In Diagram 3-14, peel motion is used because the defense has made no secondary adjustment to the swingback's motion. Therefore, the play will be run toward the motion in order to numerically block the play. Fly motion, in Diagram 3-15, has forced a secondary rotation

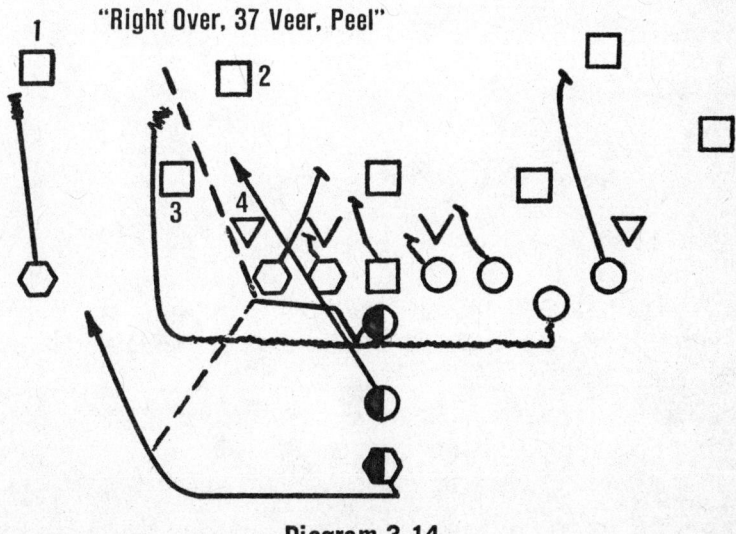

Diagram 3-14

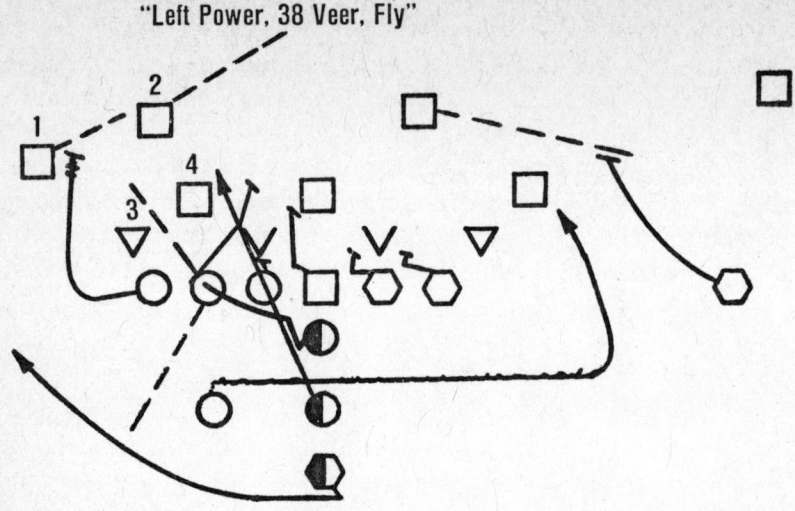

Diagram 3-15

toward the swingback. The inside veer/option is now run away from the motion because the strong safety has rotated to the deep middle and cannot effectively support either the keep or pitch from his alignment. This is especially true when motioning the swingback into the sideline and then running the play back toward the wide side of the field.

Employing the inside veer/option versus eight-man defensive fronts will be presented in Chapter 4.

BLOCKING CALLS FOR THE INSIDE VEER/OPTION

The "Chuck" call is the base tackle call for the inside veer/option. It tells the playside tackle and guard to block inside toward the center, isolating the defender on or outside the tackle's position to be read by the quarterback. A maximum split by the playside tackle further helps to isolate the defender. (See Diagram 3-16.)

The playside guard will normally block any noseman, especially if the center cannot handle him by himself. If the center can effectively single block the noseman, the playside guard will come off the LOS at a 45 degree angle and engage the linebacker.

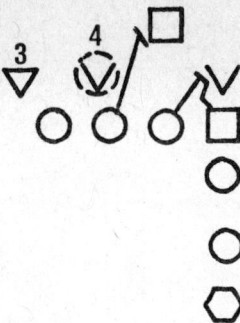

Diagram 3-16

The center steps playside to insure the playside guard/center gap and blocks any noseman or middle linebacker, or any backside linebacker.

The backside linemen seal toward the center, utilizing an inside release at a 45 degree angle. Their foremost objective is to cut off any immediate penetration and then to wall off any backside linebacker. (See Diagram 3-17.)

Diagram 3-17

"FRED" CALL

The "Fred" call is used in conjunction with most seven-man defensive fronts. It tells the playside tackle to reach release outside the defensive tackle at approximately a 45 degree angle, trying to influence the tackle to come outside with him. The playside guard and center come off at a 45 degree angle and are looking for a defensive stunt toward them. (See Diagram 3-18.)

If the defensive tackle influences outside, the tackle employs a reverse crab or shoulder block, swinging his hips upfield while establishing a solid blocking position between the defender and the fullback.

If the defensive tackle disregards the tackle's outside release and stays home to cancel the fullback, the tackle continues around him and picks up the linebacker. (See Diagram 3-19.)

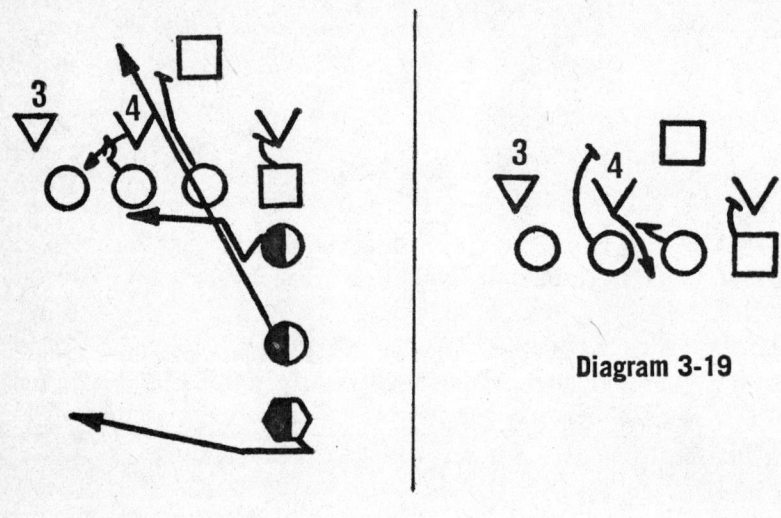

Diagram 3-18

Diagram 3-19

If the defensive tackle continually disregards the reach block by the playside tackle, complementary I-back plays will be used, especially the power off tackle and the toss sweep, to take advantage of his reactions.

We have seen a great deal of the 5-2 stunt shown in Diagram 3-20. The "Fred" call enables the linemen to effectively stop the defense's attempt at getting the extra defender to the outside that the normal veer/option blocking cannot handle. (See Diagram 3-21.)

The backside blocking scheme for "Fred" is the same as it is for "Chuck." (See Diagram 3-17.)

"WILLIE" CALL

The "Willie" call is similar to the "Fred" call. Versus a 5-2 defense, the playside guard steps out at a 45 degree angle, looking at the defensive tackle for a slant or stunt. The playside tackle steps with his inside foot toward the defensive tackle. If the slant or stunt occurs, the

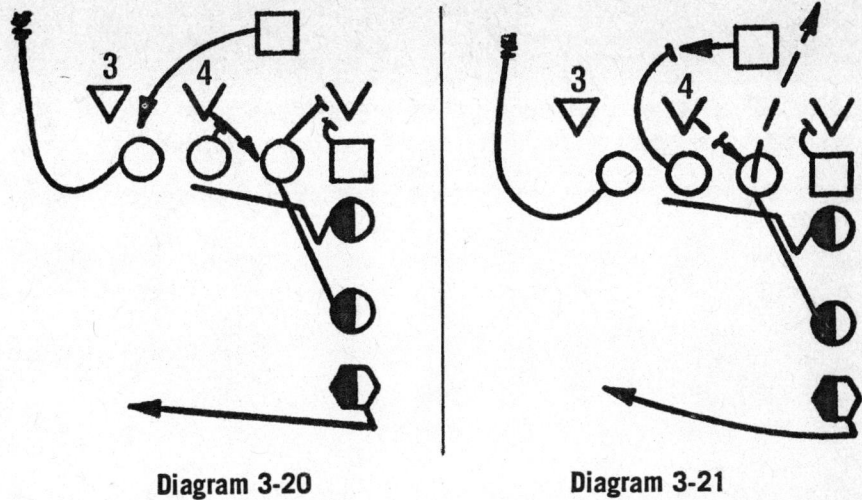

Diagram 3-20   Diagram 3-21

guard blocks out on the defensive tackle while the tackle makes contact and then passes off for the linebacker. (See Diagram 3-22.)

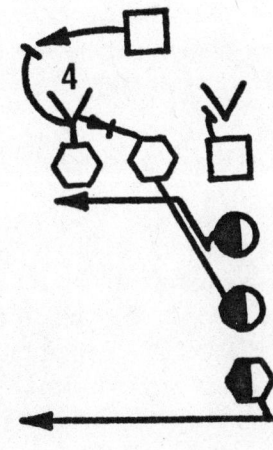

Diagram 3-22

In theory, the "Willie" call assures that we can get the ball to the fullback against defenses that are stunting inside to take away the give phase of the inside veer/option.

If the slant or stunt doesn't materialize, the tackle blocks the defensive tackle while the guard works upfield to cut off the linebacker.

The backside linemen continue to come off inside at a 45 degree angle, eliminating quick penetration first and then walling off the backside linebacker. (See Diagram 3-17.)

"TED" CALL

The "Ted" call is designed to supplement the "Fred" and "Willie" calls. If seven-man defensive fronts are getting the fourth defender to the outside that our base blocking calls cannot handle, a "Ted" call is made. With this call, the tight end or swingback (from a slot set) is assigned to block the first linebacker inside. (See Diagram 3-23.)

 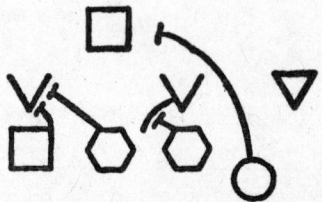

Diagram 3-23

The playside guard and tackle block their "Chuck" call while the backside linemen seal to the center.

"TOM" CALL

The "Tom" call is similar to the "Ted" call. The difference lies in the playside tackle pulling and becoming the lead blocker on the corner support. The tight end or swingback will still block the first linebacker inside while the playside guard and center block "Mike." The guard must come off at a 45 degree angle in order to collide with any hard inside rush by the number four defender. (See Diagram 3-24.)

"GEORGE" CALL

The "George" call tells the playside guard to pull and lead on the corner support while the tight end or swingback blocks the first linebacker inside. The center and playside tackle block "Mike." (See Diagram 3-25.)

Coaching the Veer/Option from the Swingback-Motion Offense

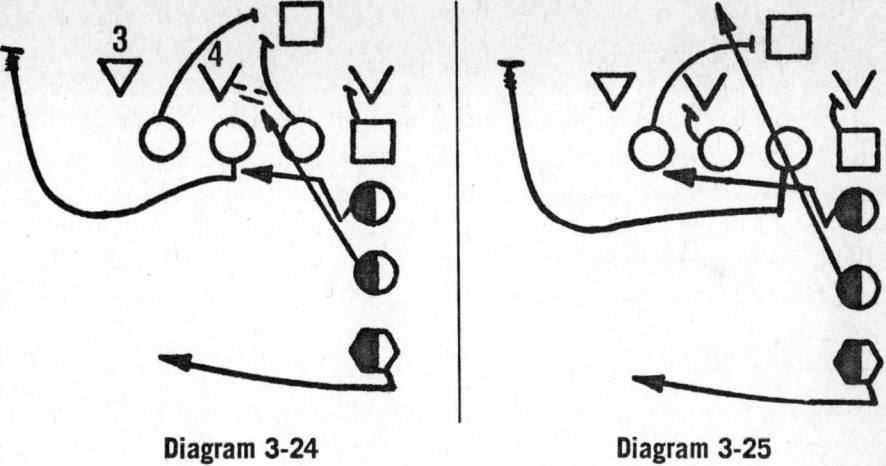

Diagram 3-24   Diagram 3-25

"George" is a very good call versus a 5-2 defense because the guard is aligned far enough to the inside so that, by the time he clears the tight end, he is clearly able to determine which defender to lead block. Any time the guard feels that the playside linebacker might blow through the guard/center gap, he automatically calls the "George" off and blocks the linebacker.

"MIKE" CALL

The final blocking call that is used with the inside veer/option is "Mike." The playside linemen block, "Out, over, linebacker," stepping out at a 45 degree angle while the backside linemen seal to the center before working upfield to wall off any backside linebacker pursuit.

Regardless of the blocking call made by the playside tackle, the quarterback goes through his normal veer/option read of the number four defender. If he is being isolated (Chuck) or influenced (Fred), or if he is being blocked (Mike), the quarterback reads his reaction and decides whether to give the ball to the fullback or to disconnect it.

RECEIVER BLOCKING TECHNIQUES FOR THE INSIDE VEER/OPTION

One of the more important factors in the success of the inside veer/option play in the Swingback-Motion Offense is the ability of the receivers to block. In essence it is, for the most part, not really a block but, rather, a shielding process in which the receiver positions himself between the ball and the defender and acts as a barrier that the defender must penetrate if he is going to make the tackle on the pitchman.

As a result of this technique, smaller players can be used at split end because finesse rather than strength is involved.

The blocking technique is termed stalking, and the techniques used will be discussed according to the position of the receiver with regard to the strength of the formation.

OUTSIDE RECEIVER

The split end, or swingback in a pro set, accelerates off the LOS with a slight outside release, forcing the secondary coverage to commit itself.

If the corner maintains his cushion and keeps backpedalling to protect his outside one-third (sky coverage from four-deep), the wideout continues sprinting downfield. Once the defender breaks down to support the run, the wideout breaks down and assumes a good football position, lowering his hips as he begins stalking the corner.

In the stalk block, the receiver patiently mirrors any move that the corner makes while establishing two leverage points. The first point keeps the defender in front of him. Second, the receiver works to keep the defender inside, playing "cat and mouse" with him, moving his base of support while remaining square to the LOS.

Every stalk block begins with the receiver working to establish these two leverage points. Then, as the defender chooses which course of action to take, the receiver adjusts his technique accordingly. However, regardless of the technique he uses, the receiver must demonstrate patience as his number one guideline when stalking. (See Diagram 3-26.)

The two leverage points afford the wideout the opportunity to execute the type of block that he is physically capable of making.

Once in position, the wideout continually tries to remain square while working his headgear to the outside armpit of the defender. As the defender reacts to the ball, the wideout establishes contact and works to keep in front of him, avoiding the clip or block below the knees. He is coached to leave his feet only as a last resort.

Coaching the Veer/Option from the Swingback-Motion Offense

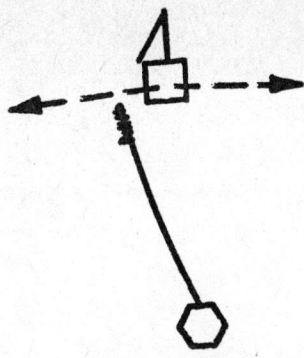

Diagram 3-26

Your tailbacks must be coached in, and actually practice, setting up the wideout's block. The wideout knows where the ball is by the defender's reaction. The tailback has to help make the stalk blocker's job easier.

The defender may choose to physically attempt to run through the receiver. In this situation, the wideout earns his keep. As the defender approaches, the wideout should deliver a blow with his inside forearm and shoulder and then recoil. As he recoils and gathers himself, he chops or roll blocks the defender. His head and shoulders are thrown across the defender's path in the direction that the defender is moving.

Third, the defender can support the pitch from the outside to the inside.

The wideout has two alternatives. First, he can widen with the defender, keeping square to the goal line while keeping the defender in front of him. Once the defender tries to come through the blocker to the ball, the wideout uses his hit, recoil and chop technique. (See Diagram 3-27.)

Second, the wideout can turn his butt to the ball and wall the defender off from the ball. He now establishes his two leverage points, with the defender's outside armpit being the one furthest upfield. (See Diagram 3-28.)

The last defensive reaction that the wideout works on is the one used when a defender attempts to beat him quickly to the inside.

In this situation, the wideout must establish a position whereby he can wall off the defender to the inside. The defender will come hard to

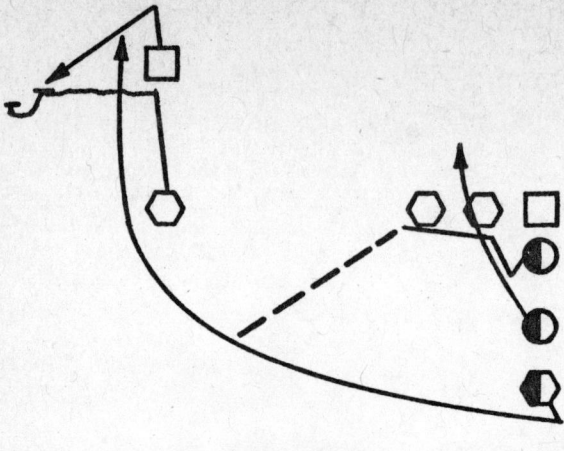

Diagram 3-27

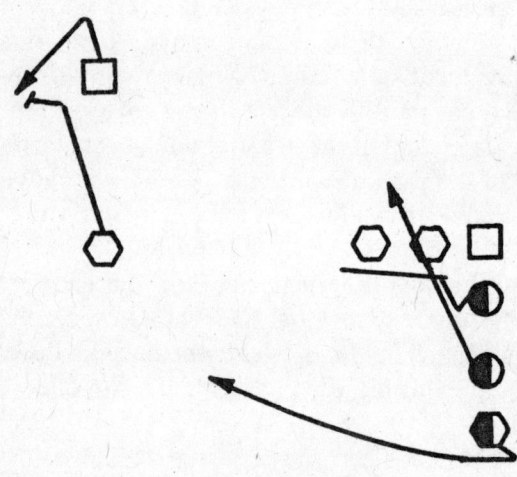

Diagram 3-28

the inside if he feels that he is quicker than the wideout or if the ball carrier runs inside. The wideout must quickly recognize the situation and be prepared to take the proper angle that will enable him to keep the defender inside without clipping him. The wideout must give ground back toward the line of scrimmage in order to remain in front of the defender.

If the secondary coverage is a corner roll (cloud support), the wideout collides with the corner to impede his progress upfield. This enables the inside receiver to achieve the proper position. After the collision, the wideout releases inside, continuing upfield to stalk the safety who is now responsible for the outside one-third. (See Diagram 3-29.)

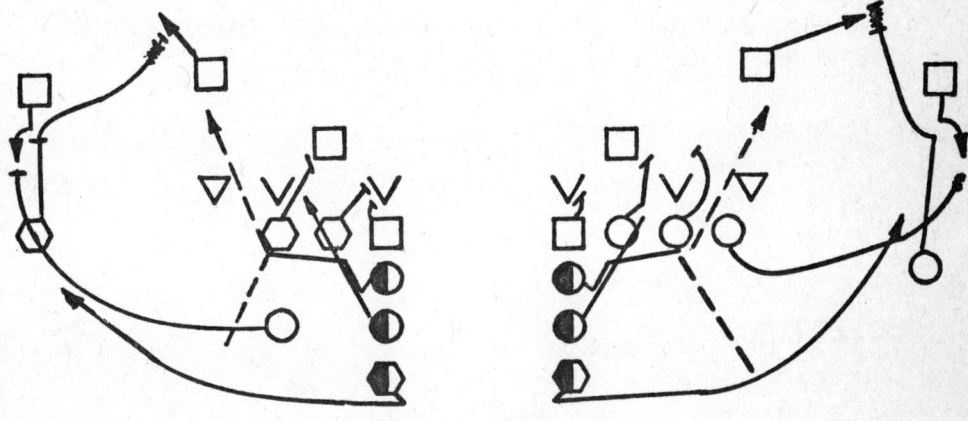

Diagram 3-29

By releasing inside off the collision with the corner the wideout is able to achieve his two leverage points while protecting the inside seam.

INSIDE RECEIVER TECHNIQUES

The inside receiver (blocker) may be the swingback, tight end, or tailback. It is their responsibility to block the defender who is assigned to support the pitch (number two defender or whoever becomes number two).

On the snap of the ball, they key the playside safety to determine the type of secondary rotation (sky or cloud). The tight end, or swingback in a slot or over set, takes an outside release and drops off the LOS approximately two or three yards in order to establish the proper ball carrier/lead blocker relationship. This arc release also affords the blocker the time needed to determine the secondary support scheme while enabling him to get his shoulders square to the LOS.

If the swingback is in the full I, open, or power set, he utilizes a three to four yard lateral channel course to establish his lead blocker/ball carrier relationship. This course must not be too wide, (which would force the play toward the sideline) and, yet, it cannot be too short (which would create an improper blocking angle). The inside blocker must be heading straight upfield when he makes his block. (See Diagram 3-30.)

Once the defensive support scheme develops, the inside receiver drives downhill for the outside knee of the number two defender. He should not overextend and leave his feet until he has made contact with the defender. (See Diagram 3-31.)

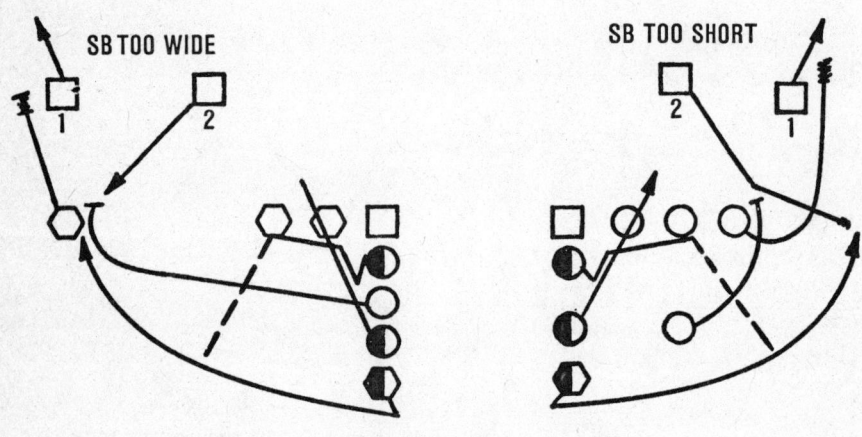

Diagram 3-30

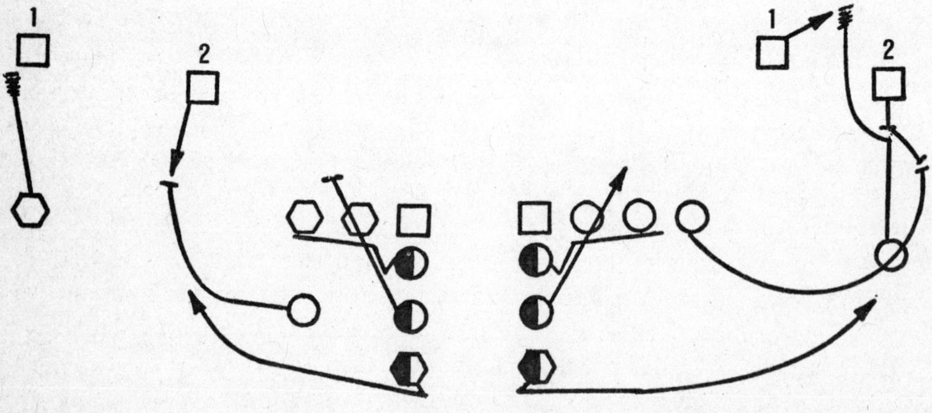

Diagram 3-31

Versus certain secondary schemes, the inside blocker will release, get his shoulders square to the LOS and simply stalk the corner support in the same manner he would if he were outside. Both techniques depend on the physical capabilities of the blocker and the type of corner support we're getting.

The major coaching point for the inside blocker, is to work his shoulders square upfield. This enables him to recognize the support and to attack the defender in whatever direction he approaches. Although we don't encourage the blocker to throw an uncontrolled roll block, we do expect him, once he squares his shoulders, to get as close to the defender as possible if he is going to cut him.

If the pitchman is in the proper ball carrier/lead blocker relationship, the fallen defender should not be able to get up and make the tackle. By emphasizing a specific body part to be eliminated (outside knee), we have found our inside blockers taking the time to break down and give the ball carrier a controlled, effective block.

If, during safety support (sky rotation), the safety supports too quickly for our inside blocker to reach his proper squared up blocking position, a "change-it" call between the inside and outside receiver is used. (See Diagram 3-32.)

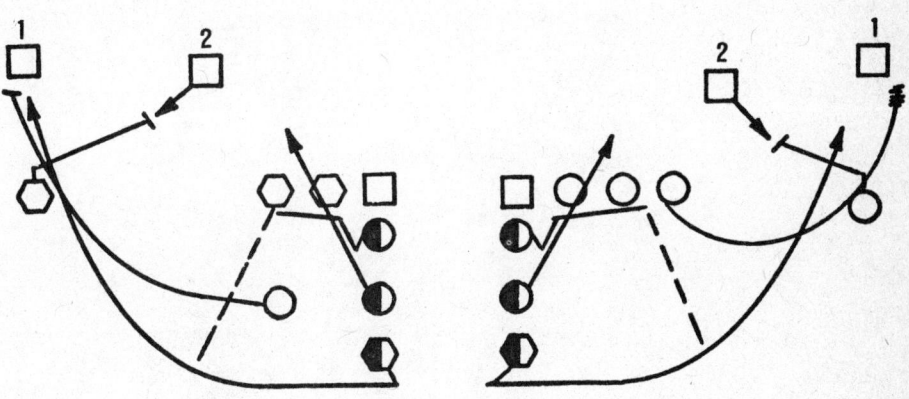

Diagram 3-32

Change-it makes the outside receiver the lead blocker while the inside blocker becomes the stalk blocker. The outside receiver uses a crack/stalk technique to block the safety. He breaks down and establishes a legal blocking position on the defender. As the defender approaches, he drives his headgear across the defender's chest and shoulder blocks him to the inside. If there is the slighest clipping possibility, the blocker shuffles quickly to the inside, trying to get squared up in front of the defender.

Change-it can be very effective, especially out of a pro set with defenses playing quick corner support with their strong safety.

Another alternative, used to cope with quick safety support, is to throw the quick post or goal pattern to the outside receiver or the seam route to the inside receiver. A more detailed discussion of the veer/option play action passes will be presented in Chapter 8.

If your tight end is having difficulty blocking the support man, the veer/option should be run with the swingback occupying a backfield position. His position affords more time and distance to adequately recognize the quick support and to achieve a better blocking position on him. (See Diagram 3-33.)

Diagram 3-33

Three-deep corner rotation is handled as corner or cloud support. The outside receivers are coached to take maximum splits to discourage this type of rotation and/or to spread the three-deep secondary.

OFFSIDE RECEIVER(S) IN THE VEER/OPTION PLAY

The key to successfully cutting back against the pursuit of an aggressive defense lies in the determination of the offside receivers to get downfield and attack the safety. Little technique is involved. Desire on the part of the receiver to hustle downfield and throw the "TD" block is the only requisite.

The offside receiver must first reduce his split without making it too obvious. Then he flattens his course out so that he can get up inside of the defender and block him without clipping him. If he releases downfield, he will be chasing nothing but the back of the defender's jersey, leading in most cases to a potential clipping situation.

If two receivers are employed away from the play, the one closest to the safety is responsible for him while the remaining receiver drives up inside the corner and walls him off from the play. (See Diagram 3-34.)

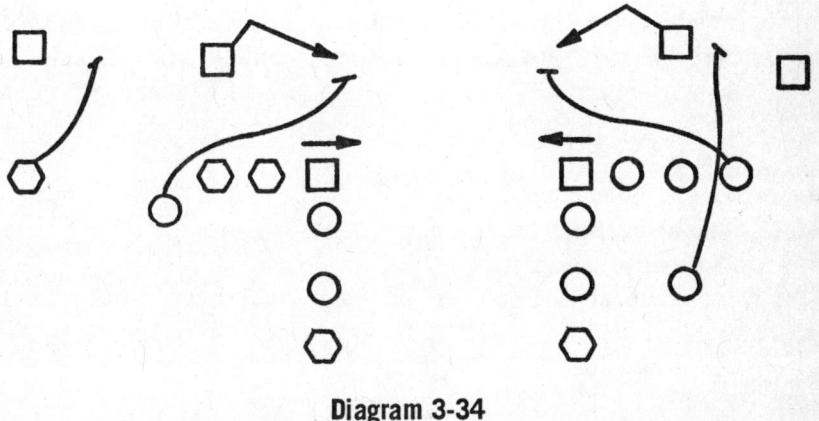

Diagram 3-34

TAILBACK/SWINGBACK TECHNIQUES AS PITCHMEN

In the Swingback-Motion Offense, the tailback and swingback can both be used as the pitchman in the veer/option play. The base 37/38 Veer employs the tailback as the pitchman, while adding the letter "Z" (37/38 Veer Z) employs the swingback in the same role.

From the tailback's initial alignment, we found that, when he simply sprinted to the outside on the snap of the ball, he either got too far ahead of the quarterback (and hence destroyed the proper pitch relationship), or he would slow down and receive the pitch while moving at half speed.

Therefore, the tailback uses a quick counterstep away from the play, creating the proper pitch relationship while the quarterback and fullback mesh. He then sprints playside, paralleling the path of the quarterback, working to get three to four yards in front of the quarterback and approximately five yards away from him. This is called the proper leverage or pitch relationship.

It is critical to the success of the play that this pitch relationship is maintained. If the tailback gets too far in front of or too far away from the quarterback, a bad pitch will result. If the tailback decreases either dimension of the optimal pitch relationship, the quarterback's pitch in most cases becomes too difficult to handle. The tailback, therefore, is coached to turn upfield only when the quarterback does.

The tailback is solely responsible for establishing the pitch relationship. We want the ball pitched out, and not back. He must strive for consistency on every play. This consistency creates confidence between the quarterback and tailback. As a result, the ball will be pitched more often when it should be. Too often, quarterbacks (especially young ones) lose faith in the pitch phase of the play and keep the ball rather than risk the pitch.

Once the quarterback turns upfield, the tailback sprints upfield, establishing a new pitch relationship four to five yards from the quarterback and slightly behind him.

The swingback becomes the pitchman on 37/38 Veer Z when he lines up in the open or slot sets to the quickside or in the power or over sets to the strongside. (See Diagram 3-35.)

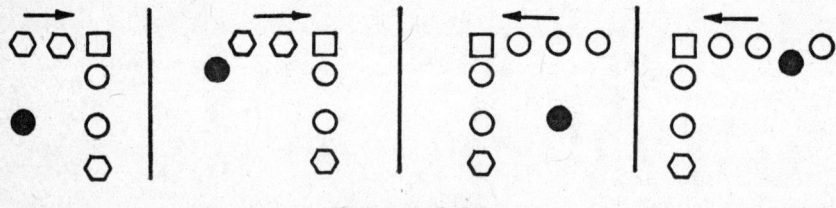

Diagram 3-35

He does not use a counterstep because of his initial relationship with the quarterback. He must sprint playside if he is to achieve the proper pitch relationship. Short peel motion may be used if he is having difficulty in reaching the desired position. This motion is especially beneficial when the play is run to the quickside with the potential hard number three read on the quarterback.

The tailback in the Veer Z countersteps to present the same key to the defense as on the veer/option and also to establish a better ball carrier/lead blocker relationship. He then runs a lateral channel course and blocks the defender supporting the pitch.

Regardless of which back is being used as the pitchman, the mesh period for the inside veer/option should be conducted with the receivers as soon as possible. This allows the pitchman to work on setting up the receivers' blocks while affording the latter the opportunity to stalk and lead block against reacting defenders.

OUTSIDE VEER/OPTION

In an attempt to force changes in defensive responsibilities of the basic inside veer/option play, the Swingback-Motion Offense employs the outside veer/option. It is designed to be run outside of a double-team block and is directed one hole wider than the inside play (See Diagram 3-36.) Because of the need for a double-team at the point of attack, we will only run the play versus opponents who use a 5-2 or 4-3 defense or a defense that positions a defender on or outside the playside tackle (4 or 5 technique).

The base outside veer plays are 35/36 Veer. In most instances, a slot set must be used to effectively run 35 Veer. The open set is a possibility if your quick tackle can stop the defensive tackle until the swingback arrives, or if there is a predicted stunt to the inside by the defensive tackle. (See Diagram 3-37.)

To the strongside, 36 Veer can be run from any set in which the swingback is aligned to the strongside, from the full I, or any time the swingback is sent in motion toward the strongside.

As the outside veer/option is practiced, the quarterback realizes that the number four defender, who normally takes the fullback, is being blocked. If the number three defender fails to recognize the difference and supports on the quarterback or pitch, the fullback must get the ball. The play, therefore, attempts to force the number three defender to become number four.

If the number three defender closes to cancel the fullback, the quarterback disconnects and turns upfield with the ball, reacting to the

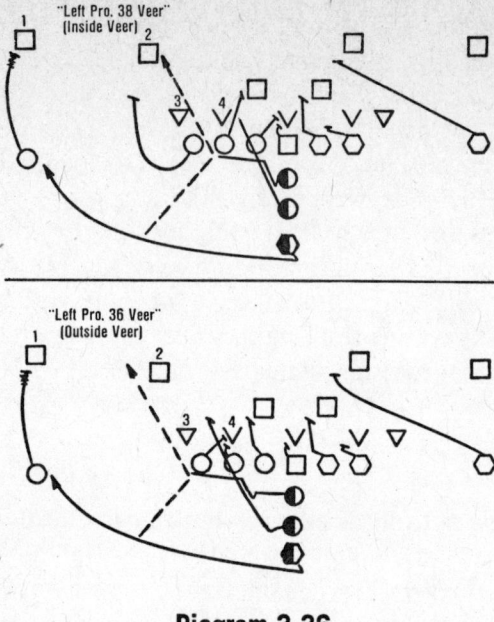

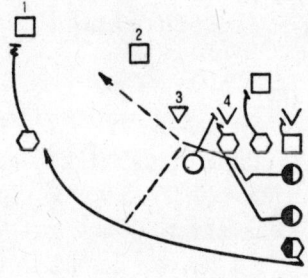

Diagram 3-36

Diagram 3-37

number two defender. In approximately 97 percent of all outside veer plays, either the fullback or quarterback ends up with the ball. The pitch is very seldom executed, except on a delayed, downfield basis.

As the quarterback continues outside, the number one and two defenders are forced to support a phase of the veer that they normally do not consider. (See Diagram 3-38.)

If the defense only partially adjusts to the outside veer, the quarterback reads his way out and exploits the phase left unsupported.

Coaching the Veer/Option from the Swingback-Motion Offense 93

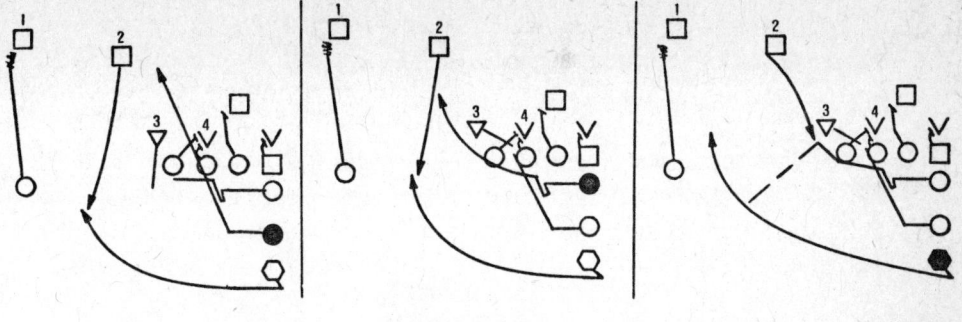

Diagram 3-38

The same logical, well-organized coaching progression that is the core of executing the successful inside veer/option must also be used when introducing and practicing the outside veer. The mechanics are repeated until the flaws are eliminated. Then the reads are introduced, starting with the simplest and advancing to the most complex.

MECHANICS OF THE OUTSIDE VEER QUARTERBACK

On the snap, the quarterback places the ball in his "third hand" (in front of his stomach), and opens up playside with a short, six-inch controlled step parallel to the LOS. His first step is followed by a crossover step which he pushes off of, stepping out and slightly back toward the mesh point with his third step. (See Diagram 3-39.)

As he steps out and back toward the mesh point, the quarterback extends the ball back toward the fullback with his arms straight. Once the mesh is begun, the quarterback uses his normal inside veer/option mechanics, riding the fullback and either giving the ball off or disconnecting.

The fourth step (adjustment step) is actually a swinging, pendulum-like step as the quarterback keeps the ball in front of the fullback until his decision is made.

In order to effectively execute either the outside or inside veer, your quarterback must play with his knees flexed. A straight-legged quarterback severely limits his ability to accelerate. Explosive acceleration can come only from a bent-knee football position.

Upon reading "give," he pulls the hand between the ball and the fullback's stomach, hands the ball off, and then brings his hands together in front of his stomach and accelerates down the line.

Upon reading "disconnect," the quarterback withdraws the ball to his stomach and accelerates past the number three defender and turns upfield. His acceleration here is vital in order to avoid the number three defender playing off the fullback's block.

The number two defender is the quarterback's next read. If he takes the quarterback, the ball is pitched. If number two supports the pitch, the keep and potential delay pitch situation is present. (See Diagram 3-40.)

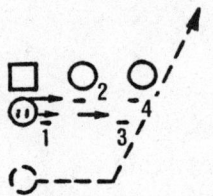

Diagram 3-39

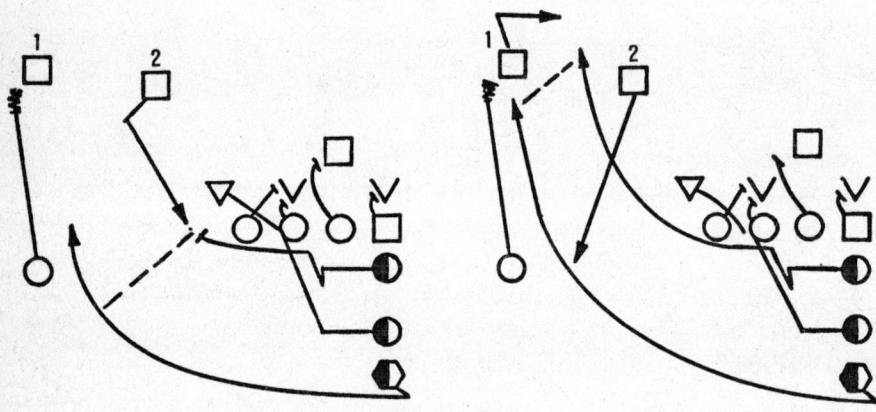

Diagram 3-40

FULLBACK

On the snap, the fullback takes a short six to eight-inch lateral step to the playside so that he can drive off of it as squarely toward the hole as possible. He must also deepen his initial alignment slightly. This will enable him to hit the hole with his shoulders, as close to square to the LOS as is feasible, from his alignment directly behind the quarterback.

He then drives off this lateral step, and aims his headgear for the outside hip of the playside tackle, who has taken a minimum split to help achieve a better mesh point.

As with the inside veer, the mesh responsibility lies with the fullback. As he drives for his landmark, the fullback raises his inside elbow and presents a pocket for the ball, giving it a soft squeeze as he continues on his course.

It is imperative that your fullback remain as close as possible to the double-team, forcing the number three defender to make a distinct inside move if he is going to cancel the fullback.

Once the quarterback disconnects, the fullback blocks the number three defender, eliminating him from getting outside to support the keep or pitch. He drives his head and shoulders across the outside knee of the defender while getting his butt heading straight upfield. If he begins to lose the block, your fullback must scramble or crab block the defender, tying up his legs to immobilize him.

TAILBACK

The tailback's mechanics are the same as for the inside veer. He must understand that, as soon as the quarterback disconnects, he will be turning upfield. The tailback must be ready to turn up with him and establish a delay pitch relationship.

RECEIVERS

The outside receiver assumes the same role that he plays in the inside veer. He stalks the defender responsible for the outside one-third.

The tight end (36 Veer) and the swingback (35 Veer) block the playside tackle's call which is "Dave." (See Diagram 3-41.)

If the defensive tackle to be doubled slants to the inside, the tight end or swingback deepens straight upfield and looks for the linebacker

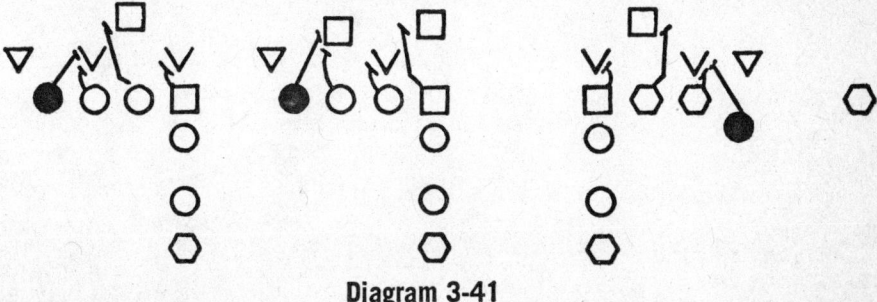

Diagram 3-41

or defender stunting to the outside. This blocking technique is called "scraping." (See Diagram 3-42.)

Diagram 3-42

When the swingback is not being used as a blocker at the point of attack, or as an outside receiver, he follows the same rules that he employs as a lead blocker on the inside veer. (See Diagram 3-43.) He will always, however, pass up the defender supporting the pitch, and will drive upfield on the defender responsible for the outside one-third.

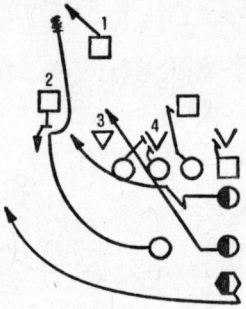

Diagram 3-43

The defender supporting the pitch, theoretically, cannot be right. If he takes the quarterback, the pitch is open. If he supports the pitch, the keep is open. (See Diagram 3-44.)

QUARTERBACK READS FOR THE OUTSIDE VEER

Even though the mesh phase in the outside veer begins one hole wider, the quarterback begins his active read of the number three

Coaching the Veer/Option from the Swingback-Motion Offense 97

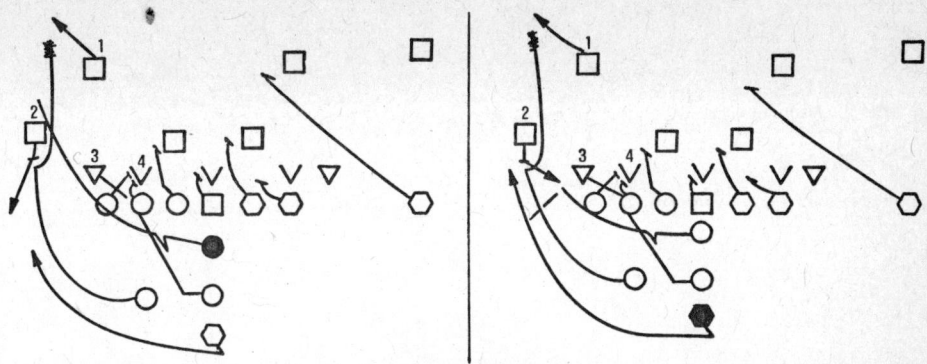

Diagram 3-44

defender as soon as he receives the snap. (His passive or pre-snap read can indicate possible perimeter change-ups due to alignment variances.)

He begins with the plan of giving the ball to the fullback. Then, as the mesh phase begins, he selects his plan based on the actions of the number three defender.

His read of the number three defender is exactly like his read of the number four defender in the inside veer. If he does not make a definite move inside to cancel the fullback, the quarterback gives the ball to the fullback.

The quarterback is coached to look for any part of the numbers on the front of the defender's jersey. If he sees any part of the numbers, the ball should go to the fullback.

There is still the chance for a positive football play if the quarterback misreads number three and gives the ball off. The play becomes your fullback against their number three defender. If the outside veer is to be misread, this read is the least costly. (See Diagram 3-45.)

If the quarterback disconnects, even though the number three defender has not committed himself to the fullback, the play has very little chance for success. The defense has created an overlap to the outside that will theoretically cancel both the keep and pitch phases of the outside veer.

Defensive change-ups between the perimeter and secondary defenders do not present the same problem for the outside veer as they do for the inside veer. These change-ups are a basic capability of the seven-man fronts and are aimed at allowing the secondary defender, usually the safety, the time and distance necessary to determine which back has the ball. (See Diagram 3-46.)

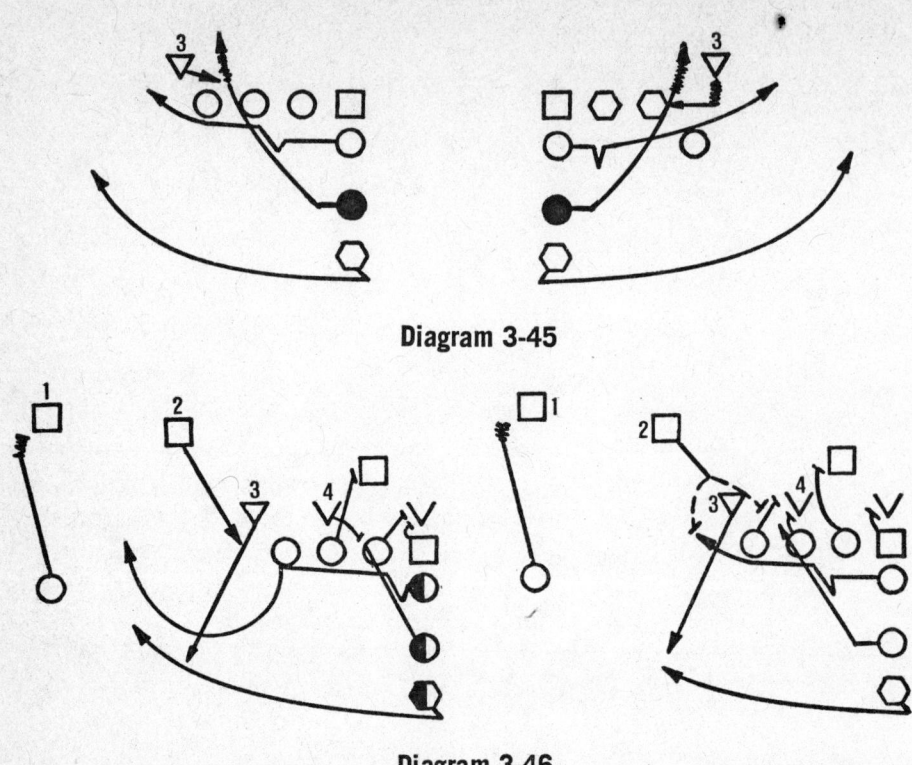

Diagram 3-45

Diagram 3-46

The quarterback is given a read to give the ball because the original number three defender is moving upfield to take the pitchman. It has been our experience that the smallest defenders on most high school teams man the safety position(s). The quarterback goes through with his original plan, leaving the ball with the fullback to test the mettle of the eager safety. Before too long, the fullback should begin to wear down the safety and chase the defense back into a more conventional scheme for defending the play.

Another consideration for the defense is the similarity in the blocking schemes of the outside veer and power off-tackle plays. As the power play becomes successful, and the number three defender, who has been eliminated through the fullback's block, begins to stay at home, the pitch or keep phase of the outside veer becomes exploitable. (See Diagram 3-47.)

The key to the outside veer is for the quarterback, once he disconnects, to get upfield into the Hero Lane, running away from the pursuit

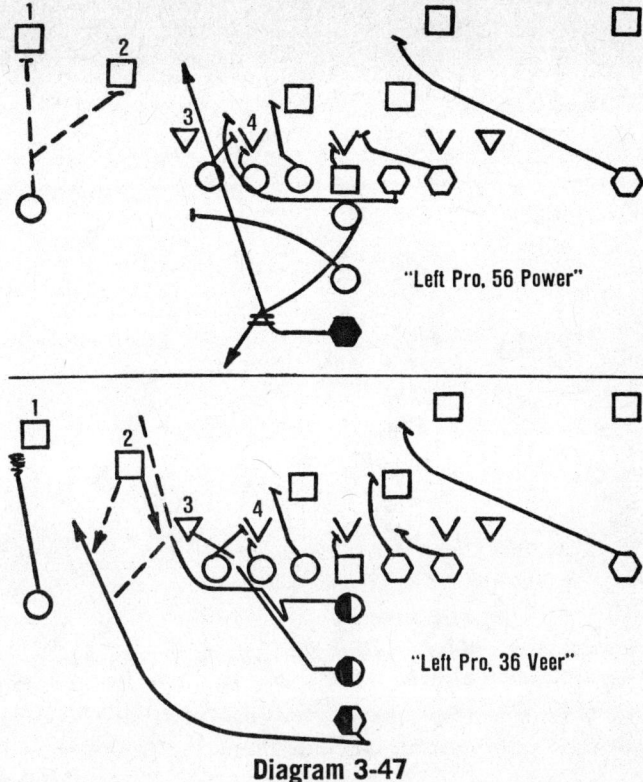

while facing the remaining defenders who can play him. (See Diagram 3-48.)

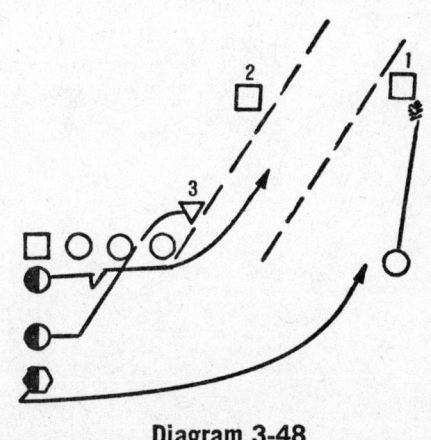

Diagram 3-48

4

**RUNNING THE VEER VERSUS
EIGHT-MAN FRONTS WITH THE
SWINGBACK-MOTION OFFENSE**

As the Wishbone and Houston Veer Offenses emerged as dominant forces in college and high school football, coaches realized the need for a defensive scheme that could successfully cope with the four phases (give, keep, pitch and pass) that both offenses presented.

As a result, the Split 6 Defense was revised and a new system, the Split 4 or 40 Defense, has become the most common and widely used eight-man front aimed at stopping the Wishbone and Veer offenses. Last year, on our 11 game schedule, seven teams employed the Split 4 Defense.

Penn State, Auburn and Texas are three major college powers that have enjoyed success with the flexible Split 4 front. Although many schools are using the 50 Defense or Oklahoma front, because of its ability to provide perimeter change-ups from the secondary from a 4-deep scheme of pass defense, the Split 4 still presents problems for veer/option teams that must be considered.

The Split 4 calls for four linebackers with only two down linemen and two ends in front of a three-deep secondary. (See Diagram 4-1.)

As an eight-man front, the Split 4 has three defenders outside the offensive tackle to both sides of the center. Therefore, as long as the safety remains in the middle of the offensive formation, it is a balanced

Running the Veer versus Eight-Man Fronts

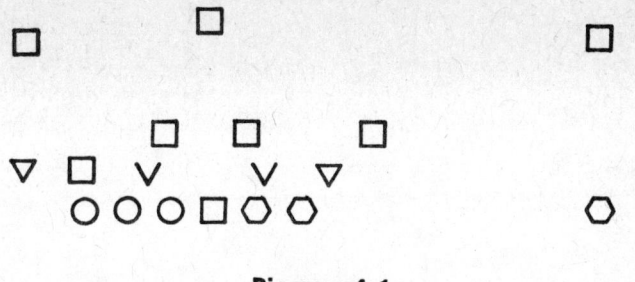

Diagram 4-1

defense capable of supporting the three running phases of the veer/option with defenders on or near the line of scrimmage.

Two other eight-man fronts that have achieved national recognition, through their use at Maryland and Georgia, are the wide-tackle or Maryland 6 Defense, and the "Junkyard" Defense, or combination wide-tackle/Split 4 defenses that the Bulldogs of Georgia employ. Considering the popularity of the Split 4 Defense, we will simply diagram and number these last two defenses and concern ourselves primarily with the Split 4 Defense in this chapter. (See Diagram 4-2.)

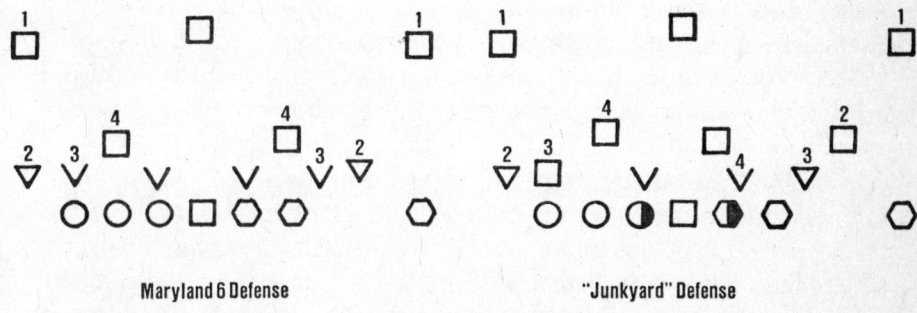

Maryland 6 Defense   "Junkyard" Defense

Diagram 4-2

An eight-man front is completely different from a defense that simply has eight defenders on or near the LOS. The major difference is that eight-man fronts normally absorb the give phase of the veer/option, with a defender that is aligned inside of the offensive tackle, leaving the three outside defenders to cancel the remaining three phases of the play (keep, pitch and pass).

In numbering the Split 4 defenders, we find number 4 aligned either in the guard/tackle gap or on the outside shoulder of the offensive guard (three technique). This position necessitates combination blocking if we are to wall off all of the defenders inside of our offensive tackle. (See Diagram 4-3.)

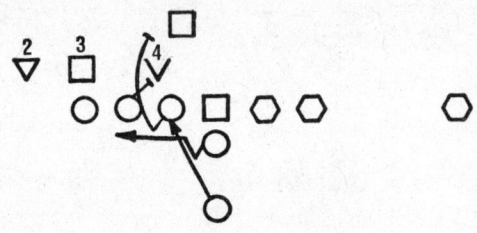

Diagram 4-3

But combination blocking against larger defensive linemen is not the strongest type of blocking scheme that we can have at the point of attack. We much prefer to double-team the defensive tackle. Therefore, we use this blocking pattern and predetermine that our fullback is not going to get the ball.

Because of the difficulties in reading a number 4 defender who is inside of our offensive tackle, and with blocking problems created by the defensive tackles in their three technique alignment, the Swingback-Motion Offense uses predetermined veer/option plays along with its outside reads of the veer, versus most eight-man fronts, and especially against the Split 4 Defense.

We will, however, return to reading the inside give if our opponent removes one of its three outside defenders to the inside to absorb the give. We feel that, unless the defense compensates by taking an inside defender (normally the linebacker), and stunts him to the outside, this is a compromising stunt because the defense has given up its inherent eight-man front capability of having three defenders outside of the offensive tackle. (See Diagram 4-4.)

The first aspect of the play to be predetermined is the keep. We do this through load blocking. Last year we loaded the veer 26 times and averaged 6.1 yards versus our Split 4 opponents.

In our load blocking scheme, the swingback will attack the number three defender, who normally has quarterback responsibility. If the perimeter defenders stunt or cross charge, the swingback reads the change-up and blocks the new number three defender.

Running the Veer versus Eight-Man Fronts 103

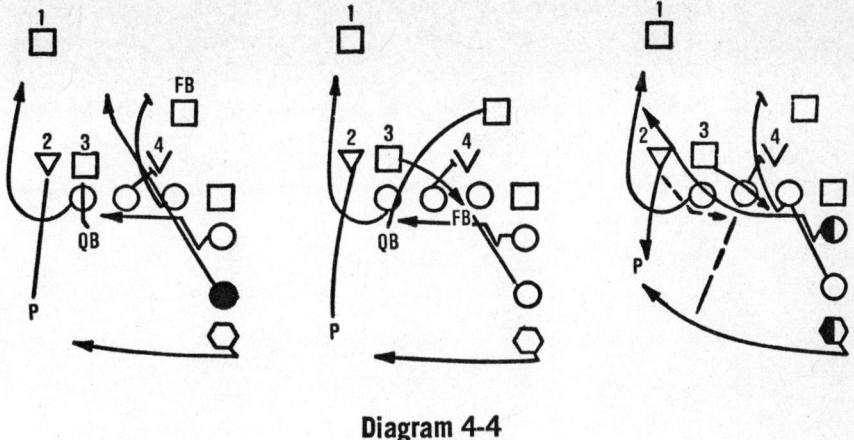

Diagram 4-4

The reasons we do not send our fullback on the number three defender and the swingback on the number two defender are twofold. First, we want to simulate, as much as possible, the inside veer so that the defenders aligned inside of our offensive tackle will remain there until they can be blocked. And second, we want to use our fullback to block the inside linebacker and help wall off the inside defenders. (See Diagram 4-5.)

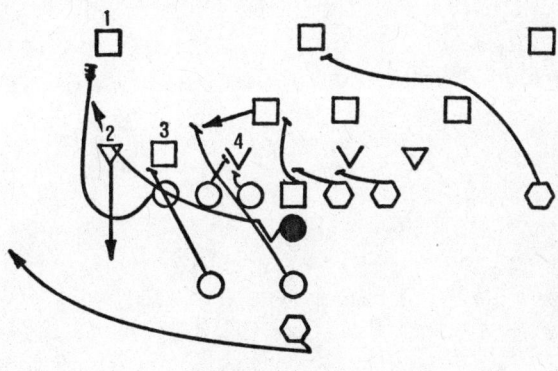

Diagram 4-5

It is important that your quarterback completely understands what is taking place on the loaded veer. He is initially predetermined to carry the ball. There is no play if he pitches the ball to the tailback, because there is no one blocking the number two defender, who we assume will support the pitch. Even if the swingback does not successfully block the number three defender, there is no pitch on the loaded veer as long as the number two defender supports the pitch.

However, if, as your quarterback is accelerating toward the Hero Lane, the number two defender aborts his pitch responsibility and decides to help out on the quarterback, the latter should execute the pitch. This is the only time he is coached to pitch the ball on the loaded veer. (See Diagram 4-6.)

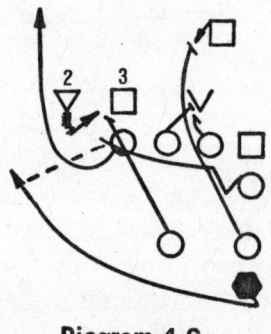

Diagram 4-6

Executing the loaded veer in this manner, although predetermining in essence only that the fullback is not going to receive the ball, allows the quarterback to determine which option (keep or pitch) has the opportunity to gain the most yardage. This decision is arrived at from the defensive reactions of the number two defender.

QUARTERBACK MECHANICS

On the loaded veer, the quarterback abbreviates or "feathers" the mesh with the fullback. We like the ball in front of the fullback to indicate veer action to the defense and, yet, we realize the need for the quarterback to get quickly outside on his predetermined course. Therefore, a "feathering" or quick mesh technique is used. The quarterback, who is not reading the give phase, merely shows the ball to his fullback while using his read or adjustment step to begin his acceleration down the line toward the swingback's load block on the number three defender.

Running the Veer versus Eight-Man Fronts

While feathering the mesh, the quarterback is keying the swingback's block. He is continually working parallel with, or slightly into the LOS so that he can get quickly upfield off of the swingback's block. (See Diagram 4-7.)

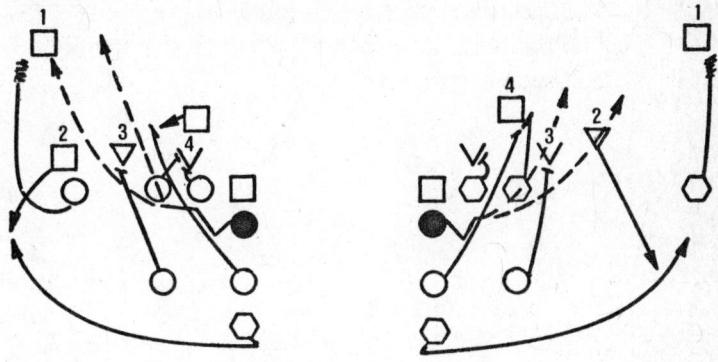

Diagram 4-7

In essence then, the quarterback's first decision as to what path to take to the Hero Lane is predicated upon the block of his swingback. If the swingback has achieved an inside/out or kickout position on number three, the quarterback comes up inside of the block. If he establishes an outside/in or log position on the defender, the quarterback goes around the block.

If the number three defender crashes hard to the inside and gains penetration, the quarterback may have to deepen his course to get around the collision point of the swingback and his block. (See Diagram 4-8.)

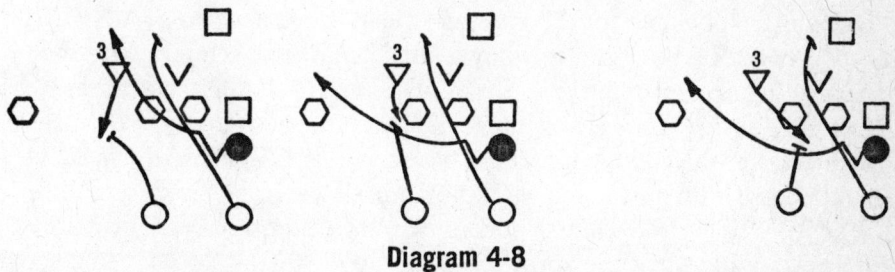

Diagram 4-8

The quarterback should arrive at the loaded area as quickly as possible so that the number three defender, who is normally somewhat bigger and stronger than our swingback, doesn't have time to play off the swingback's block. Once past the blocking area, the quarterback sprints for the Hero Lane while picking up his next key, the number two defender.

If the number two defender continues to support the pitch, the predetermined quarterback keep is executed. If, however, the number two defender recognizes the loaded play and takes the quarterback, the pitch is made. (See Diagram 4-9.)

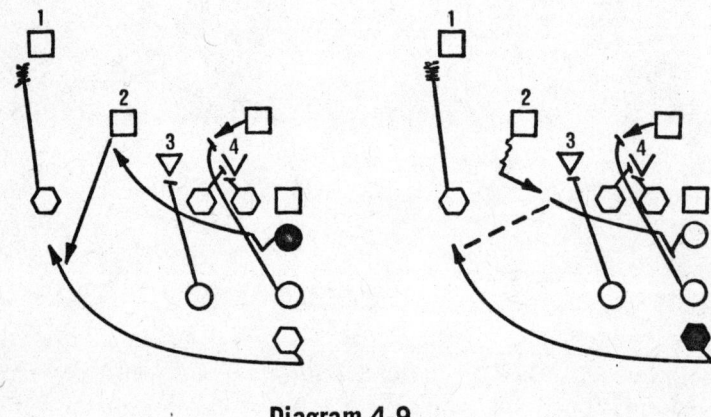

Diagram 4-9

FULLBACK MECHANICS

The fullback plays an important role in the success of the loaded veer play. Because it is predetermined versus eight-man fronts that he will not receive the ball, his block on the inside linebacker, or whoever becomes responsible for the give, is crucial to the success of the play.

Therefore, he begins the play realizing that there is no way in which he is going to receive the ball. His mesh point and landmark are the same as for the inside veer. He reads the defender that he is going to block as he drives for the outside hip of the playside guard. Because the mesh is abbreviated with the loaded veer, the fullback can leave his mesh course at anytime to block his key. Versus the Split 4 Defense, he will primarily go outside the double-team. (See Diagram 4-10.)

Since the center is stepping playside and insuring the playside gap versus a stunt, the fullback seldom blocks inside the guard/tackle double-team unless, of course, the mesh point is being seriously threatened. The design of the play is for the quarterback to get outside.

Therefore, by going outside the double-team block, the fullback is in a better position to wall off the inside linebacker.

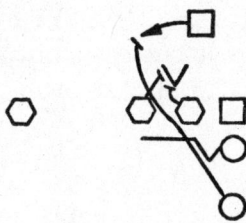

Diagram 4-10

The fullback's blocking technique depends upon the inside linebacker's reaction to the mesh. If he scrapes outside the double-team, the fullback uses his blast block technique, driving his inside shoulder into the outside number of the linebacker, establishing head position to the outside.

If the linebacker flies outside and disregards the mesh fake, our fullback is coached to try to cut him off with his blast or shoulder block technique. Many times, if the fullback is unable to establish outside position on a flying linebacker, he is able to use an outside shoulder block, establish head position to the inside, and drive the linebacker past the quarterback. The latter must be alert and cut back inside the block, then veer back outside toward the Hero Lane and away from the inside pursuit. (See Diagram 4-11.)

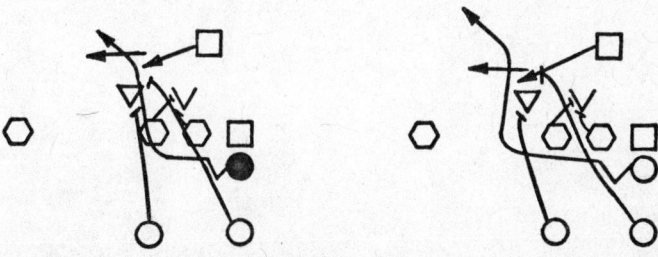

Diagram 4-11

If the linebacker and number three defender exchange responsibilities, the fullback drives his inside shoulder through the outside number of the pinching defender and log blocks him to the inside. It is imperative that the fullback attempt to block the defender up around the numbers. A low block or cut block allows the good defender to come over the top of the block and grab the quarterback. (See Diagram 4-12.) (See Chapter 6 for a detailed discussion of the fullback's blocking techniques.)

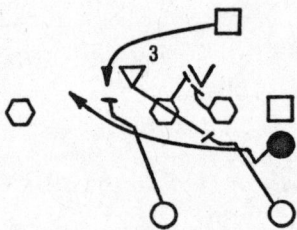

Diagram 4-12

Dave blocking, or a guard/tackle double-team at the point of attack, enables the Swingback-Motion Offense to effectively wall off the number four defender while allowing the fullback, who is our best blocking back, the time and distance needed to effectively recognize the defensive pattern and block the defender responsible for the give. Combination blocking, or a Criss call, can be employed, although we prefer to run behind the stronger double team concept. (See Diagram 4-13.)

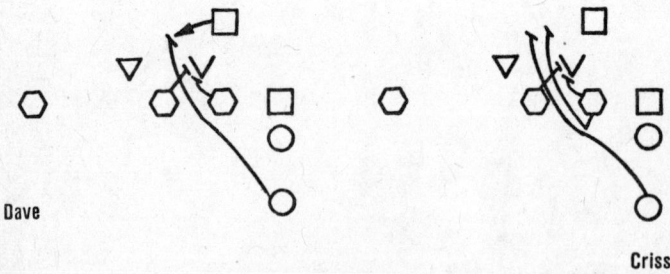

Diagram 4-13

Running the Veer versus Eight-Man Fronts   109

SWINGBACK MECHANICS

The most functional positions that the swingback can assume to load the veer are the open and power sets along with the full I position. The veer can be loaded with the swingback in a slot or over set, although these sets do not allow the swingback the optimal time or distance to recognize change-ups and make the necessary adjustments.

To help the swingback and quarterback to recognize the number three defender, while also helping to eliminate the cross charge or perimeter stunt to the tight end side, the tight end will flex his alignment to three to three and one-half yards. This flex forces the number two defender to widen with the tight end while the number three defender must align himself inside the flex. (See Diagram 4-14.)

Diagram 4-14

The most difficult type of defender for the swingback to load block is the one who pinches on a collision course for the quarterback. To effectively limit his penetration, while at the same time blocking him, we have the swingback take his initial step with his outside foot directly at the outside hip of the number three defender.

If he reads a pinch charge, the swingback drives his outside shoulder into the defender, establishing head position in front of him. He then drives him into the line using his hips and a reverse crab block if he begins to lose the defender.

Versus a slow-playing defender, the swingback continues on a course for the outside hip of the defender, letting the quarterback make the proper decision to go inside or outside of the block. If the defender widens, the swingback establishes an inside/out position and drives the defender out the line with a near shoulder block. His head position is upfield.

If the slow-playing defender commits inside, the swingback drives for his outside hip and delivers a block with his inside shoulder into the defender's outside number, establishing an outside head position.

With both blocks, we want the swingback to force the number three defender to come through his head or to run around the swingback's block. In either situation, the quarterback accelerating down the line will be past the defender.

The veer/option is difficult to load from the slot and over sets because of the proximity of the swingback to the number three defender. Defensive change-ups create problems because the swingback does not have sufficient reaction time in which to recognize the stunt and execute the appropriate block. However, the over set discourages any stunt in which the number three defender might come from the outside (dotted lines). (See Diagram 4-15.)

Diagram 4-15

From the slot/over sets, the swingback steps out at a 45 degree angle with his outside foot while keying the belt buckle of the number three defender. This first step is approximately six to eight-inches and is a control or read step. If no stunt appears, he continues reach blocking with his inside shoulder into the outside number of the defender. If the number three defender pinches, the swingback pushes off his outside foot, pivots to the inside and delivers a blow with his outside shoulder. He gains head position in front of the defender and drives him down the line. (See Diagram 4-16.)

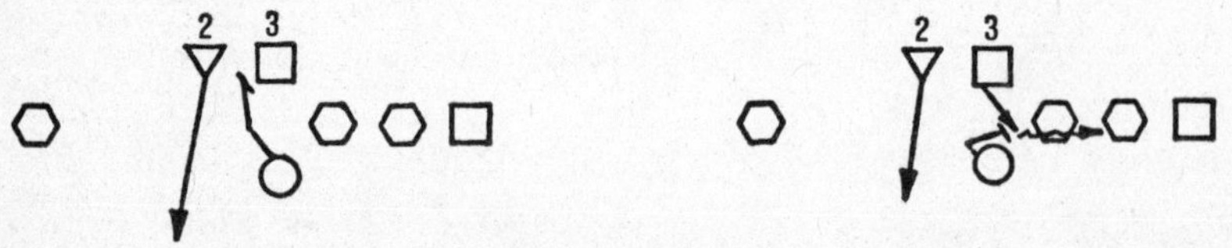

Diagram 4-16

If an outside stunt shows, the swingback turns immediately to the outside and blocks the number three defender from an inside/out position, opening up a running lane for the quarterback to the inside. (See Diagram 4-17.)

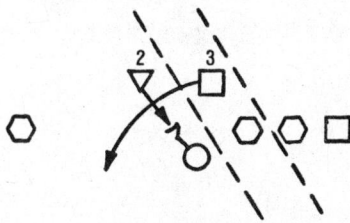

Diagram 4-17

The blocking techniques from the slot and over sets require a strong-blocking swingback who can achieve at least a stalemate on or near the LOS. Weekly scouting reports, along with an accurate evaluation of your swingback's physical capabilities, will determine how much these sets can be employed.

Probably the most advantageous Swingback-Motion offensive set from which to load the veer is the full I. From this position, the swingback has the most time in which to determine the number three defender and how he is playing the veer. It also denies the defense the opportunity to gain tendencies from the position that the swingback assumes.

The swingback uses a crossover step toward the playside, paralleling the LOS while clearing the fullback. He keys the number three defender and uses the technique based on the criteria previously discussed in this section. The swingback must attack the defender and not allow him to penetrate too close to the mesh area.

Regardless of his alignment, the swingback's read and block will normally be faster to the quickside of the formation because there is no one outside of the offensive tackle whom the number three defender must respect.

JUNCTION PLAY VERSUS EIGHT-MAN FRONTS

The "junction" play calls for the swingback to block the backside inside linebacker versus a Split 4 alignment, while the center drive blocks the playside inside linebacker out of the middle. Behind either a double-team or man blocking scheme all along the LOS, the junction play enables you to force the ball to your fullback with the aid of a predetermined lead blocker. (See Diagram 4-18.)

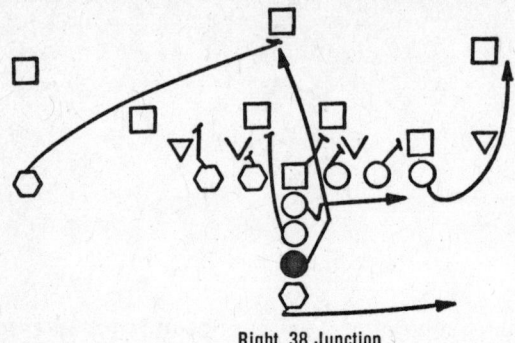

Right, 38 Junction

Diagram 4-18

The quarterback steps back playside, hands the ball deep to the fullback, and then accelerates down the line with the tailback. The swingback uses a blast block on the linebacker, establishing head position to the inside. He initially aims for the inside leg of the backside guard, staying low and getting his pads up under the linebacker. The fullback keys the blocking on the two linebackers and option runs to the open area (See Diagram 4-19.)

This play can be very effective versus the Split 4, especially when

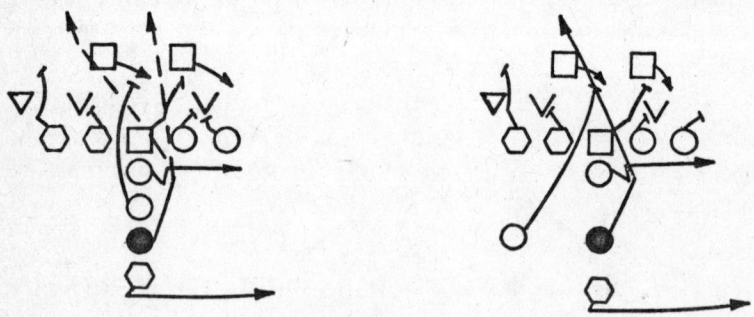

Diagram 4-19

the inside linebackers quickly scrape and shuffle to the playside. The center's block is relatively easy because he is stepping playside to insure the gap. He then drives on the scraping linebacker.

GIVE PLAY VERSUS EIGHT-MAN FRONTS

Another very effective predetermined play in the Swingback-Motion Offense's veer-related arsenal is the "give" play. Because of problems your quarterback has in reading the give phase of the veer/option versus the Split 4 Defense (give being absorbed for the most part from the inside by a linebacker off the LOS), we developed the give play where the fullback executes the read of the number four defender and reacts accordingly. (See Diagram 4-20.)

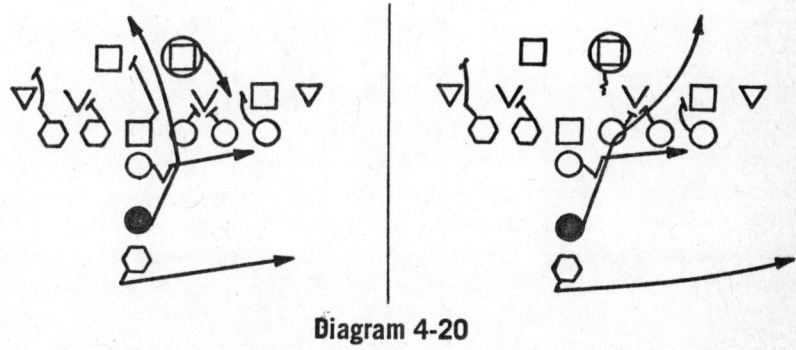

Diagram 4-20

As the fullback drives for the outside hip of the playside guard, he is reading the inside linebacker. If the linebacker scrapes outside of the double team, the fullback cuts inside and runs off of the center's block on the backside linebacker.

If the linebacker squats or supports the give by coming inside the double-team, the fullback hugs the double-team and sprints straight upfield.

The quarterback steps a little deeper on his first step, gets the ball deep to the fullback, then accelerates down the line with the tailback.

READ PLAY VERSUS EIGHT-MAN FRONTS

In order for the Swingback-Motion Offense to effectively execute the read of the inside veer versus eight-man fronts, it is necessary first to either block the tight end on the number three defender or to position the swingback as an inside blocker whereby he can lead block on the number two defender. We feel that we cannot leave the number two and three defenders, both of whom are on or near the LOS, unblocked. Immediate penetration by these defenders has the potential to disrupt the veer/option play.

The tight end's rule is to block the number three defender if he is the only receiver to the playside or if he is the inside receiver. If the tight end is the outside receiver he arc releases and stalks number one.

The swingback blocks number one if he is the outside receiver and number two if he is the inside receiver. His single exception to this rule is his responsibility to block the number three defender from an over or slot position. (See Diagram 4-21.)

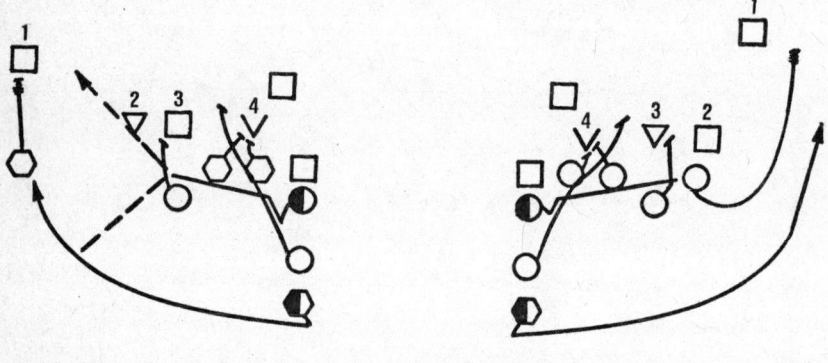

Diagram 4-21

The quarterback is coached to disregard the give, feather the mesh and read the unblocked number two or three defender. In theory, the read play is similar to the load play, although now the perimeter blocking scheme helps him to decide whether to keep or pitch. (See Diagram 4-22.)

In Diagram 4-22, from the pro set, the quarterback treats the veer as a loaded play and will keep or pitch off of the number two defender. With the power set, he accelerates toward number three and keeps or pitches off of the defender's reaction.

Running the Veer versus Eight-Man Fronts   *115*

To the quickside, the swingback must be positioned or motioned to a position whereby he can block the number two defender. (Diagram 4-23.)

In Diagram 4-23, the quarterback in both situations will execute the veer, reading the number three defender and keeping or pitching off of his reaction to the play.

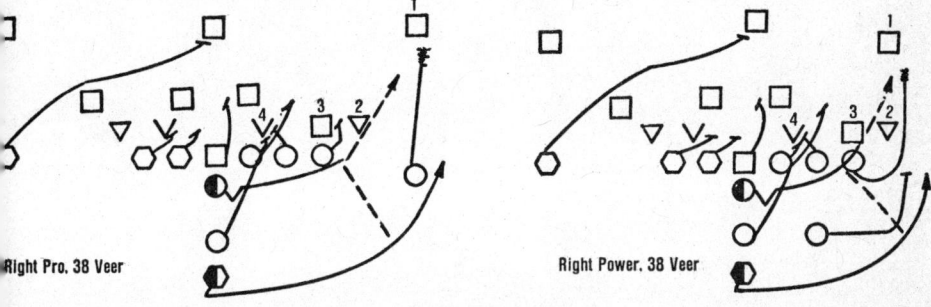

Diagram 4-22

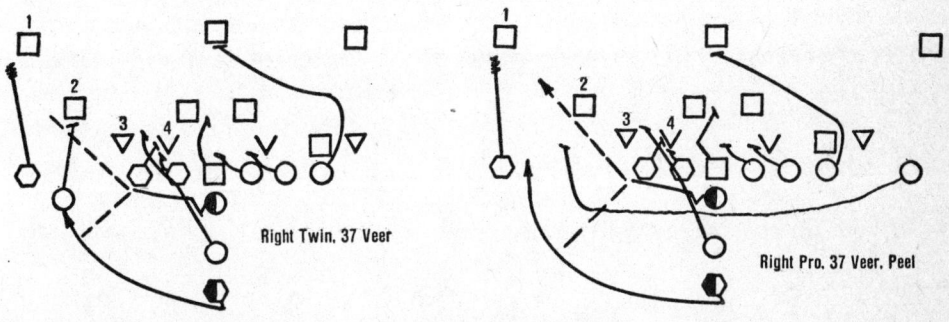

Diagram 4-23

5

USING I-BACK PLAYS TO AUGMENT THE SWINGBACK-MOTION OFFENSE

The Swingback-Motion Offense employs tandem or I-back plays, behind a flip-flopping offensive line, as its primary means of creating a solid running game. Along with the inside and outside veer/options, this offense has in its arsenal some of the basic I-back plays that the University of Southern California, with Mike Garret, O. J. Simpson, Anthony Davis and Ricky Bell highlighting them, used to gain national prominence.

We feel that the Swingback-Motion Offense must include the inside and outside veer/options, isolation, off-tackle, toss-sweep, trap and misdirection plays.

By limiting the number of offensive plays that we use, simplicity and an emphasis on execution can be maintained. Various tackle blocking calls for each play were devised to ensure that each play can be successfully blocked at the point of attack against any defensive situation.

Once the defense becomes overly conscious of the veer/option, the Swingback-Motion Offense reverts to its tailback-oriented running game, with a sprinkling of fullback and swingback plays, to capitalize on defensive adjustments and reactions.

The veer/option forces the defense to play assignment football. Each defender is given a specific responsibility regarding the various phases of the play.

Using I-Back Plays to Augment the Swingback-Motion Offense

From this basic assumption about the defense, the offense endeavors to create running plays that take advantage of the defensive adjustments and reactions to the veer/option plays. A defender assigned to support the pitch phase of the triple option will find his task complicated when he is also asked to play the off-tackle hole tough.

Any discussion of the Swingback-Motion Offense and its running game, must be prefaced by some introductory statements concerning blocking calls and the numbering of defensive techniques. This is especially needed at this time because there is no specific chapter set aside for their discussion. A detailed discussion of actual line and blocking techniques can be found in Chapter 6.

The playside tackle makes a live blocking call to his side of the LOS at any time before the quarterback begins calling his cadence. His call refers to how the linemen will block the play at the point-of-attack. Simultaneously, the backside tackle makes a dummy call to his linemen. It is important that his dummy call have some relevance to the normal code names of the blocking calls. Phony, made-up names lend no credence to the possibility of it being a live call.

Blocking calls are used to provide the linemen with optimal blocking angles against any defensive scheme. Each player has approximately three calls that can be effectively used against most defensive fronts.

Some terms also need to be defined. They will form the basis of the blocking call system:

1. *MIKE:* Man-for-man blocking. The basic rule is, "out, over, Linebacker." "Out" refers to any defender from the blocker's outside shoulder to the inside shoulder of the next offensive blocker to the outside. "Over" refers to any defender head up, on or inside of the blocker, on or off the LOS. "Linebacker" refers to any linebacker on or near the point of attack. (See Diagram 5-1.)

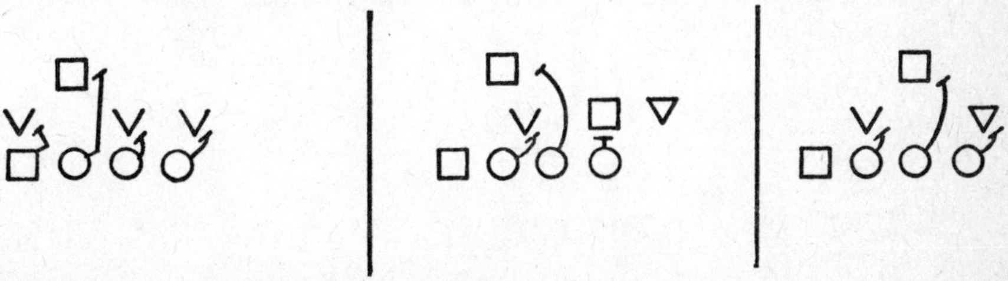

Diagram 5-1

2. *DAVE:* Double-team at the point of attack. When used at the 7/8 holes, the center must know if the defense is odd or even. Versus an odd defense, he is the post man. Versus an even defense, he will follow his backside rule. (See Diagram 5-2.)

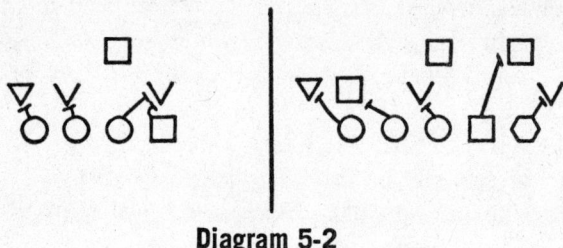

Diagram 5-2

3. *CHUCK:* Playside guard and tackle blocking inside towards the center. Everyone else blocks Mike or a special assignment. This is the basic tackle call for the inside veer/option. (See Diagram 5-3.)

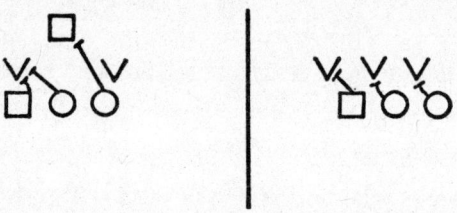

Diagram 5-3

4. *CRISS:* Cross block between the playside guard and tackle, with the tackle blocking down while the guard comes around. Favorite off-tackle call versus a split 4 defense. (See Diagram 5-4.)

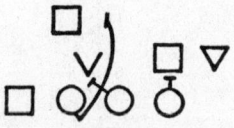

Diagram 5-4

5. *TONY:* Inside fold block between the playside guard and tackle, with the guard blocking out while the tackle comes around to the inside. (See Diagram 5-5.)

Diagram 5-5

6. *FRED:* Outside influence block by the playside tackle on any 4 or 5 technique. Everyone else blocks "Mike" or any special assignment. (See Diagram 5-6.) If the 4/5 technique is influenced, the tackle stays and blocks him. If he does not influence outside, the tackle continues around, looking for the first linebacker from the inside. (See Diagram 5-6.)

Diagram 5-6

7. *GEORGE:* Tight end (swingback) blocking first linebacker to the inside while playside guard pulls and becomes the lead blocker on the veer/option. Playside tackle blocks "Mike." Very good call versus 5-2. (See Diagram 5-7.)

8. *TOM:* Playside tackle pulls and becomes lead blocker while the tight end (swingback) blocks the first linebacker inside. Everyone else blocks "Mike." Effectively used versus a 5-2. (See Diagram 5-8.)

9. *WILLIE:* Playside guard blocks outside to pick up potential stunt. If no stunt shows, his block becomes an outside double-team with the tackle. If stunt shows, guard blocks stunt while tackle works upfield on linebacker. Effectively

used versus a 5-2 with blast play. Everyone else blocks "Mike."

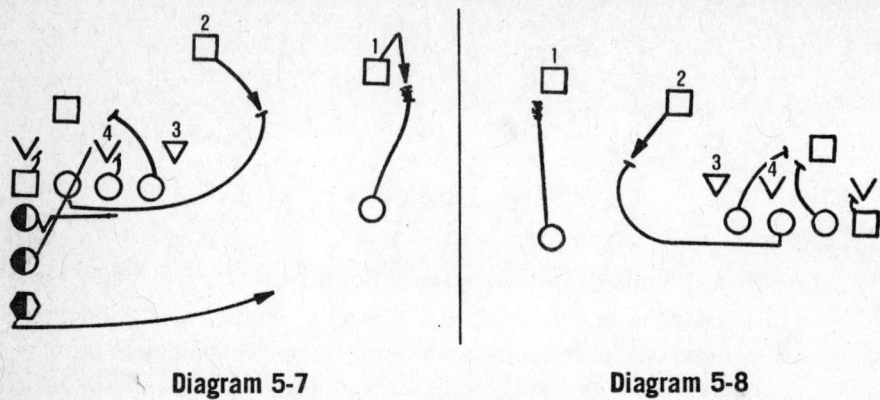

Diagram 5-7   Diagram 5-8

10. *TED:* Tight end (swingback) blocks first linebacker inside. Everyone else blocks "Mike." Effective off-tackle blocking scheme if your playside tackle can single block the 4/5 technique. (See Diagram 5-9.)

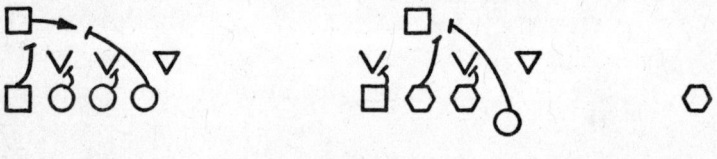

Diagram 5-9

By ascribing a man's name to every blocking call, the linemen learn a technique rather than a rule. Some of the tackle's calls are mnemonic and provide the linemen with a cue as to their assignment. Calls such as "Mike" (man), "Chuck" (center), and "Ted" (tight end first linebacker inside), are just three of these mnemonic devices.

As the season progresses from week to week, and different defenses are met, a careful selection of one or two calls, that will provide our linemen with optimal blocking angles, will be used. New calls can be used with any effective old ones to successfully combat any unique or troublesome defense.

Using I-Back Plays to Augment the Swingback-Motion Offense   121

TECHNIQUE NUMBERING SYSTEM

In an attempt to have our linemen communicate to coaches and to one another who they are to block, the Swingback-Motion Offense utilizes the Technique Numbering System that Coach Paul Bryant of Alabama (then at Texas A&M) initiated in 1956 along with A. "Bum" Phillips of the Houston Oilers (then a Texas High School Coach).

It effectively allows for a concise, simple channel of communication between coaches and linemen. It helps to eliminate any "gray" areas along the LOS. A five technique is a five technique when the lineman aligns himself on the outside shoulder of the offensive tackle. This is the only time our tackles consider a defender a five technique. (See Diagram 5-10.)

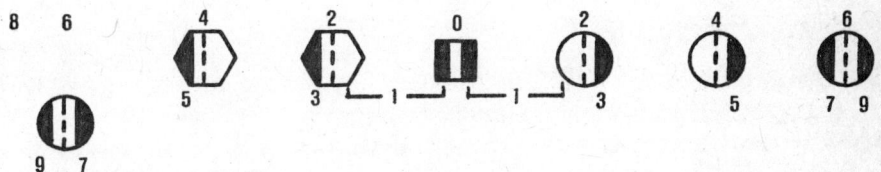

Diagram 5-10

With these ideas in mind, let us now take a look at the 12 base plays of the Swingback-Motion Offense. For simplicity, these 12 running plays involve only three different blocking schemes.

57/58 BLAST

One of the best examples of the option type running play found in the Swingback-Motion Offense is the blast. Its number designations are 57/58 Blast, but in tight goal line or short yardage situations this play will always be run to the strongside. (See Diagram 5-11.)

The Blast play is a fundamental football play whose name depicts the type of blocking pattern needed to make the play successful. The playside linemen must control the LOS to enable the fullback (swingback) to blast or drive the isolated linebacker out of the hole.

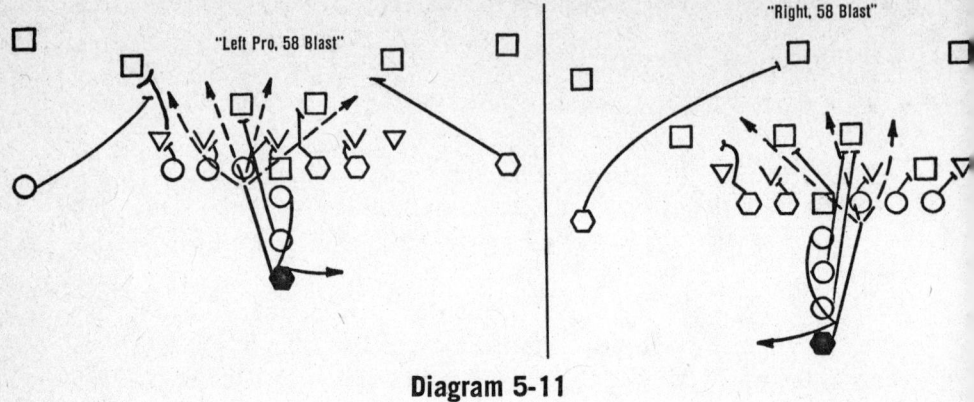

Diagram 5-11

SPECIFIC BLAST ASSIGNMNETS

- X: Near Safety.
- Y: Jam on/out to near Safety.
- SB: Wide out—near Safety.

  Running Back Position Playside: Lead on isolated linebacker; help center with noseman.

  Running Back Position Backside: First linebacker backside.

- QB: Reverse pivot, get ball to the tailback as deep as possible; boot away.
- FB: Drive hard for the butt of the playside guard, keying the guard's block versus an even defense and on the tackle's block versus an odd defense, while seeking the isolated linebacker.
- TB: Drive for the butt of the playside guard, keying the blocking scheme while receiving the ball from the quarterback; option run to the open area; accelerate.

The blast can be run out of any Swingback-Motion Offense set. The swingback can be used to bolster the blocking at the point of attack or he can be deployed or motioned in an attempt to influence the defense.

The most important factor in running a successful blast is for your quarterback to get the ball as deep as possible to his tailback. This allows your tailback to move freely and accelerate into whatever open area he finds.

Your tailback will take the handoff with his hands in front of his stomach, with his palms up, and his elbows against his side. The quarterback reverse pivots and lays the ball in the "basket" formed by the tailback's hands.

This type of handoff is simple for the quarterback and tailback to execute. It enables the quarterback to place the ball without having to find the pocket of the standard inside elbow-up handoff. It also allows the tailback to begin immediately searching for the hole he will choose while keying the first down lineman to the playside. (See Diagram 5-12.)

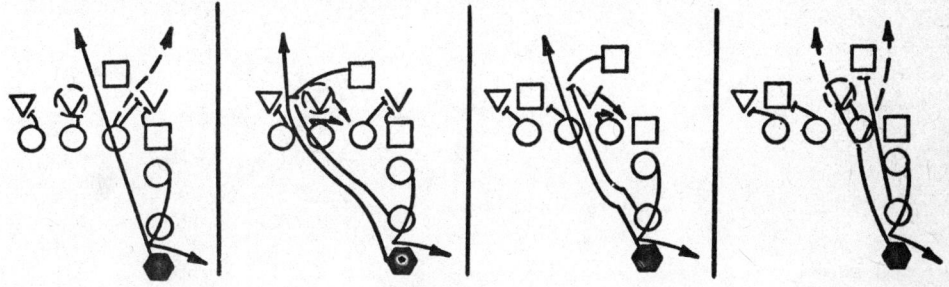

Diagram 5-12

The fullback also keys the first down lineman to the playside, adjusting his course so that he can effectively block the isolated linebacker.

Versus a 5-2 Defense, the playside guard on a "Dave" call will double-team the noseman. If he slants away from the hole, the guard will deepen and scrape off, looking for the offisde linebacker. If the noseman slants toward the hole, he is double-teamed and the backside guard, who releases toward the hole at a 45 degree angle, works upfield to block the backside linebacker. If the noseman slants backside, the backside guard and center handle him.

37/38 GIVE

A predetermined give to the fullback off of our veer backfield action, 37/38 Give exploits defenders who can more readily be blocked than read.

The quarterback moves the mesh point further back so that the fullback will get the ball sooner and will be able to option run through whatever open area he finds. The line blocking call is "Mike" versus most defenses.

SPECIFIC GIVE ASSIGNMENTS

- X: Near safety or corner.
- Y: Playside: veer release to near safety versus seven-man fronts, block anchor versus eight-man fronts.
  Backside: near safety.
- SB: Near safety or corner; slot set; versus eight-man fronts, block anchor; versus seven-man fronts, veer release to near safety.
- QB: Execute veer option, taking a slightly deeper first step in order to get ball to fullback sooner. Continue to read give key while giving ball to fullback. Accelerate down the line and upfield.
- FB: Drive for mesh point, receive ball while keying the blocking scheme. Option run through first open area and accelerate upfield.
- TB: Execute veer option. Do not look back while sprinting down the line toward your pitch relationship.

37/38 KEEP

This play is a predetermined effort to have the quarterback go outside and execute the keep or pitch. The fullback knows that he is not going to receive the ball and therefore immediately assumes a blocking role once the abbreviated mesh phase is completed. (See Diagram 5-13.)

The linemen block the defenders on the LOS while leaving the playside linebacker for the fullback. The quarterback feathers the mesh and gets quickly down the line, keeping or pitching the ball as dictated by the number three defender.

SPECIFIC KEEP ASSIGNMENTS

- X: Playside: stalk outside one-third.
  Backside: near safety or corner.

Using I-Back Plays to Augment the Swingback-Motion Offense   125

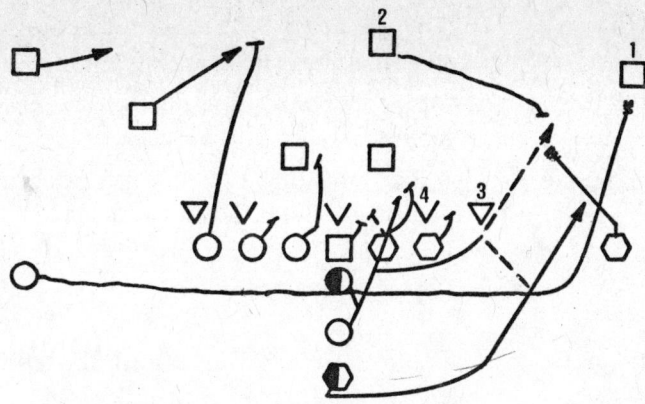

Left Pro, 37 Keep, Peel

Diagram 5-13

Y: Playside: veer release and block corner support; versus eight-man front block anchor.
     Backside: near safety.

SB: Playside:
     1. Wide/outside: stalk outside one-third.
     2. Wide/inside: block corner support.
     3. Inside: lateral channel and block corner support.
     4. Slot: veer release and block corner support; versus eight-man fronts block anchor. (See Diagram 5-14.)
     Backside: near safety or corner.

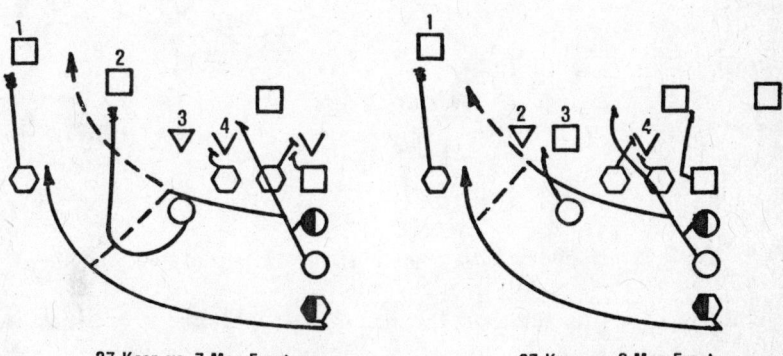

37 Keep vs. 7-Man Front   37 Keep vs. 8-Man Front

Diagram 5-14

QB: Execute veer/option, feathering the mesh and getting quickly down the line to the number three defender.

FB: Cheat up slightly, execute veer/option mesh. Block the linebacker or anyone else trying to escape from the inside.

TB: Execute veer/option, sprinting outside and establishing a good pitch relationship with the quarterback.

55/56 POWER

The off-tackle or power play, 55/56 Power, affords the tailback the opportunity to option run behind a basic block down, kick out blocking scheme. The power is another play that is more suitable to the strongside linemen's abilities. (See Diagram 5-15.)

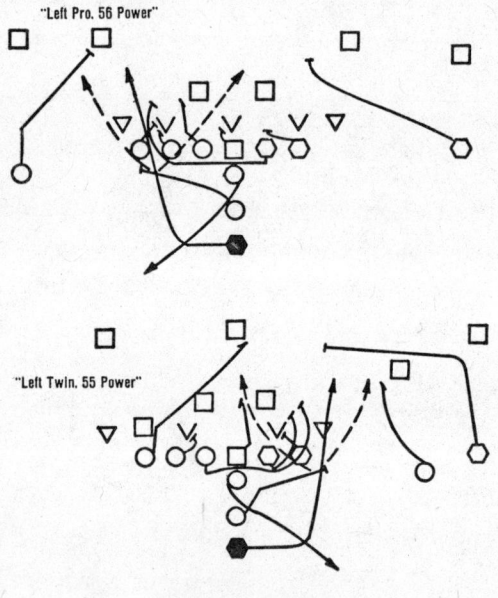

Diagram 5-15

The line blocking seals off the defenders to the inside while isolating the defender to be kicked out by the fullback. This isolation enables the tailback to key the fullback's block and make the appropriate inside or outside move.

SPECIFIC POWER ASSIGNMENTS

X: Near safety.

Y: Playside: block tackle's call.
Backside: near safety.

SB: Wide out: near safety.
Running back position playside: Influence to the outside of the defender to be blocked by the fullback, then turn upfield and block the first defender to show.
Slot/open Position: block tackle's call.
Backside: near safety.

QB: Reverse pivot, get ball to tailback as deep as possible, then fake play action pass by dropping back and setting up.

FB: Take one step with foot away from the play toward the butt of the playside guard, then turn outside and block the defender on or outside the tight end/swingback.

TB: Three-step lateral route (jab, crossover, lead) to the playside, getting shoulders parallel to the LOS as you angle the lead step toward the hole. Receive ball from quarterback while keying the defender to be kicked out.

To the strongside, the Power can be run from any Swingback/Motion Offensive set. To the quickside, versus a 4/5 technique defense (seven-man front), the swingback should possibly be employed as a slot or possible an open position in order to double-team with the quick tackle.

Versus an eight-man front, such as the Split-4 or Maryland 6, where there is no need for a double-team block, the swingback can deploy to any offensive set. The twin-set, in which the outside linebacker will be influenced to walk away with the swingback, is a good set from which to run the quickside power. (See Diagram 5-16.)

To run a successful power play, the fullback must first take the proper inside/outside angle in order to prepare himself for the most difficult block he will have to make, which is the crashing or squeezing defender.

If the defender plays the power by any other method, the fullback's inside/outside course prepares him to make the necessary adjustment and make the block.

The proper course affords the fullback the time needed to determine how the defender is playing the power and what type of block to use.

If the defender crashes, the fullback drives his head past the defender's knee and attempts to pin or log him to the inside. (See Diagram 5-17.)

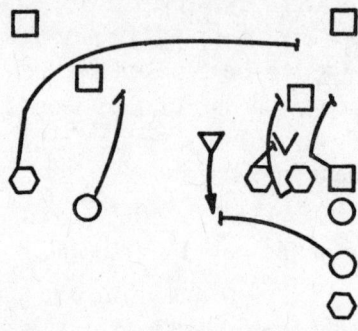

Diagram 5-16

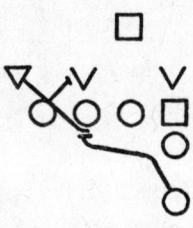

Diagram 5-17

If the defender closes with the down block and sits in the hole, the fullback works to the defender's inside hip and drives him out the line.

The easiest block for the fullback is when the defender comes straight upfield and neither crashes nor closes. The fullback works to the inside hip and drives the defender out the line.

The tailback receives the ball as he does on the blast, with his palms up and hands forming a basket in front of his stomach.

Scraping will occur when the defensive tackle in a seven-man front slants to the inside. The tight end or swingback will push straight upfield off his inside foot, looking for the linebacker stunting to the outside. (See Diagram 5-18.)

Diagram 5-18

11/12 OPTION

In keeping with the Swingback-Motion Offense's basic philosophy of attacking on a broad front with multiple options, the 11/12 option fits nicely into the offense's playbook. It can be run from any strongside set, while to the quickside versus a seven-man front, a slot or open set is needed. (See Diagram 5-19.)

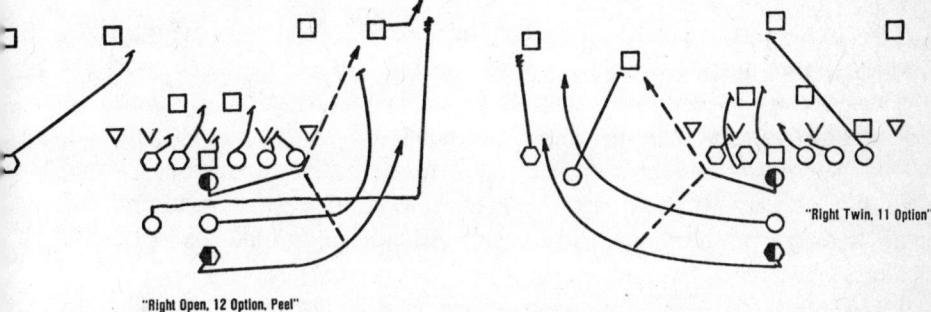

"Right Open, 12 Option, Peel"   "Right Twin, 11 Option"

Diagram 5-19

This basic option play is a speed option in which the fullback is going to become the lead blocker. By using him in such a role, the offense can declare or motion the swingback away from the play without losing the numerical advantage at the point of attack.

SPECIFIC OPTION ASSIGNMENTS

X: Playside: stalk outside one-third defender.
   Backside: near safety.

Y: Playside: block tackle's call; versus Split 4 block anchor.
   Backside: jam on/out to near safety.

SB: Playside Slot/open: block tackle's call; versus Split 4 block anchor.
Runningback Position/twin: lead blocker.
Wide out: stalk outside third defender.
Backside: near safety.

QB: Pull away from center and drop off LOS a yard and a half, attempting to hold the inside linebackers wtih a simple pass fake. Then sprint playside for the inside hip of the end defender on the LOS; option him.

FB: Take a three or four yard parallel course to the LOS, then start a downhill pull and attack the force defender's outside knee.

TB: Counterstep backside, then sprint playside establishing a good pitch relationship wtih the quarterback. As the quarterback turns upfield, turn upfield and establish a delay pitch relationship with him.

The quarterback's momentary hesitation as he drops off the LOS serves three purposes. First, it temporarily holds the inside linebackers who are not quite sure whether the play is a pass or a run. By then, the guards have established position on them.

Second, it enables the fullback to clear the quarterback's and tailback's path. If the quarterback were to receive a fast read and not hesitate, his pitch in many instances would hit the fullback as he ran his lateral course.

Finally, by hesitating, the quarterback does not stretch the play into the sideline when the play is begun from a hash mark. By delaying, he arrives at the number three defender later than he would if he opened up and sprinted down the line. It is imperative to the success of the play that your tailback have enough field to adequately maneuver once he receives the pitch from the quarterback.

11/12 COUNTER OPTION

As the inside veer/option play begins to dominate the defense, the counter option play is called to capitalize on defensive compensations to stop the inside veer.

The play begins as an inside veer/option away from the designated playside. A 12 Counter Option would initially resemble a 37 Veer play. (See Diagram 5-20.)

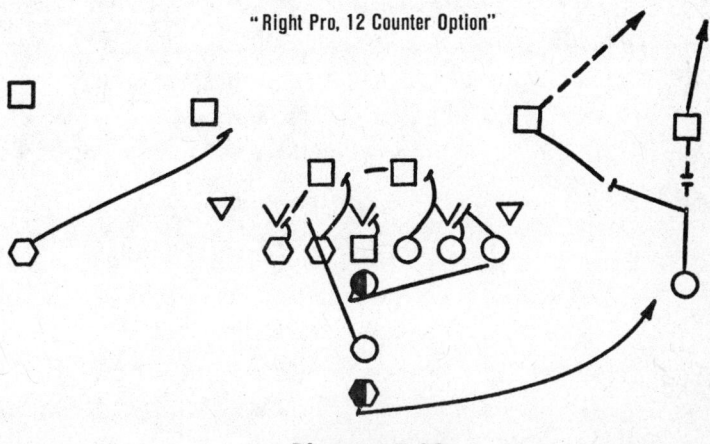

Diagram 5-20

An 11 Counter Option necessitates employing the swingback in a slot or open set versus most seven-man fronts in order to double-team with the quick tackle. (See Diagram 5-21.)

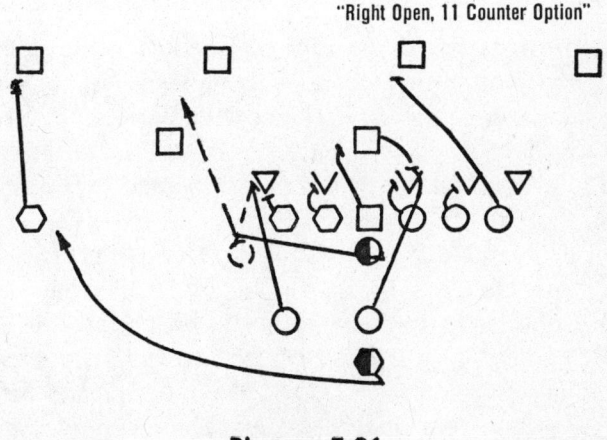

Diagram 5-21

SPECIAL COUNTER OPTION ASSIGNMENTS

- X: Playside: block outside one-third defender.
  Backside: near safety.
- Y: Playside: block tackle's call; versus Split 4 block anchor.
  Backside: jam on/out to near safety.
- SB: Playside/wide: block outside one-third defender.
  Playside/inside: lead on corner support.
  Playside Slot/open: block tackle's call; versus Split 4 block anchor.
  Backside: near safety.
- QB: Step backside, show ball to fullback, pivot back to the playside and accelerate to the inside hip of the number three defender, keeping or pitching off of him.
- FB: Drive hard for the inside leg of the backside guard; take the mesh fake and attack the first linebacker to show; sell the veer/option first.
- TB: Counterstep to the backside, then sprint playside, establishing the proper pitch relationship with the quarterback.

The quarterback's footwork must be exact so that when he fakes the mesh with the fullback, he is able to get quickly to the outside with the play. His first step is a short, six-inch step with his backside foot. He then steps through with his playside foot, pushing and pivoting back towards the playside.

A certain amount of acceleration may be lost by the quarterback as he executes his countermovements. Although acceleration is essential, the mesh fake that threatens the backside with the veer/option and elicits linebacker reactions toward the backside is the key to the play.

The basic double-team at the point of attack seals off any line penetrations. As the fullback fakes the mesh of the inside veer/option, the linebackers must either pursue in that direction (as the defense tries to gain the extra defender to the outside) or hold their ground and take on the blocker. Either of these situations that the play creates are beneficial.

After the brief but valuable mesh fake, the quarterback must pivot so that he is heading into the LOS toward the original position of the inside hip of the number three defender. If the defender gets too far upfield, the quarterback stays on this course and gets upfield.

Using I-Back Plays to Augment the Swingback-Motion Offense   133

This path forces the number three defender to commit himself. Eye contact by the quarterback with the number three defender is essential to the play. The latter must be forced to do his assigned job, and must not be allowed to string the play out.

21/22 OPTION

Diagram 5-22 shows an outside option play run off of a quick trap fake to the swingback. It is called 21/22 Option and is a much better play when it is executed to the quickside of the formation. The fullback is the lead blocker and the split end acts as the stalk blocker.

Because it is run better to a split end, 21 option is ideally the play to be run versus a Split 4 or Maryland 6 defense. No double-team is needed and there is still a lead blocker (fullback) and a stalk blocker (x). Unless we have an exceptional blocker at tight end, the play will not be run to the strongside against either eight-man front because of the time that the tight end must sustain his block on the anchor.

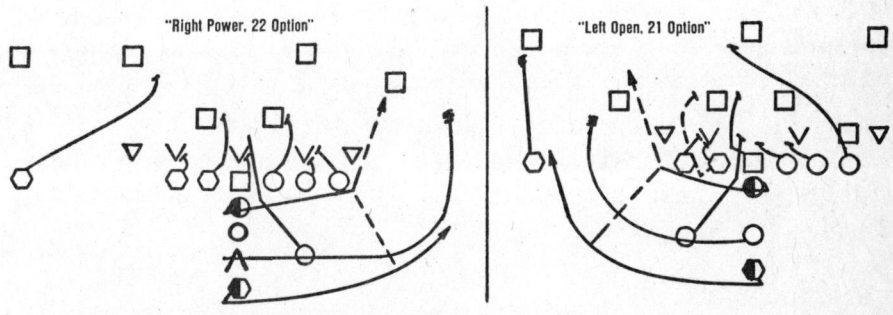

Diagram 5-22

SPECIAL 21/22 OPTION ASSIGNMENTS

X: Playside: Stalk outside one-third defender.
    Backside: Near safety.
Y: Playside: Block tackle's call.
    Backside: Jam on/out to near safety.
SB: Drive for the playside hip of the center, inside arm up, faking

the trap and blocking the first linebacker that shows; it is up to you to be tackled.

QB: Counter-pivot backside as you would on the counter option, show the ball to the swingback, then drive for the inside hip of the number three defender; keep or pitch; expect a fast read on the 21 option.

FB: Run a three to four yard course parallel to the LOS, then begin downhill pull toward the force man's outside knee; turn upfield as soon as you can to avoid stringing the play to the sideline.

TB: Counter step backside, then sprint playside establishing a good pitch relationship with the quarterback; expect a quick pitch when 21 option is called.

The swingback, faking the quick trap in the middle, should force the linebacker to freeze momentarily, enabling the blocking scheme of the interior linemen to adequately handle him.

As your quarterback starts down the line, he must maintain a position heading into the LOS. This can be accomplished only if he executes the proper counter-pivot and finishes his fake to the swingback by running through him. There will be times when penetration will force him off the line, but he must work at reestablishing himself on the proper course toward the inside hip of the number three defender.

All that is needed for the play to gain the corner is for one perimeter defender to commit to the inside, giving the fullback the outside blocking angle. (See Diagram 5-23.)

BLOCKING CALLS

Versus most seven-man fronts, the playside tackle's call on 21/22 option will be "Dave," or a double-team on the 4/5 technique. Therefore, it will be mostly run to the tight end side (22 option), or to the quickside (21 option) if our quick tackle can effectively single block the 4/5 technique ("Mike" call).

Any time there is a three technique to the playside, the call can be "Criss" or "Dave" or "Mike."

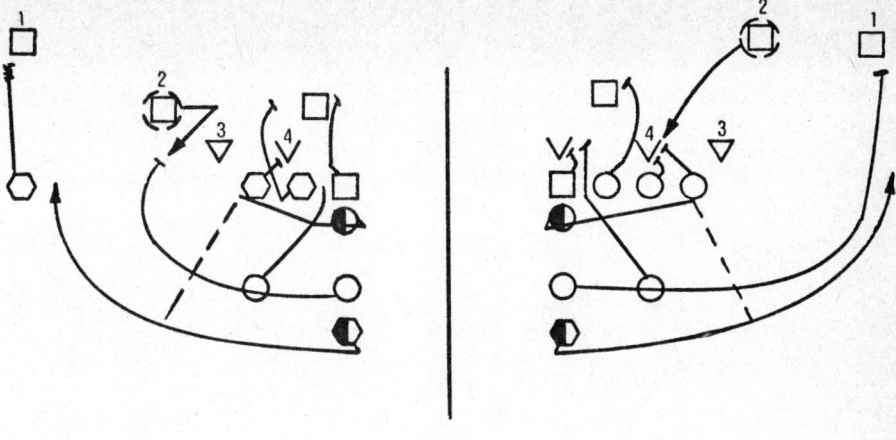

Diagram 5-23

OFFENSIVE SETS

Because the swingback is needed to fake the inside trap, the 21/22 option will be run only from the power (strongside) and the open (quickside) sets.

There is the possibility of running the play from the over and slot sets, although the quarterback will be precariously close to the number three defender after his fake to the swingback.

TRAPS

The Swingback-Motion Offense employs three different backfield actions behind one basic trap rule when running its trap plays. This simplified approach allows you to effectively trap any defensive front in which the defenders lend themselves to being trapped because of the technique they are employing. (See Diagram 5-24.)

The standard trap rule for our linemen considers most defensive possibilities and can successfully block them. In conjunction with this trap rule, and also of flip-flopping of offensive linemen, our quick guard will do 80 percent of the trapping. The regular trap rule is "Randy," and will be called on the LOS by the tackle to the side of the trap.

136   Using I-Back Plays to Augment the Swingback-Motion Offense

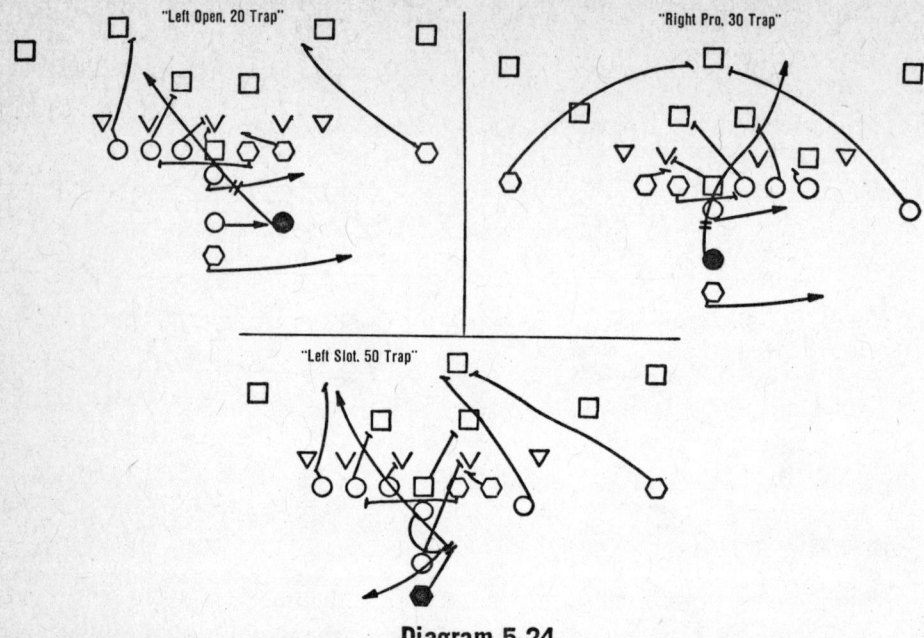

Diagram 5-24

SPECIFIC TRAP RULE FOR LINEMEN
   C:
     #0 on LOS; backside on LOS.
     Playside Guard: Inside, man on, influence and block out.
     Playside Tackle: First linebacker on or inside.
     Backside Guard: Pull and trap the first man on or outside the strong guard.
     Backside Tackle: Seal to the center.
   Y:
     Jam on or outside to near safety (four-deep) or corner (three-deep); versus Split-4, block the anchor.

Versus defensive fronts using a four or five technique, a special influence rule for the playside tackle and tight end/swingback can be used in place of the standard rule. The influence trap rule is "Jake" and will be called on the LOS by the tackle to the side of the trap.

SPECIAL INFLUENCE TRAP RULE
   C:
     Same as "Randy" trap rule.
     Playside Guard: Same as "Randy" trap rule.
     Playside Tackle: Influence and block out.

SB/Y:
First linebacker inside.
Backside Guard: Same as "Randy" trap rule.
Backside Tackle: Same as "Randy" trap rule.

By changing two blocking rules, the trap can now be set up by influencing the defender to be trapped to come across the LOS. (See Diagram 5-25.)

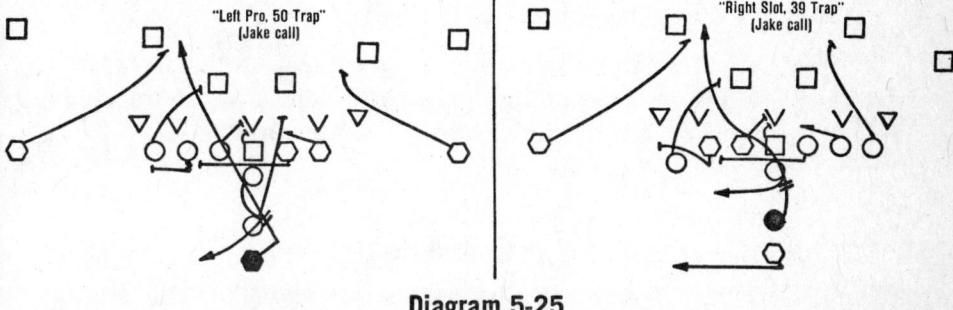

Diagram 5-25

In order to influence the nine-hole trap, the swingback must be in a slot position so that he can effectively eliminate the first linebacker to the inside.

Whenever a defense presents a walk-up defense that indicates a possible stunt or a near impossible block for playside tackle for the linebacker, a call for a "railroad" block will be made on the LOS by the linemen. "Railroad" can be used on any running play, although it best serves its purpose on the trap play. (See Diagram 5-26.)

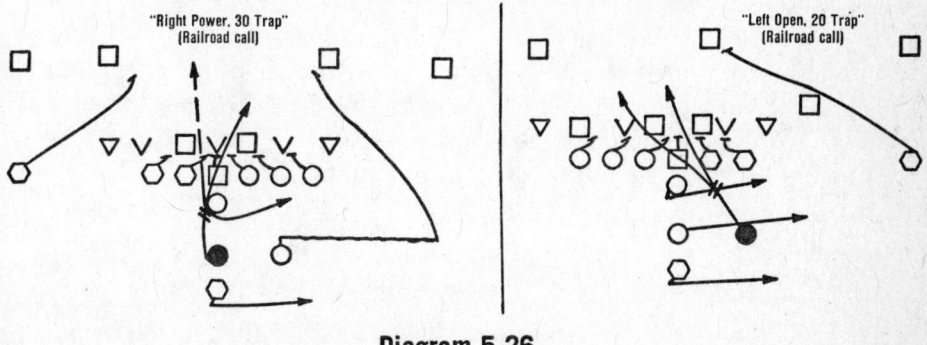

Diagram 5-26

On a "railroad" call, all linemen and the tight end/swingback wedge block to the center, working to eliminate penetration along the

LOS. Upon hearing the call, the ball carrier knows that he must search the area for a hole and accelerate low and hard through it. This is not the time for sliding along the line looking for a hole or gingerly prancing about, waiting for a break in the line.

SPECIFIC TRAP ASSIGNMENTS

20 Trap

SB: Drive for the playside hip of the center, inside elbow up. Receive handoff while keying the block of the trapping guard. Once through the hole, turn upfield and avoid running laterally.

FB: Begin lateral course and fake 21/22 option.

TB: Counter-step backside and fake 21/22 option.

QB: Counter-pivot backside, reach back with ball and hand it to the swingback, then fake 21/22 option.

30 Trap

SB: Block trap rule (influence rule) or near safety.

FB: Drive for backside leg of quarterback, receiving ball while keying the trapping guard's block. Versus a 5-2, deepen your initial alignment to read the double-team block on the noseman.

TB: Counter-step backside, then sprint playside, faking the toss-sweep.

QB: Open up backside by dropping your backside leg behind your playside heel, giving the ball to the fullback as deep as possible, then fake the toss-sweep. The handoff and fake pitch should be done in one motion.

50 Trap

SB: Block trap rule (influence rule) or near safety.

FB: Drive for the backside leg of the center, filling inside/out for the trapping guard. If no one lineman to block, attack first linebacker backside as you would the blast.

TB: Two-step course begun with a crossover step toward the backside blast hole, then veering back behind the trapping guard. (See Diagram 5-27.) Receive the handoff as you would on the blast or power. (Palms up in front of the stomach.)

QB: Reverse pivot as on the blast, get ball to tailback as deep as possible; look for him to be veering back behind the trapping guard, boot away.

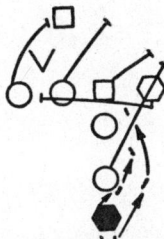

Diagram 5-27

20/29 SCISSORS

Along with 20/29 Traps, 20/29 Scissors are used to provide the Swingback-Motion Offense with those extremely valuable misdirection plays. The scissors is run off of a power fake and is designed to induce linebacker pursuit that will take them out of the play. For simplicity, the same trap rules are employed, only the backside tackle will do the trapping because of the distance that the swingback must travel. (See Diagram 5-28.)

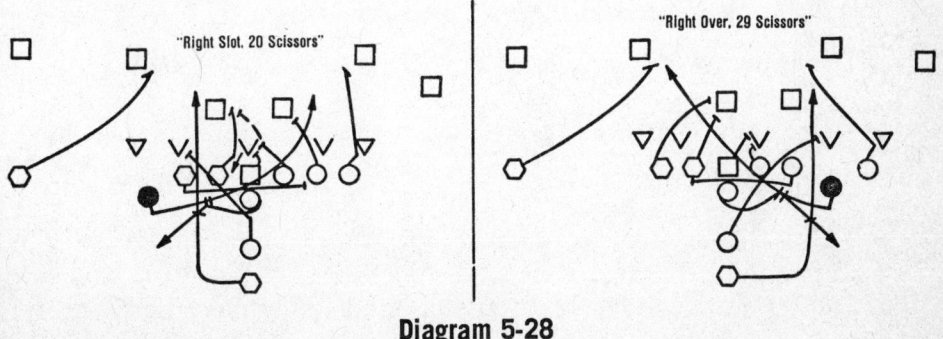

Diagram 5-28

In order to run the scissors, the swingback must be aligned in the power/over sets (29 scissors), or the open/slot sets (20 scissors). We favor the 20 scissors because of our line personnel flipping, our quick tackle is more suited for pulling and trapping than the strong tackle.

The regular or influence trap rule can be called on the scissors play. The timing of the play is important regardless of which technique is used. For the most part, a reading four/five technique will be influenced.

SPECIFIC SCISSORS ASSIGNMENTS

X: Near safety.

Y: Playside: Jam on/out to near safety; "Jake" call, first linebacker inside.
Backside: Near safety.

SB: Slot/Over Sets: Drop step opening up to the quarterback while gaining some depth on the LOS.
Open/Power Set: Short, lateral step to the outside to allow the fullback to pass in front of you.
Drive for the butt of the center while keying the tackle's trap.
Attempt to hit the hole going north and south to avoid any unblocked secondary defenders.

QB: Reverse pivot and execute an inside handoff to the swingback, then fake power to the tailback.

FB: Drive hard for the butt of the backside guard, then veer outside and fill for the pulling tackle; no one must penetrate your area.

TB: Run power play away from the call, taking fake from quarterback and making people believe that you have the ball; attack the first defender who shows.

The success of the Swingback-Motion Offense lies greatly in its ability to run a respected power off-tackle play. The defense must be conscious of the off-tackle play, and must pursue aggressively to shut it down. Once this prerequisite occurs, the misdirected scissors play opens up a potential big play.

Your quarterback must flatten his reverse pivot somewhat in order to affect the safe exchange of the ball to the swingback. Simultaneously, the fullback must clear both the quarterback's and swingback's path and effectively seal the area vacated by the pulling tackle.

51/52 TOSS

The play that enables the Swingback-Motion Offense to get outside quickly with maximum blocking at the perimeter is the Toss. Both guards are encouraged to pull whenever they are uncovered. The backside guard will always pull. (See Diagram 5-29.)

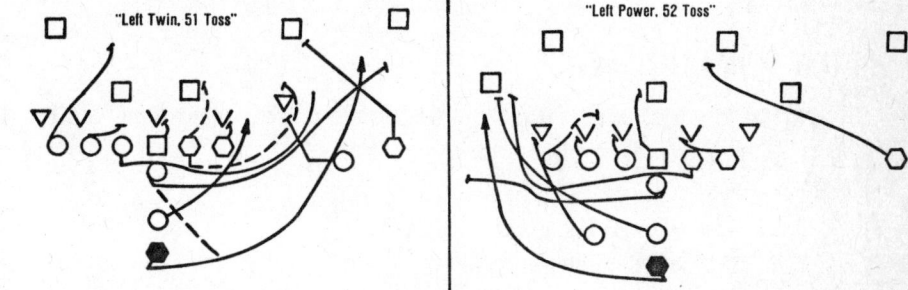

Diagram 5-29

The Toss can be run from any offensive set, and may be run away from, as well as toward, the swingback. We prefer to run it quickside (51 Toss) with the swingback aligned to the same side.

The base playside blocking call for the Toss is "Mike" (out, over linebacker), while the backside guard pulls and the backside tackle seals. With the "Mike" call the playside guard will pull when he is uncovered.

A "Dave" call is an effective blocking scheme versus a 5-2 defense when the defensive end is closing down hard to stop the power off-tackle. As he closes down, the fullback or the swingback pins him to the inside. (See Diagram 5-30.)

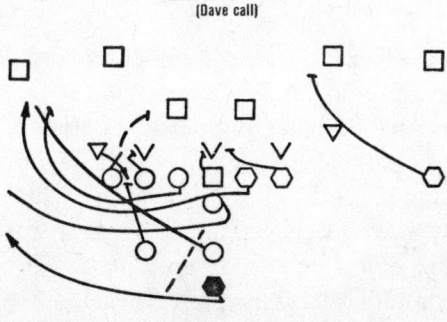

Diagram 5-30

"Dave" blocking immediately gives the tailback the corner and does not force the play to the sideline. The blocking scheme will theoretically create a running lane for the tailback to accelerate through upfield. The toss play is a vivid example of why your tailback must be able to accelerate. As the defense stretches itself to get wide quickly to defend the play, creases or cracks in its lateral containment provide excellent opportunities for a quick tailback to gain yards.

SPECIAL TOSS ASSIGNMENTS

- X: Playside: crack/stalk on near safety (four-deep) or Willie linebacker (three-deep).
  Backside: Near safety.
- Y: Playside: Block tackle's call.
  Backside: Near safety.
- SB: Playside wideout: crack/stalk near safety (four-deep) or Willie linebacker (three-deep).
  Playside: Block tackle's call.
  Backside: Near safety.
- QB: Reverse pivot, dead pitch to tailback, lead on the corner support. Chop and roll him or use a running shoulder block to eliminate him to the outside.
- FB: Chop and roll the first defender outside the tight end or slot. Attack on a direct line and eliminate him from getting upfield.
- TB: Counter-step backside, allowing the fullback to clear the pitch; sprint playside, receiving the pitch and reading the blocks of the swingback/fullback and quarterback; be ready to cut upfield quickly if the contain man forces deep.

A successful Toss play is contingent upon the fullback or swingback making his block on the contain defender. He must attack as quickly as possible and must read the defender as he moves. As with most of the backfield blocking techniques, the defender will be blocked by the fullback or swingback in the most advantageous manner.

Versus a closing defender, the fullback or swingback tries to pin him to the inside by getting his head and shoulder across the defender's outside knee. If the defender comes upfield, the blocker must now employ a running shoulder block, slipping his head to the upfield hip of the defender and simply staying with the block. The blocker's chore

Using I-Back Plays to Augment the Swingback-Motion Offense

becomes difficult when the defender squats and attempts to slow-play the fullback's (swingback's) block. The fullback/swingback still drives for the outside knee of the defender. If the defender continues to widen, the blocker turns him out and allows the tailback to read the block and cut up inside.

The Swingback-Motion Offense utilizes the Toss to augment the veer/option as a means of getting quickly to the outside. Your tailback does not need exceptional speed, but rather must possess the ability to turn the play upfield into the first crack in the lateral contain of the defense.

51/52 FLIP

Another version of the wide play potential of the Swingback-Motion Offense is the Flip. It is blocked basically the same way as the Toss, only the fullback trap is going to be faked in an attempt to hold the inside linebacker. (See Diagram 5-31.)

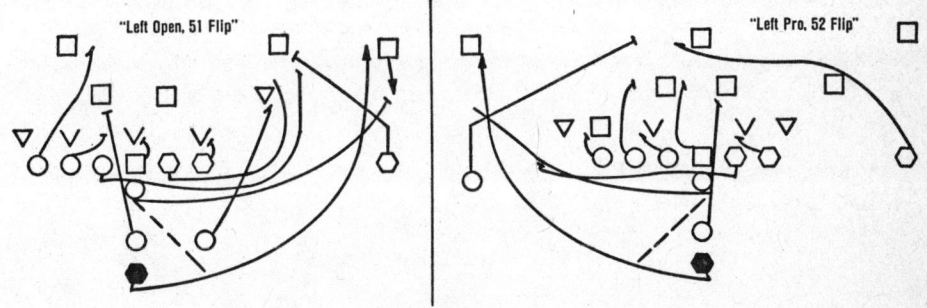

Diagram 5-31

Because the fullback is faking the trap and filling for the backside guard that pulls, the Flip is most effective when the swingback is set to the playside in a position to block the fullback's assignments. In Diagram 5-31, "Left Open 51 Flip" versus a 5-2 defense is a play in which the swingback can block the defensive end/linebacker.

SPECIAL FLIP ASSIGNMENTS

X: Same as Toss.
Y: Same as Toss.

SB: Same as Toss.

QB: Open up to the backside, show the ball to the fullback as you continue around, pitching the ball to the tailback; lead on the corner support.

FB: Aim for the backside leg of the quarterback, take ball fake and fill for the pulling guard; eliminate any penetration toward the playside, attacking any linebacker in the area.

TB: Same as the Toss, only key the block of the swingback instead of the fullback.

Both guards will pull on the Flip if they are uncovered, with the backside guard always pulling because the fullback is filling for him. The quarterback opens to the fullback and gains some depth off the LOS to enable the guard to pull past him.

COACHING PHILOSOPHY OF THE RUNNING GAME

Each play of the Swingback-Motion's running game is linked to one or more companion plays. The counter option complements the veer/option, while the Flip can be used to take advantage of the defense's reaction to the potential fullback trap.

If there are no specific running play companions to the blast and power plays, the quick screen to the split end off a blast fake and numerous play-action passes run off of a power fake adequately exploit the defense's pursuit toward stopping those plays. (See Diagram 5-32.)

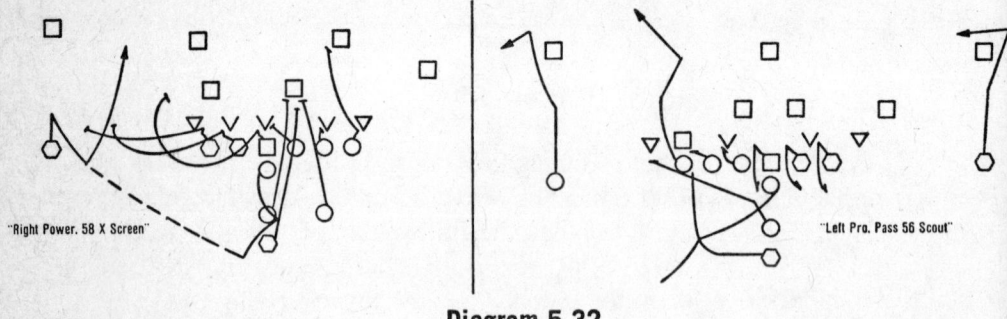

Diagram 5-32

The premium of "out-toughing" our opponents is demanded in the Swingback-Motion running game. All drills and coaching situations are erected with this premise foremost in the coaches' and players' minds. Once a defense yields an area to be exploited, a total commitment to running right at defenders and knocking them down is demanded.

Because of the tailback-oriented nature of the running game, the fullback and swingback must be praised when they successfully perform their blocking tasks. Their immediate rewards come from helping to sustain ball control, while personal rewards result when the defense compensates to stop the tailback, opening up the fullback and swingback plays.

First downs are lauded as much as, if not more than, touchdowns. Key blocks, as well as players carrying the ball, are praised in an effort to involve the entire offensive unit in working to maintain continuity through each player's doing his job on every play. No block or play assignment is considered trivial. The running game must be coached as a team concept if the Swingback-Motion Offense is to consistently move the ball.

6

BLOCKING TECHNIQUES THAT ENABLE THE SWINGBACK-MOTION OFFENSE TO SCORE

The basis for the construction of a sound offensive unit lies in a solid foundation of blocking techniques that linemen and backs execute once the ball is snapped. The Swingback-Motion Offense is no exception. By incorporating tackle blocking calls which afford the point-of-attack linemen with the optimal method of attacking any defensive front for each offensive play, the Swingback-Motion Offense is able to solidify and broaden its offensive capability.

For each tackle call there is a corresponding blocking technique for those linemen blocking at the point-of-attack. Each player listens for the tackle call made on the LOS and associates the call with the technique. Therefore, the blocker learns a blocking technique rather than simply memorizing a blocking rule.

For example, the huddle call is, "Left Pro, 56 Power." On the LOS, the strong tackle recognizes the Oklahoma 5-2 Defense and calls, "Dave." The quick tackle (backside tackle) makes a dummy call of "Fred." (See Diagram 6-1.)

Tackle call sheets (See Diagram 6-2a) and worksheets (See Diagram 6-2b) for that particular week indicated to the strong tackle that 56 Power versus a four or five technique was to be blocked "Dave." The strong tackle is the post blocker, while the tight end knows that on a "Dave" call at the six hole he is the lead blocker.

Blocking Techniques That Enable the Offense to Score

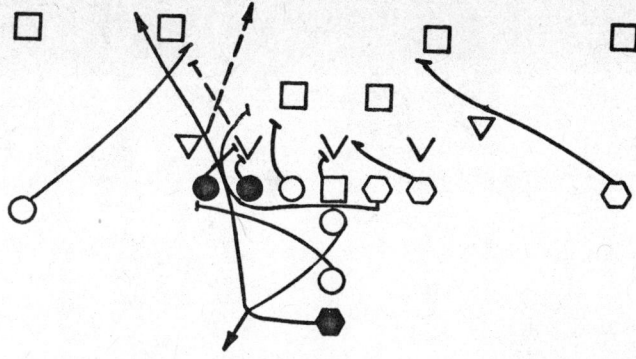

Diagram 6-1

Our tackle call sheets are normally handed out after Tuesday's practice, or as soon as our film analysis of our opponent is finished. Everyone receives both the strongside and quickside tackle calls and is encouraged to learn and understand them.

On Wednesday, or on the day after our film work is done, each player is issued a series of worksheets upon which he is to draw in his assignment for the play listed versus the defenses shown.

Quarterbacks detail each back and receiver action as well as list the probable tackle call that will be made. Tackles write their call or calls on the sheets in addition to diagramming their specific assignment.

Dropback passes, screens and draws, and play action passes that will be included in that week's game plan, are also listed on the worksheets. If a specific play is to be run only against an anticipated defense (from tendencies shown), it will be shown on the worksheets only versus that particular defense.

Our players return their worksheets to their offensive breakdown coach the following morning by 8:30 AM. Each worksheet is graded and handed back to the players to study or redo. We attempt to return their worksheets to them by Friday morning at the very latest.

Certain opponents have tried shifting their defense in an attempt to confuse our blocking calls. As soon as our tackles made their tackle call, the defense would stem, or shift to another defense. To effectively counteract this tactic, we used either a quick cadence or an extended cadence. The latter gave the tackles an opportunity to make the correct re-call.

TACKLE CALLS

Quickside

Quickside Play	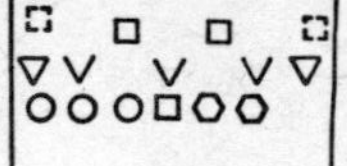 5-2 w/Rover	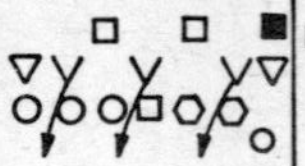 5-2 Rover Quick Slant Strong	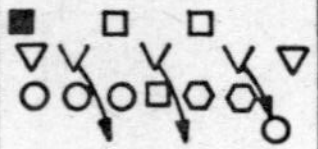 5-2 Rover Strong Slant Quick	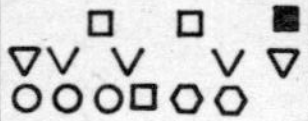 5-2 Offset Nose Strong	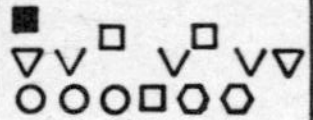 5-2 Offset Nose Quick	Comments
37 V	Chuck/Fred/Tom*	Fred/Willie/Chuck	Chuck	Chuck/Fred/Tom* Mike	Chuck/Tom*/Ted $	* QT: TOM the veer vs. any 4/5 technique. The TE (SB) will block the 1st LB inside.
57 B	Dave	Dave/Willie	Dave	Mike	Mike	
20/30/50 t	Randy/Jake	Randy	Randy	Randy/Jake	Randy/Jake	
20 S	Randy/Jake	Randy	Randy	Randy/Jake	Randy/Jake	$ TE (SB) block the 1st LB inside.
55 P	Dave	Dave	Dave	Dave	Dave	
51 T/51 F	Mike/Dave	Mike/Dave	Mike/Dave	Mike/Dave	Mike/Dave	Rover: Number 39 (■)

Quickside Play	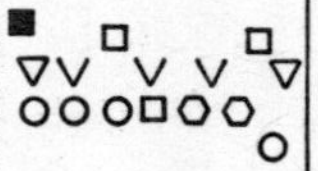 5-2 Eagle Quickside	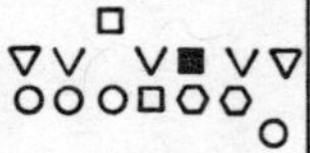 5-2 Rover Eagle Quickside	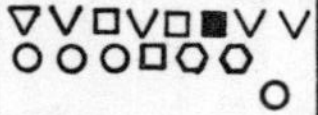 5-2 Rover Eagle Walk-up (Goal line)			Comments
37 V	Dave/Ted/Chuck	Dave/Mike	Chuck/Dave Railroad**			**Wedge blocking to the center. You, can RAILROAD any play that we have versus a walked-up or goal line defense.
57 B	Mike	Mike	Railroad**			
20/30/50 t	Randy/Jake	Randy/Jake	Railroad**			
20 S	Randy/Jake	Randy/Jake	Railroad**			
55 P	Criss	Dave	Chuck			
51 T/51 F	Mike	Mike/Dave	Chuck			

Diagram 6-2a

Blocking Techniques That Enable the Offense to Score 149

Strongside Play	TACKLE CALLS Strongside					Comments
	5-2 w/Rover	5-2 Rover Quick Slant Strong	5-2 Rover Strong Slant Quick	5-2 Offset Nose Strong	5-2 Offset Nose Quick	Rover: Number 39 (■) *SG - TE/SB scrape to LB when slant is away from play. **C block 1 technique SG block LB
38 G	Mike	Mike	Mike	Mike	Mike	
58 B	Dave	Dave	Dave/Willie	Mike	Mike	
38 K	Mike/Dave	Mike/Dave	Mike/Dave*	Mike/Dave**	Dave	
56 P	Dave	Dave	Dave*	Chuck/Dave**	Dave	
36 V	Dave	Dave	Dave*	Chuck/Dave**	Dave	
12 0	Dave	Dave	Dave*	Chuck/Dave**	Dave	
12 CO						

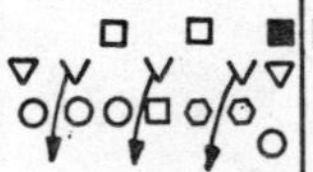

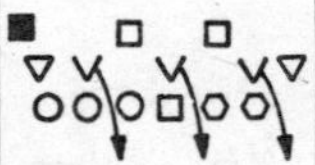

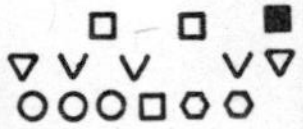

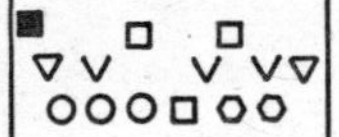

Strongside Play						Comments
	5-2 Eagle/Rover Strongside		5-2 Eagle/Rover Strongside	5-2 Rover Down Eagle Strong (Goal line)	5-2 Rover Walk-up (Goal line)	#Wedge to the center $SG/ST Dave the 3 technique while the TE (SB) blocks the 1st LB inside.
38 G	Criss/Mike	If we get off the ball and EXECUTE. This is what BENSALEM'S defense should look like!	Mike	Mike	Railroad #	
58 B	Mike/Chuck		Mike	Mike	Railroad #	
38 K	Dave		Dave	Dave	Chuck/Mike	
56 P	Ted $		Dave	Dave	Railroad #	
36 V	Ted $		Dave	Dave	Railroad #	
12 0	Ted $		Dave	Dave	Railroad #	
12 CO	Ted $					

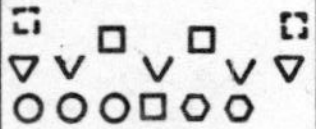

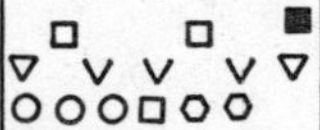

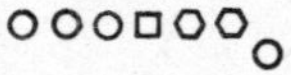

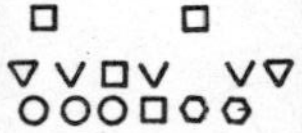

Diagram 6-2a (cont'd.)

150 Blocking Techniques That Enable the Offense to Score

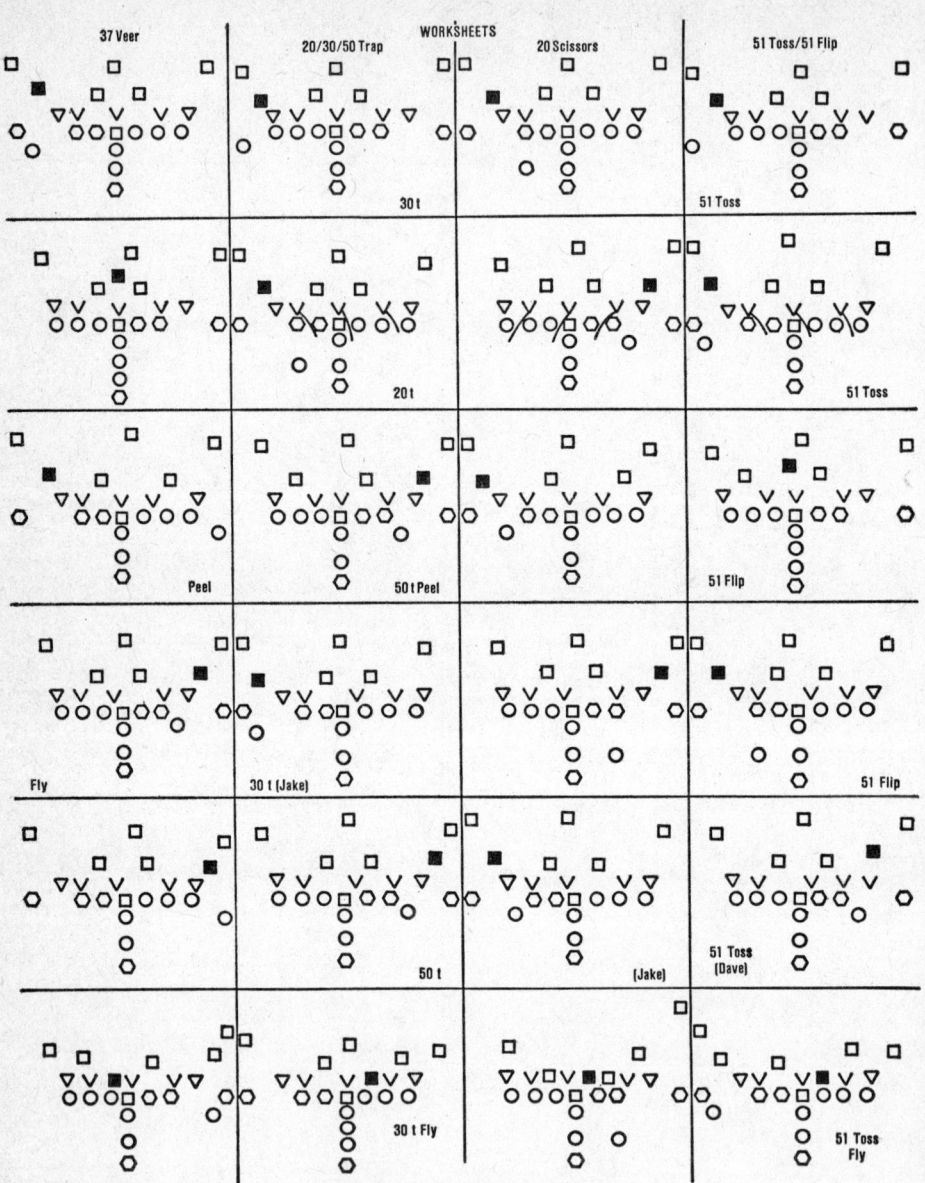

Diagram 6-2b

As your linemen become familiar with defensive fronts, stemming defenses should pose little problem. An individual defender located at each point of attack can only assume so many alignments or techniques. Even if the tackle is unable to make a new call, the blockers at the point-of-attack must recognize the realignment and employ the appropriate blocking call and technique.

BLOCKING THEORY

Because of a glaring lack of big linemen in our football program, the scramble block was adopted and modified to serve as the basis of our blocking technique. In its modification, the emphasis is placed on the blocker remaining low while exploding off the LOS, attacking the defender's hip area with as much blocking surface as possible. The scramble blocker, although firing out low, is coached to deliver a shoulder block while avoiding going into an all fours or crab position unless he is losing the block.

This version of the scramble technique enables the blocker to accomplish his task while avoiding the power area of the defender's upper body. Too often in the past, good blocking position was lost when our smaller blockers simply could not sustain their blocks against bigger defenders.

By neutralizing the defender's source of mobility, the blocker decreases defensive movement along the LOS, creating gaps or running lanes for our option-style runners, especially our tailback. These running lanes are initially created by aggressive line splits.

The key to our successful scramble blocking in the Swingback-Motion Offense is for the offensive linemen to explode off the ball. This explosion enables the blocker to immobilize the defender while gaining defensive movement off the LOS. It must be a quick uncoiling from the basic line or blocking position as their explosion captures the neutral zone.

BASIC BLOCKING POSITION

Offensive linemen in the Swingback-Motion Offense use a four-point stance. From this stance, the blocker uses the basic blocking, or "power position." His head is up in the neck's anatomically strongest position (flexion or "bulled" position), and his back is arched while his buttocks are low. The blocker's legs are well up underneath his center of gravity to help improve stability while augmenting his power.

As initial contact is made with the inside shoulder, the blocker extends into the defender, gathers his legs while streamlining his body by snapping his hips forward and throwing his head and eyes "toward the sky." This hip movement arches the blocker's back and adds power to his block.

If the blocker loses his power or blocking position, he scrambles to an all fours or crab position and works his shoulders and buttocks upfield through the outside hip/knee area of the defender, forcing the defender to play through him to the ball.

INDIVIDUAL BLOCKING TECHNIQUES

Individual blocking techniques involving a defender who is head up or offset to the playside are started with a 45 degree step toward the playside with his playside foot. While keeping low, the blocker gains an outside or playside position on the defender. His points of reference are his backside or inside shoulder across to the playside hip of the defender. This 45 degree step is designed to position the blocker at the point where the defender will be on the snap of the ball, and not where he is before the snap.

As the blocker gathers his legs, he works to square his shoulders and feet with the LOS to gain movement upfield. This position makes it difficult for a well coached defender to play through the blocker's head to the ball. The blocker tries to pin or squeeze the defender between his head and inside shoulder. (See Diagram 6-3.)

Shoulders Square   Shoulders Unsquare

Diagram 6-3

If the blocker loses his blocking position, he scrambles or crab blocks the defender, working to square his shoulders with the LOS. This squaring up is the only way that scramble blocking can be consistently effective.

Diagram 6-4

In blocking a linebacker, the lineman uses a different point of reference. He continues to release off the LOS at a 45 degree angle toward the playside, driving his inside (backside) shoulder across the linebacker's playside armpit. As he achieves this position, the blocker squares up and drives the linebacker upfield. (See Diagram 6-4.)

Considering the clip zone that extends from tackle to tackle and three yards on either side of the LOS, the blocker, as a last resort, will clip the linebacker, scrambling on all fours while rolling up the back or side of his legs.

In order to effectively block a linebacker, the blocker must explode off the LOS and drive for a point where the linebacker will be, not where he is initially aligned.

Movement upon contact, regardless of whether it is versus a down lineman or a linebacker, is gained through short, choppy, driving steps as the blocker works for balance while avoiding instability through overstriding and overextending.

REACH BLOCK

A Reach Block is designed to eliminate any defender who is aligned to the playside and who is outside of the blocker's position at the snap of the ball. It involves most odd-numbered techniques.

The Reach Block technique is basically the same individual blocking technique previously presented in this chapter. The major difference is that the blocker may have to flatten out his initial step to insure that the defender's penetration will be minimized and that the blocker will gain as much blocking surface across the defender's outside knee/hip as possible (See Diagram 6-5.)

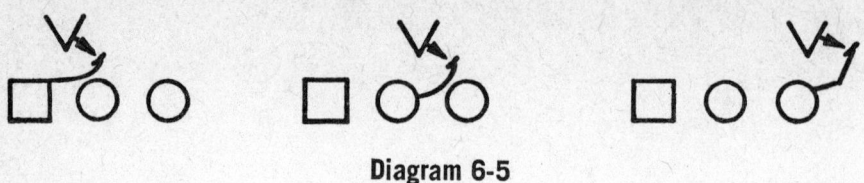

Diagram 6-5

The reach blocker's primary concern is eliminating defensive penetration while hindering the defender's movement to the outside.

DOUBLE-TEAM BLOCK

The Double-Team Block in the Swingback-Motion Offense is based on the post-lead concept in which one blocker posts or centers the defender while the other blocker leads or drives him, walling him off from the point-of-attack.

The post blocker steps off at a 45 degree angle with his outside (playside) foot, attempting to establish head position on the playside hip of the defender (reach block). The lead blocker begins his execution by stepping with his inside foot, sealing off the playside gap between himself and the post blocker so that the defender's initial charge does not split the block. Both of these first steps are short, six to eight-inch controlled steps at approximately a 45 degree angle.

Upon sealing the playside gap by stepping properly, the blockers gather their other legs, widen their base of support and establish a solid power position. They utilize short, driving steps to gain momentum and move the defender off the LOS. The double-team's force should be applied upfield, with the blockers swinging their buttocks together to further seal the gap while directing their force off the LOS. (See Diagram 6-6.)

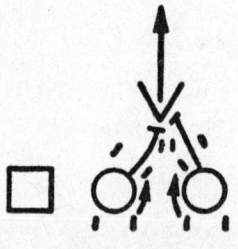

Diagram 6-6

The lead blocker makes contact with his inside shoulder on the playside hip of the defender, putting his chin in the defender's "back pocket." This position by the lead blocker makes it more difficult for the defender to spin out of the block.

If the defender does attempt to slide off of or spin out of the double-team, the lead blocker uses a reverse crab or long body block while the post blocker drives the defender over the lead blocker. (See Diagram 6-7.)

Diagram 6-7

The basis of a good double-team block lies in movement by the defender off of the LOS. In many instances, this movement will hinder linebacker pursuit. If most of the movement is down the line, however, the lead blocker is providing most of the drive to the block. (See Diagram 6-8.)

Diagram 6-8

CRISS BLOCK

A cross block between the guard and tackle versus primarily the Split 4 Defense, the Criss Block sends the tackle down inside on the three technique while the guard comes around for the linebacker. (See Diagram 6-9.)

Diagram 6-9

The tackle, whose move is first, steps inside and down the LOS toward the spot where the defender will be. He establishes head position in front of the defender while delivering a blow with his outside forearm/shoulder. If the defender tries to spin out, the tackle reverse crabs him, whipping his hips into the defender. Otherwise, he drives the three technique down the LOS, allowing little or no penetration.

The guard takes a short step that falls in between a lateral and a drop step, which allows the tackle to block down. The guard then gets upfield tight off the tackle's butt to the linebacker. It is imperative that he immediately gain a "shoulders square to the LOS" position so as to enable him to effectively block a quick scraping linebacker.

This short first step by the guard allows him to pick up the linebacker if he stunts inside. In order to effectively execute the Criss block, the guard must establish eye contact with the linebacker as he is making his short first step. (See Diagram 6-10.)

Diagram 6-10

TURNOUT BLOCK

On the Turnout Block, which is used quite extensively with our Blast or isolation play, the blocker explodes on the snap of the ball with a short six- to eight-inch step with the foot closest to the defender while driving for the inside hip of the defender. The blocker makes contact with his outside shoulder while establishing head position past the inside hip of the defender.

Once this position is attained, the blocker uses his basic individual blocking techniques, driving the defender in whatever direction possible. His primary concern is to sustain the block, either through shoulder contact or through scrambling, and also to maintain his body position between the ball and the defender.

TONY BLOCK

Used versus the 5-2 as well as the Split 4 Defense, the Tony block is a reverse Criss block. The guard blocks to the outside while the tackle comes around to the inside for the linebacker. (See Diagram 6-11.)

Diagram 6-11

The same principles for the Turnout and Criss blocks are used in the Tony block. To facilitate the guard's role in the Tony block versus a 5-2 Defense, the guard is encouraged to take a maximum split while the tackle assumes a minimum split.

SEAL BLOCK

The Seal Block is used by backside linemen as they block from their initial position to the playside hip of the center.

No defensive movement upon contact is required in the Seal Block. The premium lies in the backside linemen cutting or sealing off backside pursuit and penetration. Clipping is legal but is encouraged only as a last resort. If the blocker must clip when sealing, he probably did not execute his technique with enough quickness and enthusiasm.

Very little credit is ever given to backside blockers. In the Swingback-Motion Offense, in which the ball is on or near the LOS a great deal of the time with the veer/option, the Seal Block is carefully and methodically coached. Players who execute successful Seal Blocks that cut off backside pursuit are praised along with those linemen who were blocking at the point-of-attack.

The Seal Block consists of two basic techniques. The first involves sealing versus a down lineman. The blocker steps directly down the LOS toward the playside, in many cases employing almost a pulling movement as he attempts to establish playside position on the defender. (See Diagram 6-12).

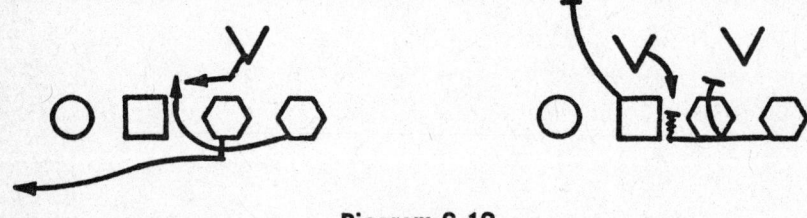

Diagram 6-12

Once the blocker establishes position, he works to get upfield on the defender, squaring his shoulders so that the defender will have to go through as much of his body surface as possible if he is to pursue the play.

The second seal technique is used versus a linebacker. The blocker comes off the LOS at a 45 degree angle toward the playside, driving upfield while working his headgear across the playside armpit of the linebacker. If the linebacker threatens to stunt, the blocker uses a flatter first step in order to achieve position in front of the linebacker.

"RAILROAD" OR WEDGE BLOCK

On all trap plays and certain inside running plays (37/38 Give, 57/58 Blast) versus a walked-up or short yardage defense, "Railroad" is a call made on the LOS by any offensive blocker who first recognizes the defense, alerting everyone else along the LOS that Wedge Blocking is now being used.

The center (on all trap plays) or either guard (on the Give or Blast plays) are the apex of the wedge. Everyone else takes a short step inside toward the apex, placing his inside shoulder on the outside hip of the next blocker to the inside. Upon contact with the blocker to the inside, the lineman swings his buttocks inside to seal the gap and begins driving or wedging upfield.

PULLING TECHNIQUES

All five interior linemen, excluding the center, will be required at one time or another to pull in the Swingback-Motion Offense. They may pull to lead the Toss or Flip plays, to influence veer/option defenders, or to trap.

Speed and balance are the two most important attributes that pulling linemen must possess. They must be quick enough to get out of their stance and yet be balanced enough upon contact to deliver an effective block.

The lineman's stance must be the same functional four-point stance that he assumes on all offensive plays. Tipping his pull and/or direction by leaning back on his haunches or cocking his stance must be eliminated through repetition. An alert defensive player can detect stance variations that provide him with early cues as to what type of play to expect and where to expect it.

Four important fundamentals are stressed in coaching pulling in the Swingback-Motion Offense:

1. *Pushing off with both hands*. From his four-point stance, the lineman pushes off the ground with both hands, starting his pull by gaining momentum through his hands and arms.
2. *Throwing the playside elbow*. The elbow to the side of the pull is thrown backwards and around the back of the pulling lineman, opening his shoulders and hips toward the direction of his pull.
3. *Taking a short, controlled, six-inch step*. This step builds the foundation for the entire pull. It must be into the LOS slightly if the player is trapping in order to achieve the proper attack course on the most difficult defender to trap. If the blocker is pulling to lead a wide play, his first step parallels the LOS so that he can gain depth off the LOS on his third and fourth steps. (See Diagram 6-13.)

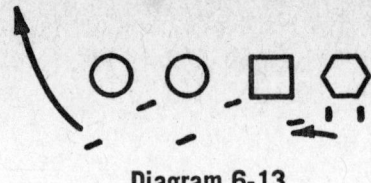

Diagram 6-13

4. *Putting the chest over the knee.* In order to achieve balance and a low hitting position, the blocker, after pushing off his hands and throwing his playside elbow back and taking a short six-inch lead step, places his chest over his lead knee. He keeps his head up and his eyes open. This position keeps him low and allows him to roll over the lead leg while gaining the momentum that is needed at the point of contact.

In trapping, the lineman uses a shoulder block that corresponds with the direction of his pull. When trapping to the left, the blocker makes contact with his left shoulder while establishing head position "in the hole." If the defender being trapped penetrates too far upfield, the lineman turns upfield and becomes a lead blocker.

When pulling on the Toss, Flip or Power plays, the guards execute the same four fundamentals that the trapping linemen employ. However, because they are pulling to lead the play and not to trap, depth is required off the LOS to facilitate their getting around the corner quickly. As the guard pulls, he gains depth off the LOS on his third step so that he can turn the corner as tight as possible to the last block along the LOS. This depth allows him to direct his momentum straight upfield. (See Diagram 6-14.)

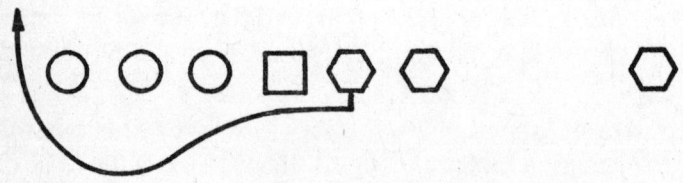

Diagram 6-14

This course enables the blocker to "hug" the corner or last inside block while eliminating running laterally and stretching the play to the sideline. (See Diagram 6-15.)

Blocking Techniques That Enable the Offense to Score

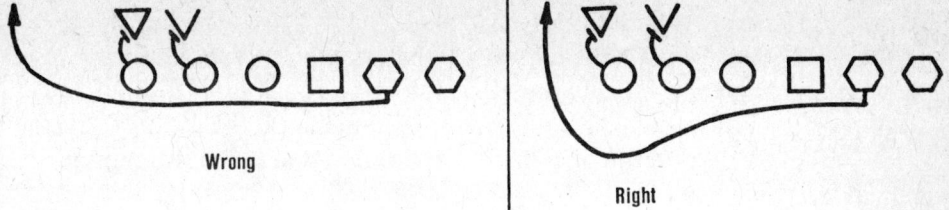

Diagram 6-15

The pulling guard is coached to look inside first, then upfield and finally to the outside. Positive yardage is insured if the ball carrier crosses yard lines instead of hash marks, and the guard must eliminate inside pursuit first if the ball carrier is to consistently gain yardage.

On our bootleg plays, the pulling guard will gain depth on his second step while gaining a square position with the defender to be blocked. (See Diagram 6-16.)

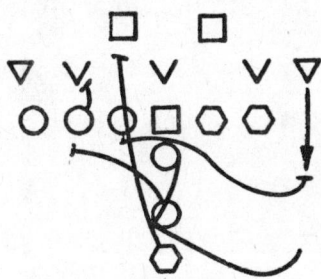

Diagram 6-16

This square position allows the guard to react to whatever position he finds the defender in. It also allows him to head straight upfield and block if the quarterback gives a "Go" call. After gaining the proper depth, which is approximately five yards off the LOS and just outside the offensive tackle, he squares up and slides, keying the defender. Since the defender is reading the quarterback, the guard reads the defender in order to know where the ball is at all times. The guard waits for the defender and delivers a combination hands and shoulder block similar to his digit protection block. If the defender is playing a waiting game, the blocker goes after him under control, attempting to keep his hands out of the throwing lanes.

As with all effective boot plays in the Swingback-Motion Offense, the quarterback must help set up the guard's block. If the defender is working outside to contain the play, the quarterback must pull up and allow his guard to block the defender to the outside. If the defender tries to make the play from the inside, the quarterback should continue outside while his guard walls off the defender to the inside.

INFLUENCE BLOCKING

Influence Blocking is used exclusively with the Swingback-Motion trapping game. There are three types of Influence Blocks used:

1. Pull Influence (see pulling techniques)
2. Reach Influence (see Reach Block)
3. Pass Influence

Depending on the type of defender to be influenced, the lineman to the side of the trap will use one of the three influence blocks to set up the defender for the trap.

In the Pull or Reach Influence, the lineman executes the initial block before blocking out on the next defender on or off the LOS. (See Diagram 6-17.)

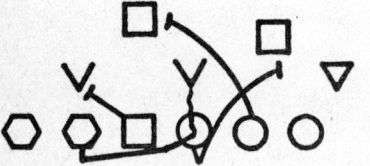

Pull Influence

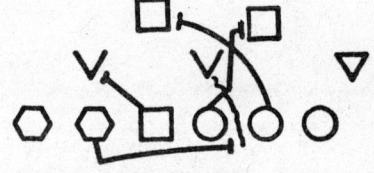

Reach Influence

Diagram 6-17

Possibly the most effective influence block that we use, especially versus Oklahoma 5-2 teams, is the Pass Influence. The offensive tackle drops off the line showing pass. He delays two counts before blocking outside on the next defender on or off the LOS. The tight end or swingback picks up the tackle's rule of first linebacker inside if the guard must help the center with the noseman. (See Diagram 6-18.)

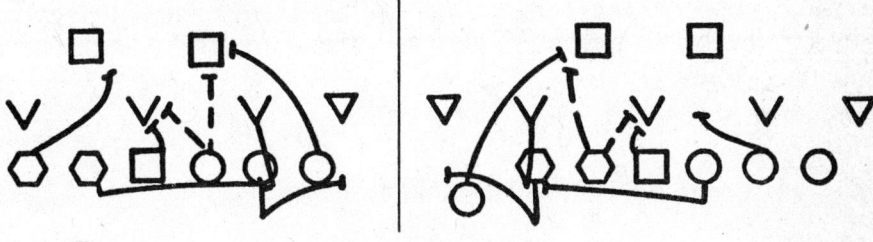

Diagram 6-18

DOWNFIELD BLOCKING

Linemen who pull and lead our wide plays, or who release from the backside to get downfield to block, are encouraged to knock the defender to the grass. Too often, the running shoulder block allows the defender to play off the block and make the tackle. For this reason, we coach the Chop and Roll Block downfield.

As the blocker approaches the defender, he breaks down in a good football position while getting close enough to the defender to step on his toes. From this position, he throws a hard right (or left) cross to the defender's belt buckle while driving his corresponding leg and hip into the man. The force behind the right or left cross will increase the leg and hip momentum into the defender.

Upon contact, the blocker rolls up the defender's legs. He must avoid lunging or jumping at the defender, but rather, drives through him. By rolling, the blocker may be able to get back up and help out elsewhere while trapping the defender's legs under him.

SEPARATION BLOCK

The Separation, or "Touchdown" Block is used to knock a potential tackler from the ball carrier. It is an extra effort block that normally occurs past the LOS, and, because of its important nature, charts are kept each week to determine those individuals who are making the extra effort to achieve a Separation Block.

The blocker selects a part of the tackler that is not in direct line with the ball carrier (normally somewhere between the defender's armpit and knee), and executes a running shoulder block. He drives through the tackler, trying to dislodge his arms and shoulders from the ball carrier.

Separation blocks often mean the difference between a mere gain and a touchdown. However, caution and common sense must be used if there is the possibility of a clip. The blocker must also avoid making contact with the ball carrier.

PASS BLOCKING

Pass blocking in the Swingback-Motion Offense encompasses aggressive blocking (quick passes and play action passes), digit protection (longer dropback passes), gap hinge blocking (backside play action protection) and screen pass blocking.

1. AGGRESSIVE "MIKE" BLOCKING

Each lineman blocks his "Out, over, linebacker" rule. When blocking a down lineman or a linebacker on the LOS, the blocker fires out with a 45 degree step into the defender's knee/hip area. He must insure that the hands of the defender are kept down out of the passing lanes.

When his Mike rule includes a linebacker, the blocker steps off at a 45 degree step at the first down lineman to the inside, while keying the linebacker. If the linebacker drops, the blocker helps block the down lineman. If the linebacker rushes, the blocker fires off his inside foot and blocks him. This short six to eight-inch step by the blocker insures his area while holding the linebacker momentarily.

The center blocks his Mike rule, including an offset noseman to either side. When his responsibility involves blocking a linebacker, he short steps at a 45 degree angle toward the quickside gap, keying the first linebacker quickside. Versus a middle linebacker, he short steps directly at him and then sets up short if he drops. (See Diagram 6-19.)

2. DIGIT PROTECTION

Because the gorilla seemingly has the best balance of all animals, we have tried to copy his stance when coaching our linemen to digit protect. The following principles are coached:

Blocking Techniques That Enable the Offense to Score 165

Diagram 6-19

a. Feet shoulder width apart.
b. Ankles, knees and hips are flexed in a posture much like the gorilla. The hip flexion especially gives the pass blocker the "waddle" look that the gorilla has when he walks.
c. Arms hang loosely in between the legs with the fists clenched.
d. Upper trunk is upright and squared to the LOS.
e. Head is erect and the eyes remain open at all times.

The most important aspect of pass blocking is the blocker's ability to gain separation quickly from the LOS. By quickly getting back off the LOS, the blocker creates a buffer that the defender must close before he reaches the blocker. As the defender closes this distance, the blocker is already set up and is able to discern what type of pass rush the defender is going to use. (See Diagram 6-20.)

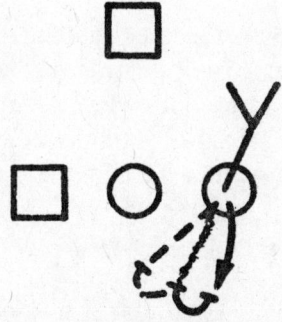

Diagram 6-20

The depth of the blocker's drop depends on whether the potential rusher is a defender on the LOS or one off the LOS. If he is on the LOS, the blocker sets up at approximately two yards and to the inside of the defender. If the rusher is off the line, the blocker sets up at approximately four yards. This extra two yards enables the blocker to move in any direction that the defender might stunt.

As the blocker sets up, he attempts to position himself on the inside hip of the rusher. He must protect the inside rush lane first because that is the shortest distance to the quarterback. As a result, the blocker will always honor an inside fake by the defender while never taking an outside fake.

The blocker's primary objective is to keep his body between the defender and the quarterback. To achieve this objective, the blocker uses a hit and recoil technique. Waiting until the defender has committed himself, the pass blocker, from his gorilla-like square stance, takes a short jab step with his outside foot while delivering a blow with his outside shoulder and hands.

It is important that the blocker not get his feet too far apart. This will destroy his balance and severely limit his mobility. Upon contact, he drives his hands up between himself and the rusher, keeping his hands up and his forearms parallel. This forearm position makes it difficult for the rusher to use the blocker's elbows as handles for turning him. The hands also act as a buffer to help absorb and impede the rusher's momentum.

If the rusher grabs the blocker's pads, the blocker, with a violent outward thrust of his forearms, is able in many cases to dislodge the rusher's grip. It is imperative that the blocker not allow his shoulders to be turned perpendicular to the LOS.

After contact, the blocker recoils from the rusher by pushing off his jab step and resets his square position to again await the rusher. He must wait for the rusher and not go out and chase him.

Digit protection is a man-blocking scheme based on a helping principle if the blocker's assigned man does not rush. Chasing defenders destroys this principle by opening up rushing lanes.

Our digit pass blockers are concerned about three basic types of pass rushers:

1. Inside rusher. The inside rusher is trying to take the shortest route to the quarterback. The blocker hits and recoils. If he cannot gain separation from the rusher after contact, the blocker uses an inverted or

Blocking Techniques That Enable the Offense to Score 167

reverse shoulder block and drives the defender to the inside. He uses short, choppy steps and avoids overstriding. If the blocker allows his center of gravity to go beyond his base of support, he becomes unbalanced and is easily shed by the rusher.

2. Outside rusher. The outside rusher presents a problem only in that he may begin outside and then attempt to defeat the rusher back to the inside.

The blocker must understand that if he remains between the rusher and the quarterback he has done his job. Versus the outside rusher he hits, recoils and maintains proper body position in a balanced posture. If the blocker cannot separate from the rusher, he forces his head from the inside to the outside and uses a reverse shoulder block to run the rusher past the quarterback. (See Diagram 6-21.)

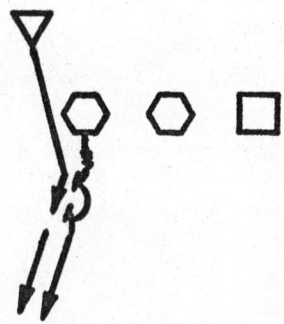

Diagram 6-21

The blocker again uses short, choppy steps while gaining control of his momentum. All too often, the rusher will stop and attempt to use the blocker's momentum to run him past the quarterback. The rusher then steps behind and sacks the passer.

The blocker must play a "cat and mouse" game with the outside rusher, waiting for him to commit himself before he delivers his block. As the game progresses, the blocker is able to determine when the rusher is trying to defeat him by going to the outside and when he is decoying his inside rush by first starting outside.

3. Straight ahead rusher. The straight ahead rusher is trying to overpower the blocker or is trying to get him turned perpendicular to the LOS so that he can defeat him to the inside or to the outside. If strong

enough, the blocker hits and recoils, hits and recoils, giving ground grudgingly but yet separating from the rusher as he recoils. He knocks the rusher's hands off of him by thrusting his forearms outward. Body position versus the straight ahead rusher is paramount to success.

Cutting the rusher is coached only as a last resort. The blocker hits, recoils and then uses a chop and roll block to knock down the overpowering defender. Cutting as a first block is discouraged because the rusher still has time to get up and assault the quarterback.

If faced with one of your blockers being overpowered, place your best pass blocker to that side by flipping your line and make whatever adjustments are needed to insure that your best blocker ends up on their best pass rusher.

3. GAP HINGE BLOCK

In the Gap Hinge Block, the linemen protecting the backside on play action passes take a short lateral step toward the playside to insure the gap. They then push off their gap step and wheel or hinge back toward the backside. (See Diagram 6-22.)

Diagram 6-22

Once the backside blockers hinge, the protection becomes a man scheme inside of a zone concept. The inside blocker protects the inside first, then helps out where needed. The next blocker to the outside protects his area, picking up anyone from his inside to his outside. (See Diagram 6-23.)

The gap hinge is likened to the swinging of a gate. Once the gate swings shut, the hinging blockers get approximately a yard apart with their backs to the passer and allow no one through the gate. They continue shuffling toward the passer with their heads on a swivel, decreasing the rusher's angle to the quarterback. (See Diagram 6-24.)

Blocking Techniques That Enable the Offense to Score   169

Diagram 6-23

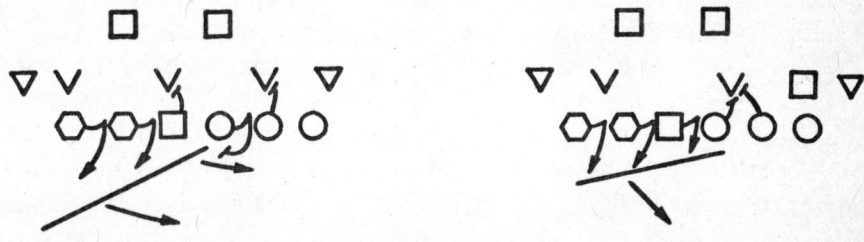

Diagram 6-24

Once a defender enters their area, the blocker employs his hit and recoil, digit protection blocking techniques. He is especially aware of the route (inside, outside or straight ahead) that the rusher is attempting to take.

4. SCREEN BLOCKING

All of the Screen plays in the Swingback-Motion Offense are for the most part quick screens run off of play action fakes. As a result, the most important aspect of our screen blocking lies in the lineman's ability to establish contact on the LOS momentarily, then slip behind the defender and sprint to the screen area. This slipping behind the defender causes him to lose sight of the blocker as he reacts to the run fake. (See Diagram 6-25.)

Everyone involved in the screen gets off at a 45 degree angle toward the screenside. If the defender is on the LOS, the blocker makes contact with the outside of the defender, delays for one count, then sprints to the screen area. If the defender is off the LOS, the blocker steps and delays a count before sprinting outside.

Diagram 6-25

The screenside tackle is responsible for driving out any defender reacting up from the outside. If no one shows, he waits for the receiver's "Go" call and leads him upfield. The screen guard is responsible for getting in front of the receiver and leading him upfield. The center gets to a position just inside the screen area (which is a point approximately equidistant from the screen receiver and screen tackle's original position) and blocks inside first, then upfield. Their technique can be either the running shoulder block or, more preferably, the chop and roll block.

RECEIVER BLOCKING TECHNIQUES

As a receiver in the Swingback-Motion Offense, the split end (X), swingback (SB or Z) and tight end (Y) are responsible for learning the following blocking techniques:

1. STALK BLOCK (X, Y, SB)

See Chapter 3 for a detailed discussion of stalk blocking principles.

2. CRACK/STALK BLOCK (X, SB)

In an attempt to gain as much advantage on the Toss or Flip plays as the crackback block affords, yet minimize the illegal blocks and clips that are inherently present in a crack situation, we use the crack/stalk block.

On the snap, the wideout takes one step upfield with his outside foot, then drives straight down the line toward the defender to be blocked.

This first step is used to push the outside defender off the LOS while the receiver disguises the play. As the receiver drives inside, he adjusts his course to that of the defender while determining whether or

Blocking Techniques That Enable the Offense to Score 171

not he can block him legally. If he can, he uses a high, running shoulder block, making contact with his upfield shoulder into the defender's armpit while establishing head position in front of the defender (See Diagram 6-26.)

Diagram 6-26

If there is the possibility of a clip, the receiver breaks down and stalks the defender in the same manner that he would on a veer play.

The receiver waits for the defender to square up to the LOS before attempting to block him with a high shoulder block. If it appears that the defender will not allow himself to be legally blocked, the receiver deepens and looks for the next defender pursuing from the inside.

3. NEAR SAFETY/CORNER BLOCK (X, SB, Y)

On running plays away, it is the receiver's task to block the near safety or corner. It is primarily a hustle block, with the emphasis lying in the proper route taken. (See Diagram 6-27.)

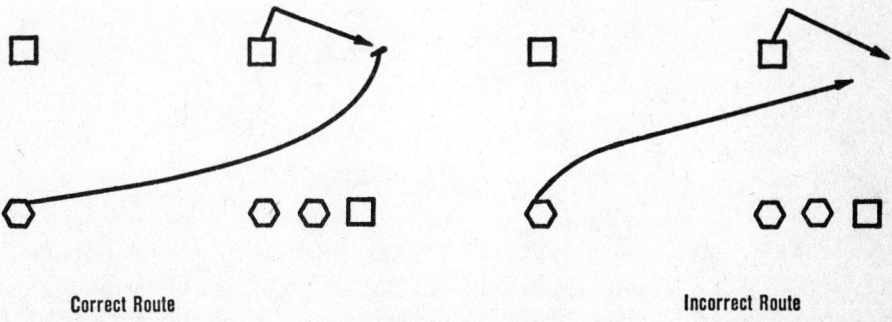

Correct Route   Incorrect Route

Diagram 6-27

The receiver must flatten out his course and sprint to a position where the safety is going to be, and not to where he is. It then becomes a simple matter of how much the receiver wants to get to the defender and make the block.

The blocking technique is either a chop and roll block, if the receiver achieves a position in front of the defender, or a running shoulder block if he is alongside of the defender. He must avoid the clip at all costs. If he has any doubt, the receiver doesn't throw the block.

As the receiver sprints to the near safety (corner), he looks for the ball. If the runner is breaking back against the pursuit, he breaks down and crack/stalks the defender.

4. JAM ON/OUT BLOCK (SB, Y)

This type of block is used by the swingback from a slot position and by the tight end. The blocker fires out toward the inside hip of the defender, delivering a shoulder/forearm block with his outside arm. He then releases upfield on the near safety or corner. (See Diagram 6-28.)

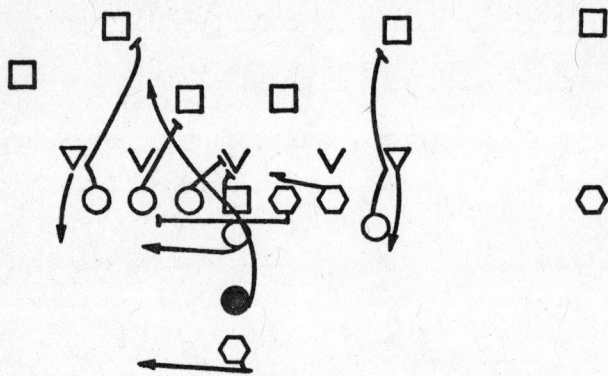

Diagram 6-28

The Jam on/out Block is used to temporarily impede a defender who, if left unblocked, could possibly make the tackle on an inside play. And yet, it is not imperative for the blocker to sustain his block. Rather, he is trying to make the defender go around his block, giving the ball carrier time to get through the hole.

BACKFIELD BLOCKING TECHNIQUES

The brunt of the backfield blocking in the Swingback-Motion Offense is borne by the fullback. John McKay, former head coach at USC and now the head mentor for Tampa Bay of the National Football League, once stated that the burden isn't on the tailback who carries the ball 28-30 times a game but, rather on the fullback who is being hit and pounded on every play.

BLAST BLOCK

In the Blast Block, the fullback (swingback) drives on the isolated linebacker and executes a shoulder block, knocking the linebacker back off the LOS. This type of block allows the tailback to option run and break into the open area. (See Diagram 6-29.)

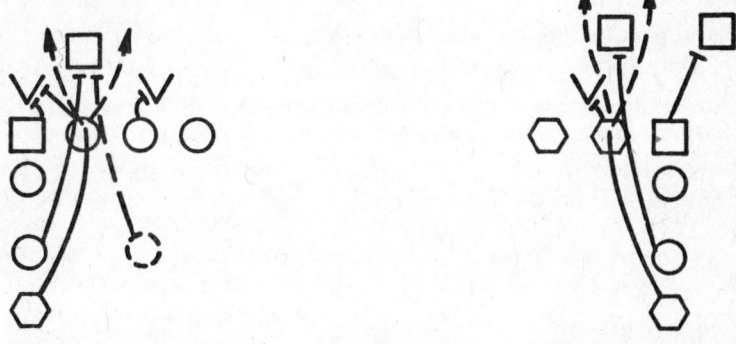

Diagram 6-29

The fullback's shoulder block is aimed at the numbers of the linebacker. The success of the block lies in the blocker getting his shoulder under the pads of the linebacker, straightening him up out of his power position. (See Chapter 5 for a detailed description of 57/58 Blast.)

KICKOUT BLOCK

The key to the fullback's block on the power play is an inside/out course that provides him with the proper angle to block the most difficult defender, one who squeezes the hole down without penetrating.

The fullback's first step is a crossover step toward the outside hip of the playside guard. This step allows him to clear the quarterback's reverse pivot while establishing an inside/out course on the defender to be kicked out. He mentally approaches every power play by working from the toughest (1) to the easiest (3) defender. (See Diagram 6-30.)

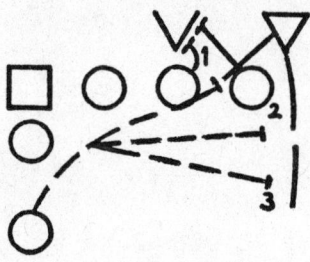

Diagram 6-30

As he approaches the defender, the fullback gathers himself and delivers a shoulder block while establishing head position to the inside. He uses a right shoulder block when the play is going to the right, and vice versa for a power play to the left.

LOG (PIN) BLOCK

Many times on the power play, the fullback will be confronted with a pinching defender, making it most difficult for him to kick the defender out. Therefore, the fullback is coached to log or pin the defender to the inside, with the tailback reading the block and taking the play to the outside. (See Diagram 6-31.)

In the Log Block, the fullback starts out on his normal inside/out power course. As he nears the defender, he drives his inside shoulder into the outside hip/knee of the defender, then whips his hips into the man, pinning him to the inside. He goes into an all fours crab position if needed, to keep the defender inside.

The Log Block is also used on the Toss and other outside plays versus a pinching or crashing defender.

FILL BLOCK

Filling for a pulling lineman requires the back to carry out his fake or assignment while attaining proper body position at the LOS. It is

Blocking Techniques That Enable the Offense to Score   175

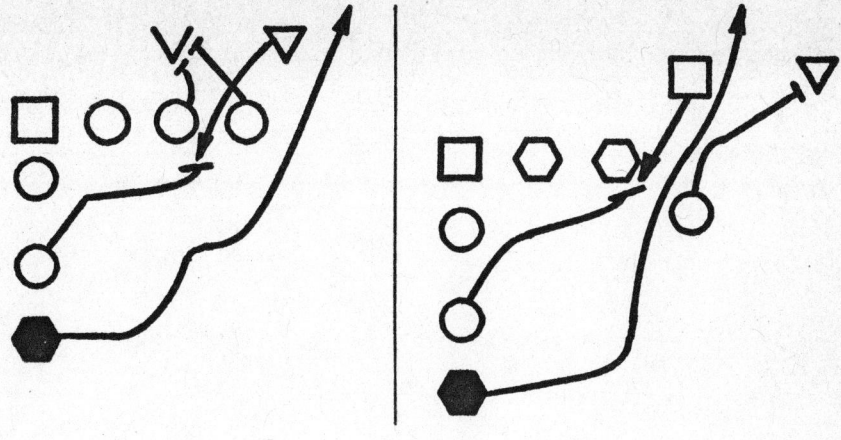

Diagram 6-31

imperative to his success that the back begin inside (playside) and work to the outside (backside) when establishing his blocking angle.

The back must force the defender, by body position alone, to come through him if he is to get to the ball. He runs the play that is being faked as quickly as possible, delivering a block with his backside shoulder/forearm while establishing head position between the defender and the ball.

CHOP AND ROLL BLOCK

See Linemen/Downfield Blocking in this chapter for a detailed discussion of the Chop and Roll Block.

INFLUENCE/TURNOUT BLOCK

Primarily a block used by the tight end and/or swingback on the power play versus a Split 4 Defense, the Influence/Turnout Block involves influencing the anchor defender before blocking or turning out on the next defender to the outside.

The blocker steps with his inside foot directly at the anchor, then pushes off to the outside. He immediately establishes inside/out position and walls the defender off. As he makes contact with his downfield shoulder (shoulder closest to the ball), he slides his head upfield. Because his block is not at the point of attack (the anchor he influences is being kicked out), the tight end and/or swingback is more concerned with body position and with sustaining the block than with driving the defender down the line.

The Influence Block can also be effectively used when the swingback is in a power or open position. He attacks the defender to be kicked out on a lead or reach course. As the defender reacts outside to the influence, the swingback turns out or goes upfield on the safety or corner. (See Diagram 6-32.)

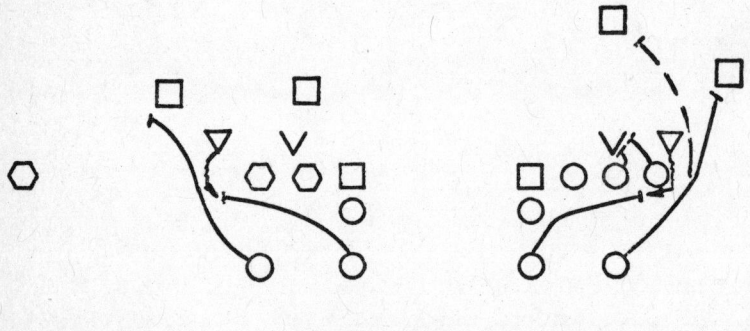

Diagram 6-32

LEAD BLOCK

See Chapter 3 for a detailed discussion of lead blocking on the corner support. This block is used on the Toss/Flip, Veer and all option plays as the Swingback-Motion Offense captures the corner.

BACKFIELD PASS BLOCKING TECHNIQUES

Running backs in the Swingback-Motion Offense must be able to pass block on dropback and sprint out passes as well as on play action passes.

1. AGGRESSIVE MIKE BLOCK

The fullback and tailback use an aggressive Mike block on all 90 series passes (quick passes). They are responsible for attacking their man and forcing him to keep his hands down out of the throwing lanes.

The back drives for the outside knee of the defender. The key lies in the back attacking as though the play were a run. This forces the defender to engage the back instead of looking for the pass.

Versus seven-man fronts, the fullback (strongside) and the tailback (quickside) block the end defender on the LOS. Versus eight-man fronts, the full back checks the first linebacker to the strongside before blocking the end defender. If the linebacker stunts, the fullback attacks him and blocks him low in an attempt to keep his hands down. The tailback continues to block the Willie linebacker.

2. DIGIT PROTECTION BLOCKING

In Digit Protection, the fullback is always responsible for blocking the first linebacker strongside, excluding any Mike or middle linebacker. The tailback always blocks the quickside end or linebacker (Willie). (See Diagram 6-33.)

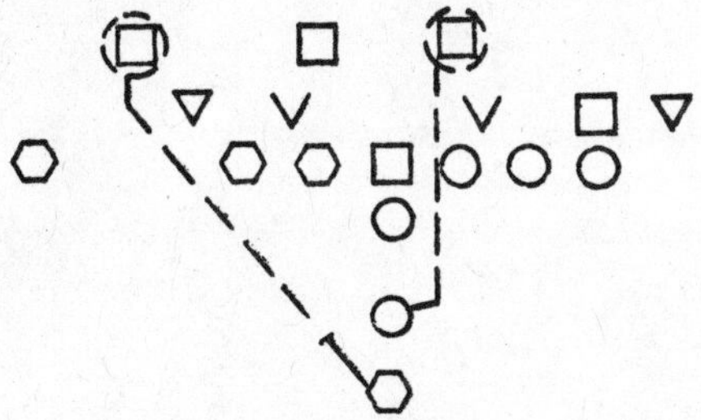

Versus a Split 4 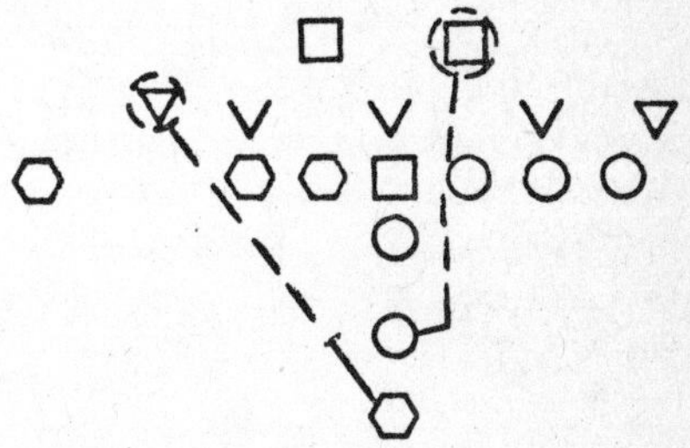   Versus a 5-2

Diagram 6-33

On the snap, the backs step directly at their defender while moving laterally to allow the quarterback to drop. As they step, the fullback and tailback key their defender. If he stunts, the back moves toward the area he is stunting to and blocks him with a high shoulder block. As with the linemen, the backs are conscious of protecting the inside route to the quarterback.

If their defender stunts, the fullback and/or tailback approaches him on a slight inside/out course, achieving solid body position between the rusher and the quarterback. The back then uses the hit and recoil blocking technique, and will cut the rusher only after contacting him first with a shoulder block. (See linemen digit protection techniques in this chapter.)

If no stunt develops, the fullback and tailback square up to the LOS and provide help from the inside to the outside. (See Diagram 6-34.)

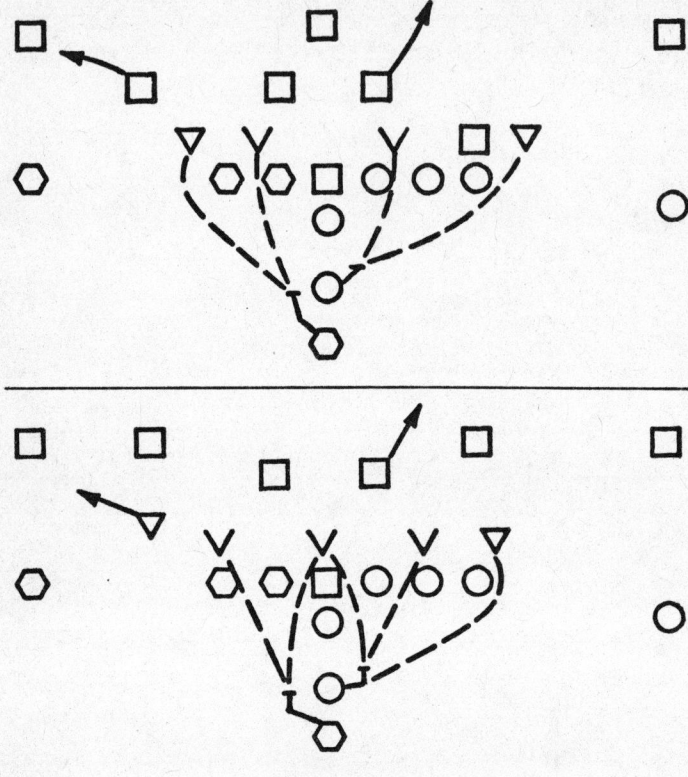

Diagram 6-34

Their heads are on a swivel as they work on not giving up ground which could impede the quarterback's passing motion. Being cognizant of the defensive front being used by our opponent, and also of their strongest pass rushers, aids the fullback and tailback in determining where their help is most needed.

3. SPRINT/JET PROTECTION BLOCKING

The back who is responsible for blocking the number three defender or contain man, drives for the outside knee of the defender and uses a chop and roll block. He must not leave his feet too soon but, rather, establish solid contact with his inside shoulder on the outside knee/hip of the defender, driving through it before he rolls.

When the tailback is assigned to block playside, he keys the fullback's block on the number three defender. He helps the fullback if needed. Otherwise, he checks inside to backside while awaiting the quarterback's "Go" call. (See Diagram 6-35.)

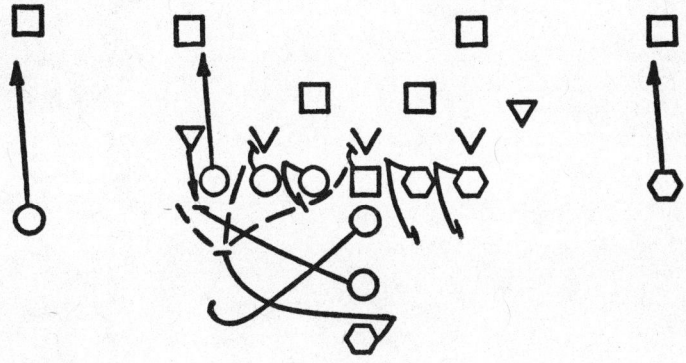

Diagram 6-35

If the tailback is assigned to block backside, he establishes an inside/out position, protecting the shortest route to the quarterback, and employs digit protection blocking techniques.

PASS 37/38 TAILBACK BLOCKING TECHNIQUES

The tailback plays a very important role in the successful execution of Pass 37/38, which, to us, has been one of the most important play action passes in the Swingback-Motion Offense. His blocking technique must be aggressive on the number three defender, and it must keep the defender's hands out of the quarterback's passing lanes.

While counter-stepping, the tailback establishes visual contact with the number three defender. This eye contact helps him to determine the type of technique that the defender will be using.

The tailback then formulates which route he must take in order to achieve proper body position between the defender and the quarterback. (See Diagram 6-36.)

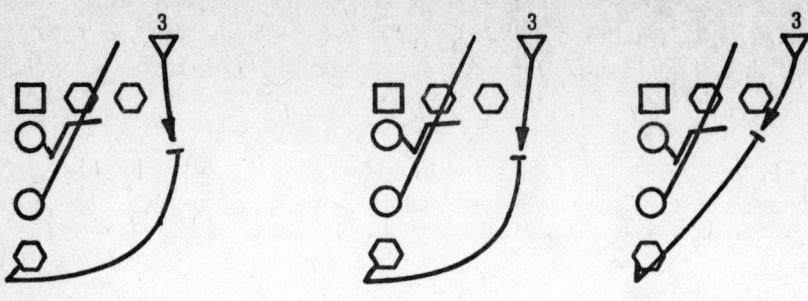

Diagram 6-36

His blocking technique is a shoulder block into the hip of the defender while establishing head position to the inside. However, versus a pinching defender, the tailback uses a log block, pinning the defender to the inside as the quarterback moves to the outside around his block. (See kickout and log blocking techniques in this chapter.)

7

INCORPORATING A SIMPLIFIED PASS OFFENSE INTO THE SWINGBACK-MOTION SYSTEM

The Swingback-Motion Offense can readily employ any type of passing game that your personnel dictates. The simplicity of the pass offense lends itself to either dropback or sprint out action, depending on the abilities of your quarterback and linemen.

With the defense occupied, making continual adjustments to the swingback and his motion capabilities, the passing game becomes a valuable weapon on any down.

Maximum protection, as well as a flare control series, allows the Swingback-Motion Offense to effectively throw the ball against virtually any scheme imaginable.

RECEIVER LEGS

The entire Swingback-Motion passing attack is based on timing the receiver's pattern to the quarterback's action. To accomplish this all-important aspect of passing, receiver legs were developed.

Each leg is six yards in length and has a definite purpose. The first leg is the speed leg. The receiver explodes off the line of scrimmage and makes the defensive back in his area believe that a deep pattern has been called. On the second leg, the receiver tries either to get the defensive back head up if the secondary coverage is man-for-man, or he attempts to decoy his pattern. In conjunction with most second legs, there is a gathering phase in which the receiver gains control over his momentum and prepares to catch the football.

QUARTERBACK DROPS

As the receiver is running his legs, the quarterback is making his drop. In the dropback attack, his drops are at one, three, five and seven steps, depending on which aspect of the dropback attack is to be run. A right-handed quarterback is coached that whenever his right foot hits the ground, he is in a drop position of the pass offense. Conversely, a left-hander knows that when his left foot strikes the ground he is at one of the four drop areas.

The sprint out passing game utilizes both a seven-step half sprint as well as a full sprint out. Both of these passing actions will be discussed in detail later in this chapter.

The emphasis on timed passing is to have the receiver finishing his legs as the quarterback is completing his drop. The quarterback uses a "no reset" method of passing, completing his drop on a semi-flexed back leg so that he can push off while releasing the ball. There is no stepping forward or resetting with his back foot. He plants his back foot and steps forward with his front foot and delivers the ball.

This timing is aimed at eliminating needless quarterback sacks because of the quarterback's taking too much time to reset and throw. It also helps cut down on the quarterback's waiting for the receiver to make his break, which allows the defender time to close on the receiver and the ball.

If defensive teams try and disrupt the timing of the receiver's release off the line of scrimmage, motion will be employed by the swingback to insure that at least one wide receiver will get off the line without being duly harassed.

INTRODUCTION TO THE 90/70 SERIES

The 90 and 70 Series are the base dropback passing series of the Swingback-Motion passing game. They can be run from nearly every offensive set, although the pro set, or motioning the swingback from one set to his pro set position, is the ideal formation. Since the pro set is used

Incorporating a Simplified Pass Offense Into the System

approximately 55-60 percent of the time, the defense is unable to obtain any real tendency as to when it might expect a pass.

90/70 SERIES MECHANICS

The 90 Series is the short or quick passing game. The line will block aggressive Mike (out, over, LB) along the line of scrimmage, firing out low to keep their defender's hands down and out of the passing lanes. It is a maximum protection series. Both the fullback and tailback will stay in and block.

The 70 Series is an extension of the 90 Series. It is the two-leg passing game incorporating three-receiver patterns with maximum protection provided by the line, fullback and tailback. The line uses drop-off blocking techniques with man-for-man principles called digit protection. Digit protection affords the coach immediate answers as to whose man sacked the quarterback.

The split end (X) and swingback (SB) will run mirrored routes, and their routes will be one leg in length (90 series) or two legs in length (70 series). In both series, the receivers must drive off the line of scrimmage, forcing the defense to either respect the deep threat or to commit its coverage immediately. Both of these objectives aid the quarterback in making an intelligent decision as to which receiver to throw to.

The first digit in the 90/70 series designates the line and backfield blocking while the second digit indicates the route to be run by the split end and swingback.

Even-numbered routes (except 90) are run to the outside while the odd-numbered ones are run to the inside. (See Diagram 7-1.)

90/70 SERIES PASSING TREE

Diagram 7-1

ROUTE DESCRIPTIONS OF THE 90/70 SERIES

Each route in the 90/70 series is also given a name so that the receiver can associate the number with the name, making it easier for them to learn the system:

90—Hitch: two to three steps, turn in and face the ball. Give the quarterback a stationary target.

91—Snap: one leg, curl inside and face the ball.

92—Quick: one leg, break outside outside on quick out move, coming slightly back toward the line of scrimmage. Avoid rounding off the 92. It only serves to close the distance between the receiver and defender. (See Diagram 7-2.)

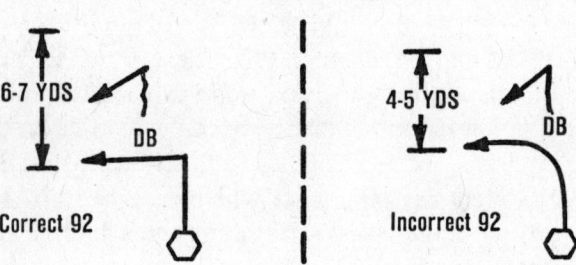

Diagram 7-2

99—Goal: one leg, take a definite step toward the flag, then break for the middle of the goal posts. Avoid bringing the 99 across the field into another defender's zone. Take it right to the posts. (See Diagram 7-3.)

73—Curl: two legs, curl inside and look for the ball.

74—Wide: two legs, turn outside sharply and work slightly back toward the line of scrimmage because the ball is in the air longer. As with the 92, avoid rounding off the 74.

75—In: two legs, turn inside sharply and continue across the field, getting between the linebackers.

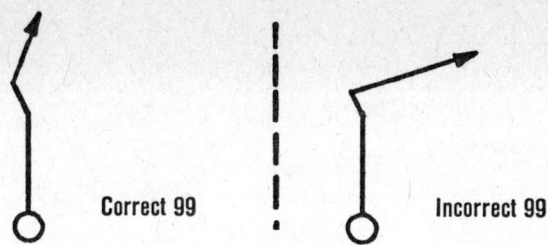

Diagram 7-3

76—Flag: two legs, with the second leg being run to the inside at approximately 60 degrees. Turn back outside and run to the flag. Avoid flattening out the extension of the second and running to the sideline instead of the flag. (See Diagram 7-4.)

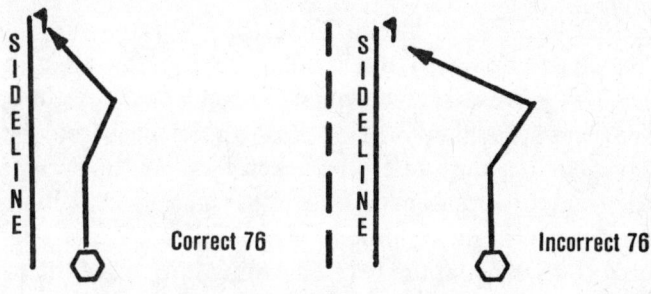

Diagram 7-4

77—Post: two legs, breaking for the middle of the goal posts or between the safeties as the second leg is extended. As with 99, avoid crossing the field. Get upfield to the posts.

78—Streak: two legs, extending the second leg up the field, keeping it outside away from the safety. (See Diagram 7-5.)

As diagrammed, the second leg on all 70 series routes except 76 works to the outside at approximately a 60 degree angle in an attempt to make each pattern look the same and hence decoy the intended route.

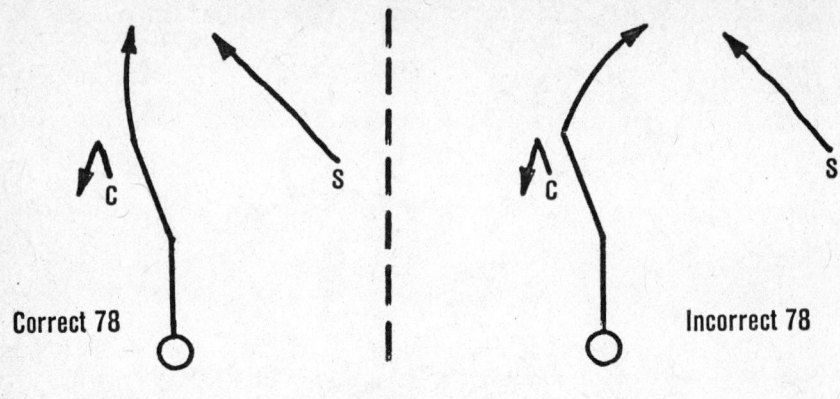

Diagram 7-5

TIGHT END/HOT CURL MIDDLE

The tight end (Y) in the 90/70 series will run a hot curl middle route. His first step is to the inside, keying the first linebacker strongside. If the linebacker disappears or stunts, the tight end yells, "Hot" and turns straight upfield to take the quick pass from the quarterback, who is keying the same linebacker.

It is extremely important that the tight end runs straight upfield and not across the field. By running straight upfield, it puts him on the shortest course to the goal line while keeping him out of the path of the other linebacker. (See Diagram 7-6.)

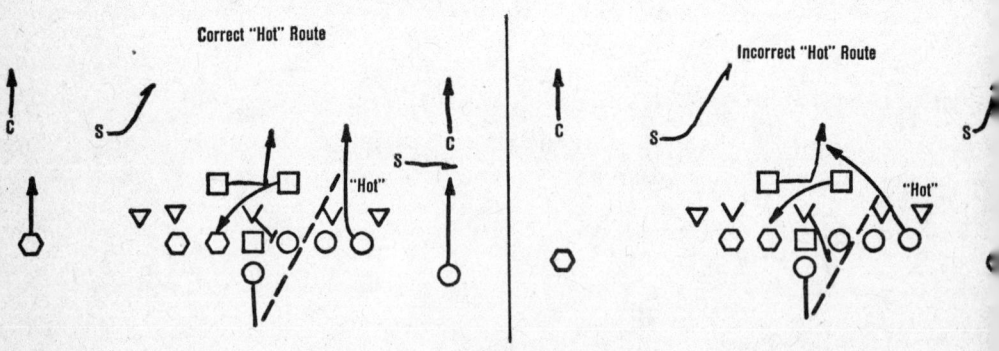

Diagram 7-6

Incorporating a Simplified Pass Offense Into the System 187

If the linebacker doesn't disappear or stunt, the tight end continues upfield and curls in the middle at six yards in the 90 series and at 12 yards in the 70 series. The quarterback now knows that if for some unforeseen reason both wide receivers are covered, he always has the tight end curling in the middle, a zone which many defensive schemes leave open.

QUARTERBACK ACTIONS IN THE 90 SERIES

The quarterback will make a three-step drop on all 90 series routes except 90. On 90 he will take a one-step drop and throw. The 90 pattern is also the only pass in which the quarterback will determine which wide receiver he is going to throw to before the ball is snapped. He simply looks at the defenders and throws to the receiver whose man is playing off of him the furthest. The rest of the 90 series reads will be covered later in this chapter.

QUARTERBACK ACTIONS IN THE 70 SERIES

In the 70 series, the quarterback will make a seven-step drop on every route except 74. On 74 he will drop five steps because of the time and distance that the ball is in the air.

90 SERIES PROTECTION

The base protective scheme for the 90 series will be aggressive Mike, which is out, over, linebacker. (See Diagram 7-7.) The blocking techniques were discussed in Chapter 6.

90 SERIES PROTECTION RULES

C —#0 on or off the LOS; 1st LB quickside.
SG—Out, over, LB.
ST —Out, over, LB.
QG —Out, over, LB.
QT —Out, over, LB.
FB —Check 1st LB strongside to perimeter contain man (defensive end).
TB —First man outside quick tackle (Willie).

The 90 series blocking scheme enables the offense to pick up and block the "hot" key linebacker. However, the ball will still be thrown to the tight end because the underneath coverage to that side has been eliminated by the stunt, leaving only a safety standing between the tight end and the goal line.

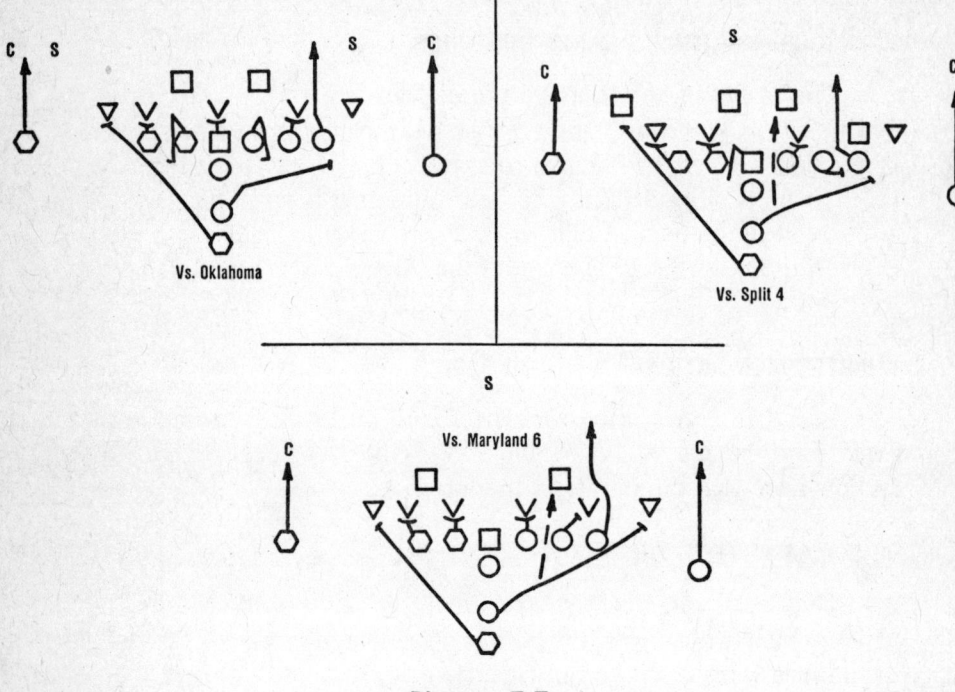

Diagram 7-7

70 SERIES PROTECTION

The pass protection scheme for the 70 series will be digit protection, in which the line counts men, drops off the line of scrimmage and blocks the man they counted. (See Diagram 7-8.) The blocking techniques for digit protection were discussed in Chapter 6.

70 SERIES PROTECTION RULES

    C —#0 on or off LOS; 1st LB quickside.

    SG —#1 on the LOS.

    ST —#2 on the LOS.

Incorporating a Simplified Pass Offense Into the System

QG —#1 on or off the LOS. (Split 4 exception: #2.)
QT —Covered.
FB —1st LB strongside excluding Mike (MLB).
TB —Willie LB.

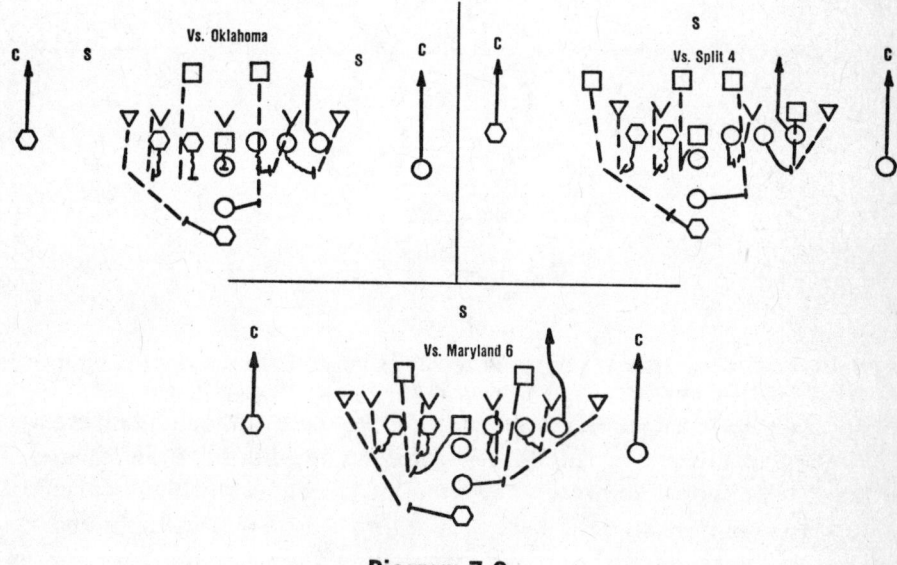

Diagram 7-8

QUARTERBACK READS IN THE 90/70 SERIES

The quarterback's initial read in the 90/70 series is the "hot" key, which is the first linebacker strongside including Mike (MLB). He does this on his first step away from center. If the key disappears or stunts, he dumps the ball to the tight end who is also reading the same key.

If the "hot" key drops off, the quarterback now picks up the safety in his line of sight. If the quarterback is right-handed, it would be the defensive left safety in a four-deep secondary. At the high school level, it is minor that he is the strong or weak safety. Most high school teams employ some form of zone coverage, rolling or inverting the zone to either the two-receiver side or to the wide side of the field. By reading the safety in the line of sight, the quarterback is able to determine the basic coverage and as a result throw away from the strength of the zone.

For example, let's look at, "Right slot, 74 Peel." (See Diagram 7-9.)

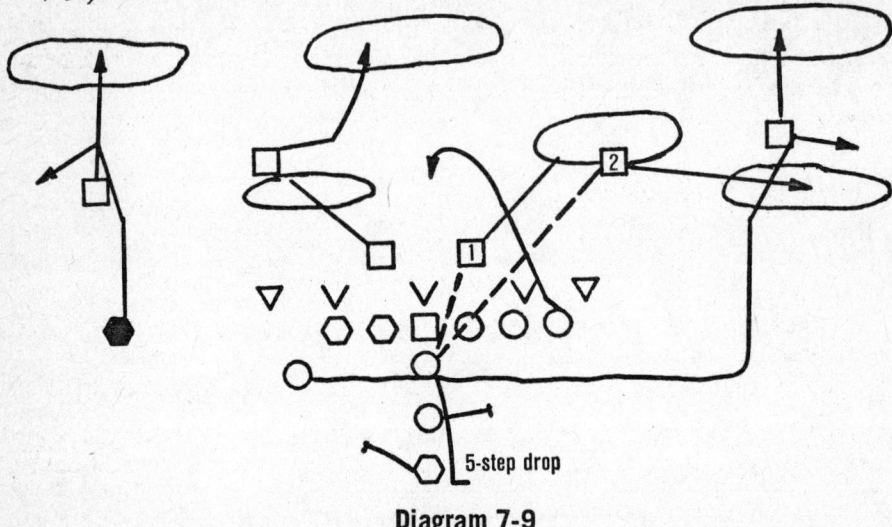

Diagram 7-9

The defense adjusts to the swingback's peel motion and inverts to the two-receiver side. The "hot" linebacker key drops off. The quarterback now knows to throw away from the direction in which his safety read is moving. Therefore, he would throw the 74 to the split end.

In this defense, the secondary is rolling its zone to the quickside as well as to the wideside of the field. The quarterback's "hot" key drops. The ball should be thrown to the swingback, because he is the wide receiver, away from the direction that the safety in the line of sight read is moving.

INTRODUCTION TO THE 60 SERIES

The 60 series is the flare control series of the Swingback-Motion passing game. The tailback and/or fullback will be sent out into the basic three-man pattern in an attempt to influence the defense's underneath coverage as well as to flood a specific zone. This very important phase of

Incorporating a Simplified Pass Offense Into the System 191

the passing game can be run from any set, and in theory will be run mostly from the basic run formations, i.e., open, power, over sets in an effort to catch the defense playing the run first.

In keeping with the offense's basic simplicity and philosophy of execution, the 60 tells the offensive line to use digit protection while the second digit designates the flare control scheme to be used. A word is added to describe the patterns to be run by the three primary receivers, for example, "61 Whirl," "62 Scout."

FLARE CONTROL NUMBERING

60—Both backs block. Maximum protection. (Same as the 70 series).

61—Tailback check assignment and release quickside if he drops; Fullback block assignment.

62—Fullback check assignment and release strongside if he drops; Tailback block assignment.

63—Both backs check assignment and release to their respective side if their man drops. (63 Wheel is the only automatic release of both backs).

This simple numbering system can very easily be extended to include automatic releases by both backs, as well as having one back release and the other back pick up his assignment, to having both backs release to the same side. All that is needed is to assign a number to the specific backfield action desired.

TAILBACK/FULLBACK ROUTES

If the tailback and/or fullback release, they run complementary routes with the three primary receivers. From week to week, certain 60 series patterns work better than others. Therefore, if only three or four 60 series patterns are to be used, the backs simply learn their routes for only those patterns. Here are the three basic patterns that the backs run (see Diagram 7-10).

Flare: Take one or two steps to the side, keying your assignment while allowing the quarterback to drop; then swing away from the line of scrimmage, looking over your inside shoulder for the ball.

Shoot: Take one or two steps to the side, key your assignment, then aim for a spot approximately one yard outside the offensive tackle. Once across the LOS, turn outside to the flat and deepen the route to 3-4 yards. Look over your outside shoulder for the ball.

Circle: Take one or two steps to the side, key your assignment, then aim for a spot approximately one yard outside the offensive tackle. Once across the LOS, turn straight upfield and look over your inside shoulder for the ball. Avoid taking the circle too much to the inside. Find the seam and accelerate upfield.

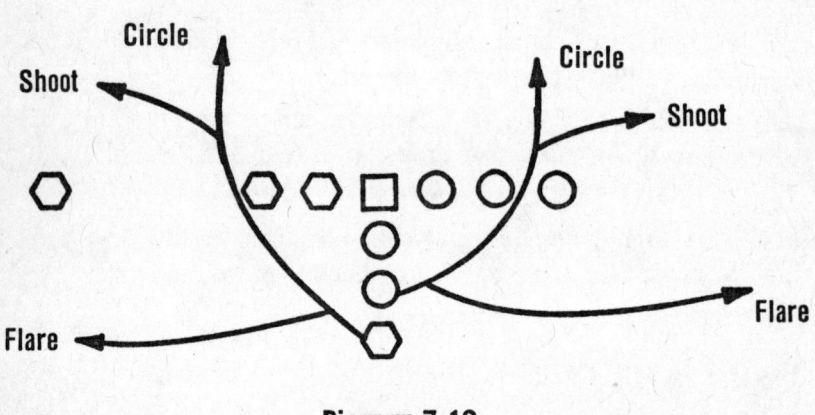

Diagram 7-10

PASS ROUTES IN THE 60 SERIES

The 60 series is broken down into five quickside (x) and five strongside (Y-SB) routes. All 60 series routes beginning with the letter *W*, except Wipe, are designed to have the split end as the primary receiver. Routes beginning with the letter *S*, except Strike, are intended to hit either the tight end or swingback.

Releasing the tailback quickside and the fullback strongside helps to achieve this objective. However, by using the swingback in both the

Incorporating a Simplified Pass Offense Into the System 193

tight end as well as in the split end side of the formation, the primary receiver can be changed.

If the defense will roll or invert its secondary to the two-receiver side most of the time, the Swingback-Motion Offense, in theory, can predetermine which receiver will be open simply by declaring the offensive set and/or motion that will accomplish this end.

60 SERIES QUICKSIDE ROUTES

(See Diagram 7-11.)

Route Name	QB Drops (steps)	X	Y	SB	TB	FB
Whirl	7	Curl (73)	Curl (73)	Post (77)	Flare, shoot or circle	Flare, shoot or circle
Wide	5	Wide (74)	In (75)	Curl (73)	Flare or circle	Flare or shoot
Wag	5	Goal (99)	Seam	Quick (92)	Flare or shoot	Flare or circle
Wheel	5	Slo-Goal (99)	Straight	Goal (99)	Circle	Circle
Wipe*	7	Post (77)	Drag	Flag (76)	Flare	Flare or shoot

*Tight end primary receiver

Diagram 7-11

Let's look at a few of the quickside routes from two of the Swingback-Motion Offensive sets. (See Diagram 7-12.)

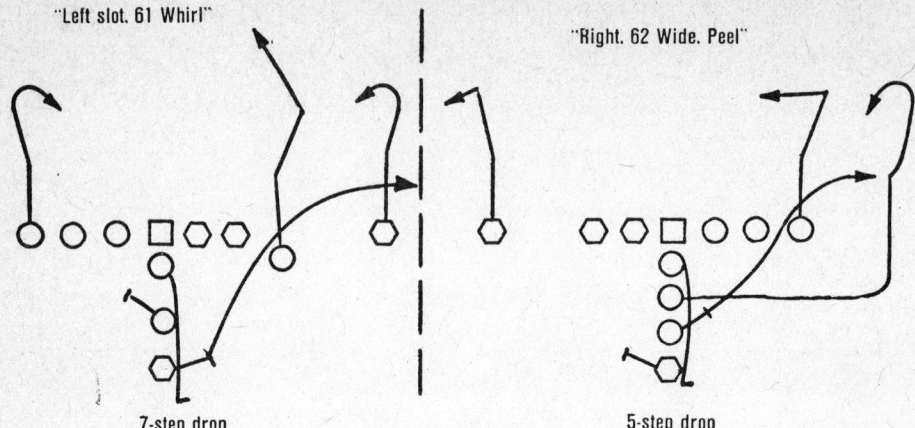

Diagram 7-12

60 SERIES STRONGSIDE ROUTES

(See Diagram 7-13.)

Route Name	QB Drops (steps)	X	Y	SB	TB	FB
Stop	7	Streak (78)	Quick (92)	Curl (73)	Flare or shoot	Flare or circle
Steel	5	In (75)	Wide (74)	Streak (78)	Flare, shoot or circle	Flare or circle
Strike*	7	Slo-drag	Post (77)	Streak (78)	Flare or shoot	Flare or shoot
Sag	5	In (75)	Quick (92)	Goal (99)	Flare or shoot	Flare or circle
Scout	5	Flag (76)	Flag (76)	Wide (74)	Flare or circle	Flare or shoot

*Split end primary receiver

Diagram 7-13

Incorporating a Simplified Pass Offense Into the System   195

Here are two strongside routes from a power and pro set. (See Diagram 7-14.)

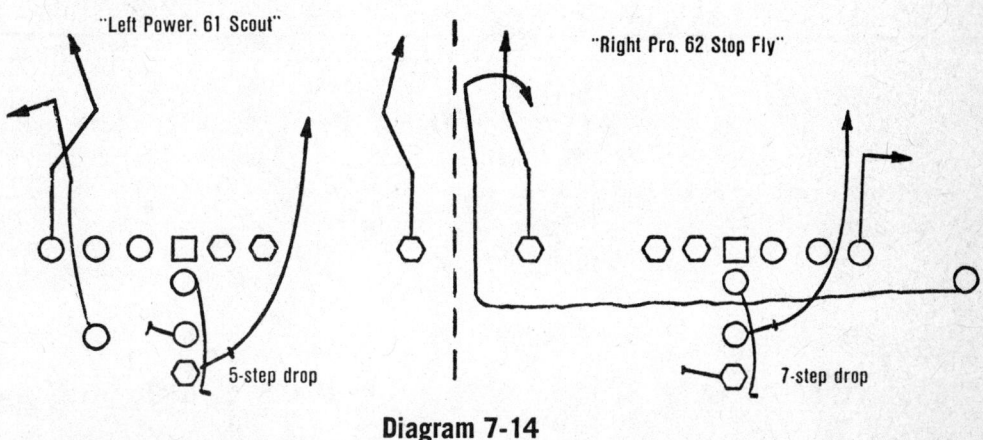

Diagram 7-14

60 SERIES PASSING TREE

(See Diagram 7-15.)

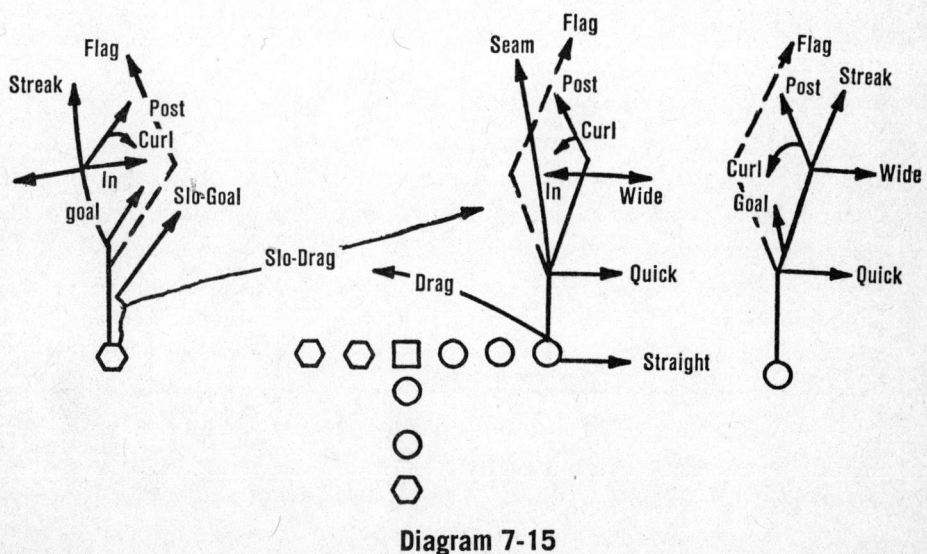

Diagram 7-15

60 SERIES PROTECTION

The 60 series pass protection is digit or 70 series protection for the line. If it is imperative to the success of the play that either the tailback or fullback automatically release into the pattern, the center must hear the flare control digit (second number) so that he can help out to the side of the releasing back if his man (the center) drops off into the underneath coverage.

We have used the twin and open sets in looking at the blocking scheme and routes for two 60 series plays. (See Diagram 7-16.)

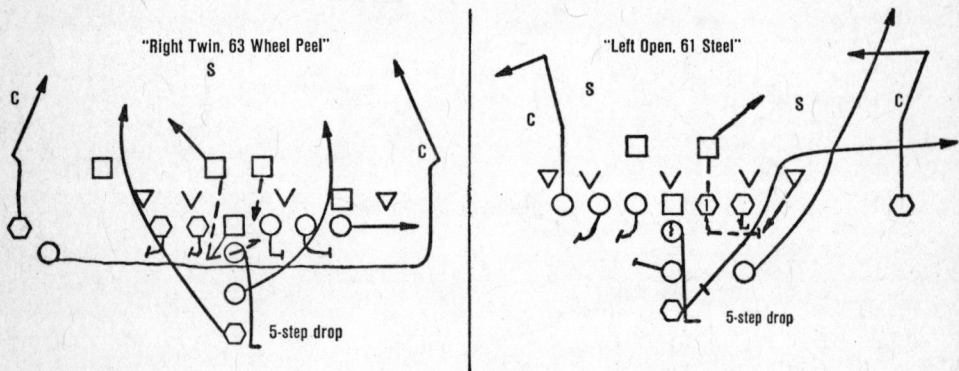

Diagram 7-16

Digit protection rules in both the 60 and the 70 series enables the offense to adequately block a four-man rush to the quickside of the formation. However, it leaves one man free when the defense sends four rushers to the strongside. No blocking scheme short of complicated changes can solve the problem. Therefore, if the defense has a tendency on certain downs of sending four rushers strongside, a 70 series route would be called and the tight end "hot" principle would be applied to the situation. (See Diagram 7-17.)

QUARTERBACK READS IN THE 60 SERIES

Since the 60 series does not utilize the "Hot" principle, and since digit protection is able to cope with the "hot" linebacker if he stunts, the quarterback focuses his attention on the safety in the line of sight as he moves away from center.

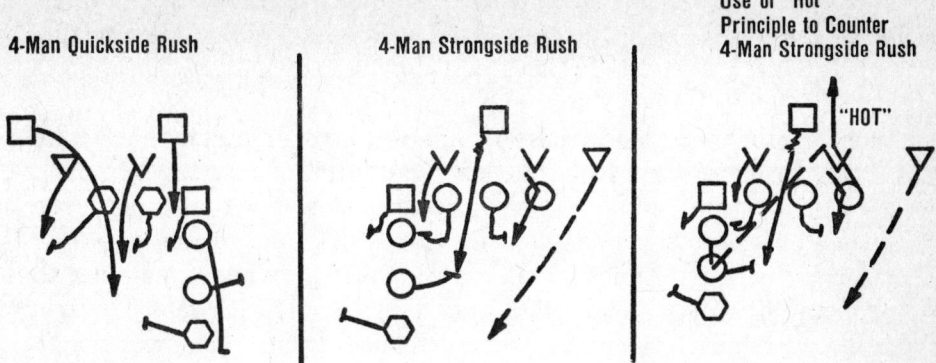

Diagram 7-17

INTRODUCTION TO THE 80 SERIES

The 80 series is the sprint out passing game of the Swingback-Motion Offense. It should again be noted here that the entire passing game from this offense more than likely will not be used in one season. A careful analysis of the capabilities of the quarterback, as well as of the offensive line, must be completed first. Then, those facets of the Swingback-Motion passing game which best suit the individual players must be selected and practiced. The point to be made by presenting the entire passing game is that the tremendous flexibility and versatility of this offense lends itself to adapting to its personnel through a basic, simplistic approach. This series, like all of the previous ones, can be run out of any offensive set.

80 SERIES MECHANICS

There are two distinct actions in the 80 series. The first is the sprint action, in which the quarterback opens up playside and sprints for a spot approximately five yards deep behind the playside tackle. As the quarterback is sprinting out, he is reading the safety or rover (four-deep secondary), or the outside linebacker (three-deep scheme) to that side. Once he arrives at five yards, he turns upfield, parallels his shoulders to the line of scrimmage, and either runs or throws the ball.

The quarterback is instructed to throw from anywhere along his five-yard course, and not just after he reaches the spot behind the playside tackle. His ability level will determine whether he throws the quick, short pass on the move or whether he first pulls up. It is a difficult pass any time the quarterback does not have his shoulders parallel to the LOS, let alone when he is moving away from the receiver.

The sprint action will be used against teams whose perimeter defenders get knocked off their feet easily or against teams who drop their perimeter people into their pass coverage while attempting to contain the play with someone from the inside. If necessary, the tight end or swingback can block on the defender coming from the inside to contain the quarterback.

Blocking the tight end or swingback may be all that is needed to get the ball thrown deep or to allow the quarterback to turn the corner. Many defensive backs are taught to come and support the run if the inside receiver blocks, in this case severely exposing their area of pass defense.

The second 80 series action is jet. The quarterback opens up playside and sprints for a spot approximately seven yards deep behind the playside tackle, reading the safety or rover (four-deep) or outside linebacker (three-deep) to that side. Any time along that seven-yard channel that he sees a receiver open, he pulls up and delivers the ball. The quarterback is instructed to pull up and set his feet rather than having him try to throw the ball on the move.

Jet action will be used against teams who read the quarterback's sprint action and quickly revolve their zone to that side. Jetting enables the quarterback to pull up at any time to throw and also affords him the opportunity of throwing backside away from the strength of the zone. This half-sprint action allows the offense to attack the entire width of the field, as in the dropback attack, while presenting to the defense the possibility of forcing the corner, as in the full-sprint action. Once the sprint out action begins, the defense must either commit itself to the playside or protect the entire field before it is able to determine whether the spring (full) or jet (half) action is being used. Diagram 7-18 shows two 80 Jet passes from an open and power set.

80 SERIES HUDDLE CALLS

The 80 series will be called in the huddle as follows:

80 Sprint at one (quickside) + a 60 series route.

80 Jet at two (strongside) + a 60 series route.

Incorporating a Simplified Pass Offense Into the System 199

The odd and even numbers correspond with the offensive hole numbers for the wide plays in the running game. Both sprint and jet action can be employed to either the strongside or quickside of the offensive set.

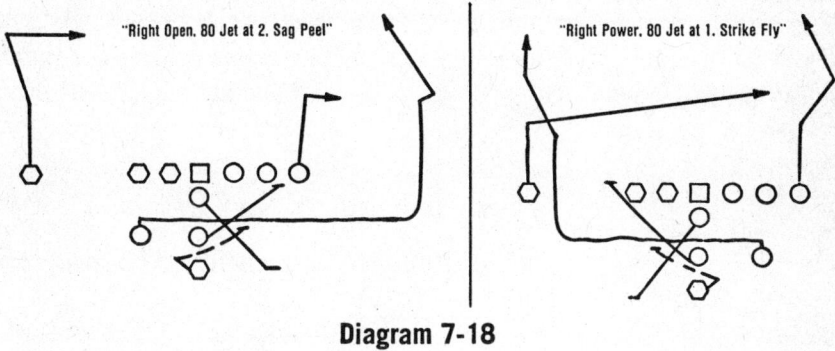

Diagram 7-18

80 SERIES ROUTES

Sixty series word descriptions are used after the type of sprint out action called to tell the three receivers what routes to run. (See Diagram 7-19.)

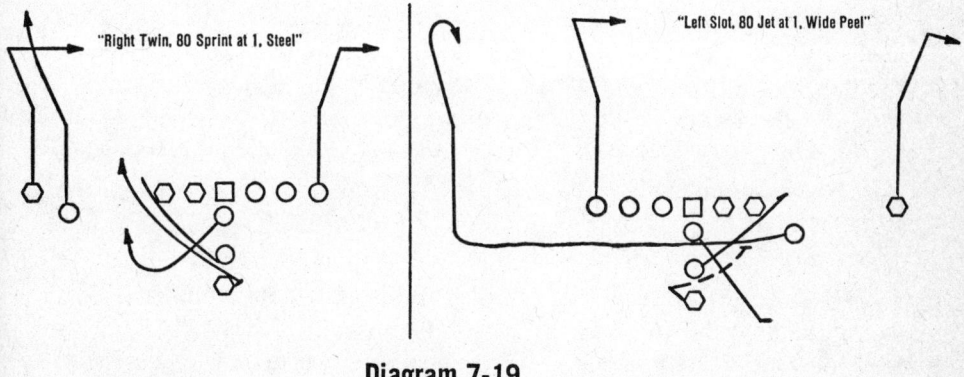

Diagram 7-19

QUARTERBACK THOUGHT PROCESSES IN THE 80 SERIES

In the 80 sprint action, the quarterback is thinking of running the ball first and passing only if the fullback or tailback fails to eliminate the perimeter contain man or if he is sure of getting either the first down or the touchdown via the pass. If the quarterback sees any seam in the lateral contain of the defense, he accelerates into it and gets yards upfield. Anytime the quarterback decides to run the ball he yells, "Go" to alert his lead blockers that they should now cross the line of scrimmage.

The quarterback's thought process in the jet action is the converse of the sprint action. He is looking to pull up and complete the pass rather than running for yardage.

80 SERIES SPRINT PROTECTION

The playside linemen in the 80 sprint action will use basically the same aggressive Mike techniques that they employed in the 90 series. The emphasis is on keeping the defender from getting upfield or from getting lateral movement toward the quarterback. If the blocker loses his man, the defender must be made to go completely around the blocker to the ball.

The backside linemen will use a pull/seal technique. The guard will try to get out in front of the quarterback while the tackle will block any penetration along the line of scrimmage. The latter is instructed to clip if necessary because he is within the legal clip zone.

In the 80 sprint pass, the fullback will chop and roll the man responsible for perimeter contain while the tailback will first step backside and check for any immediate threat in the form of a linebacker stunt or a hard defensive end rush. The tailback will then slip underneath the quarterback and aim for a spot approximately two yards outside the fullback's block, chopping and rolling the first defender to show. He must work upfield unless immediately confronted, and must not concern himself about looking inside until he crosses the line of scrimmage. The quarterback is thinking of running the ball first and his course might be impeded by the tailback slowing down to look for someone.

If the quarterback is a better passer than runner, the line blocking on the backside can be changed to "gap hinge" protection, a backside block that will be used on most play action passes that will be discussed in Chapter 8. The quarterback's thought process now would be, "throw first, run second." (See Diagram 7-20.)

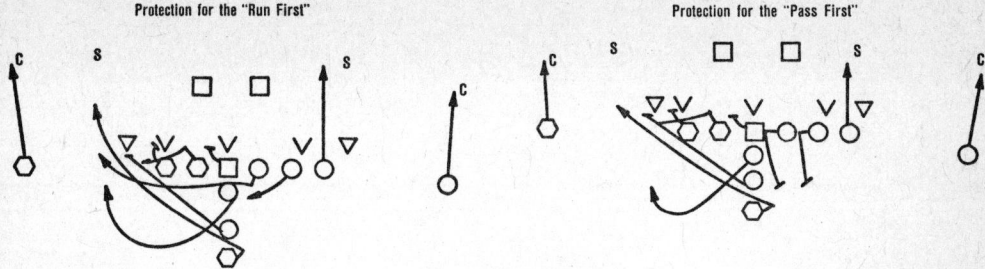

Diagram 7-20

80 SERIES JET PROTECTION

Because the quarterback is thinking, "pass first," and in many cases pulling up short of the seven-yard position behind the playside tackle, the backside linemen will gap hinge while the frontside will use an aggressive Mike block.

The fullback will continue to drive at the perimeter man and will chop and roll him, keeping his hands out of the throwing lanes to the playside.

The tailback continues to check the backside, helping out when needed. Otherwise, he will drop underneath as the quarterback passes in front of him and will block from the inside to the playside.

The center will always step playside to insure the playside gap against a stunt or slant. If none, and there is no one head up on him, he will extend the gap hinge backside. (See Diagram 7-21.)

FLARE CONTROL IN THE 80 SERIES

As in the 60 series, the second digit in the 80 series will control which back is to release and which one is to block. Both backs cannot be sent out at the same time.

80—Both backs block assignment.
81—Tailback release playside; Fullback block assignment.
82—Fullback release playside; Tailback block fullback's assignment.
83—Tailback release backside; Fullback block assignment.

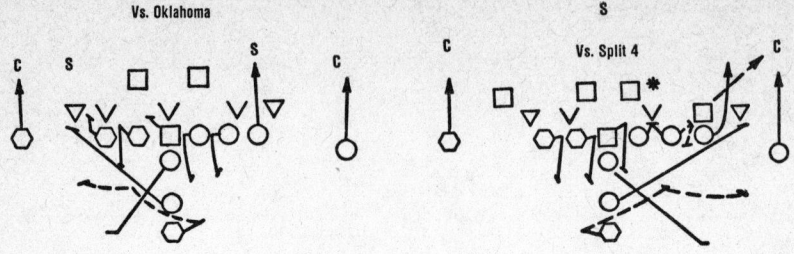

*If playside three technique in gap, and guard unable to reach on him, tackle will help out.

Diagram 7-21

Let's look at the flare control out of two Swingback-Motion Offensive sets. (See Diagram 7-22.)

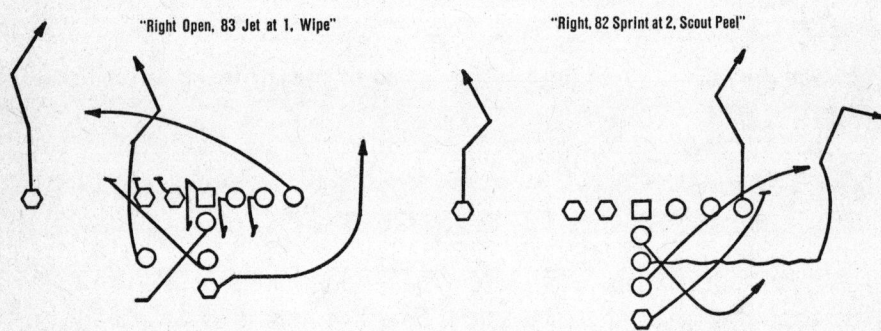

Diagram 7-22

8

PLAY ACTION PASSES, SCREENS, DRAWS AND SPECIAL PLAYS OF THE SWINGBACK-MOTION OFFENSE

PLAY ACTION PASSES

Swingback-Motion Play Action Passes are run off of its most successful running plays, plays that the defense is forced to respect. The offensive unit must make the pass play look as much like the run play as possible. Because of its potent running attack, the Swingback-Motion Offense and its play action passes play an integral role in every game plan.

There are two types of play action passes in the Swingback-Motion Offense. The first is called "Pass." The word "Pass" precedes the called running play to be faked and tells the quarterback and line that, after the play fake is made, the quarterback will continue moving to, or will set up to, the side of the line where the fake went. (See Diagram 8-1.)

The second type of play action pass is called "Boot." The word "Boot" precedes the running play to be faked while telling the quarterback and line that, after the play fake, the backside guard (guard to the side of the fake) pulls and leads the corner protection while the quarterback is going to move away from the side of the fake. (See Diagram 8-2.)

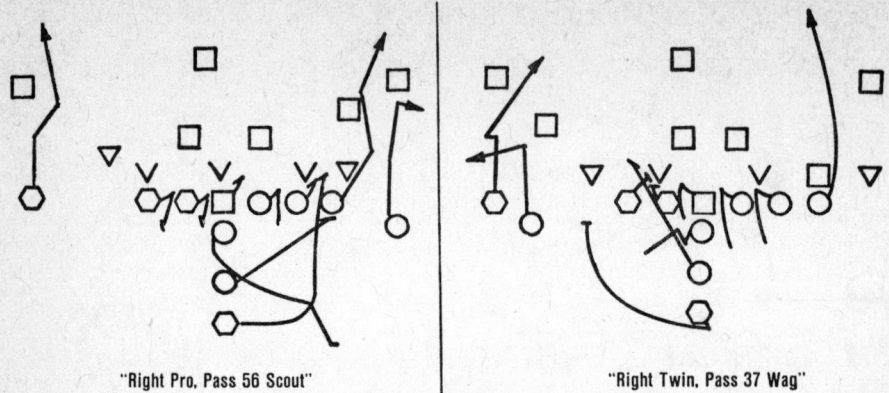

Diagram 8-1

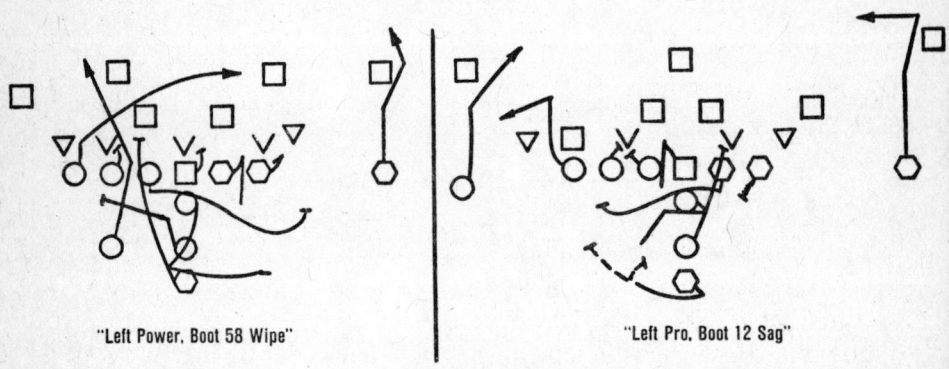

Diagram 8-2

MECHANICS OF THE PLAY ACTION PASSES

The quarterback adds the word "Pass" or "Boot" to the beginning of his huddle call, alerting the offensive line to the pass play.

Receivers automatically lengthen their legs at least one yard so that the base pattern for all play action passes will either be seven or 14 yards. By lengthening their legs, the receivers afford the quarterback enough time to properly fake the running play and still be able to time up the pass with the receiver.

Sixty series routes are used to denote the patterns to be run. The

Play Action Passes, Screens, Draws and Special Plays

complete play action passing game revolves around the quarterbacks and receivers learning the 12 (six strongside and six quickside) routes of the 60 series.

PASS 11/12

Pass 11/12 are play action passes off of our lead option. As the quarterback comes down the line, he reads the corner support scheme and throws to the open receiver. (See Diagram 8-3.)

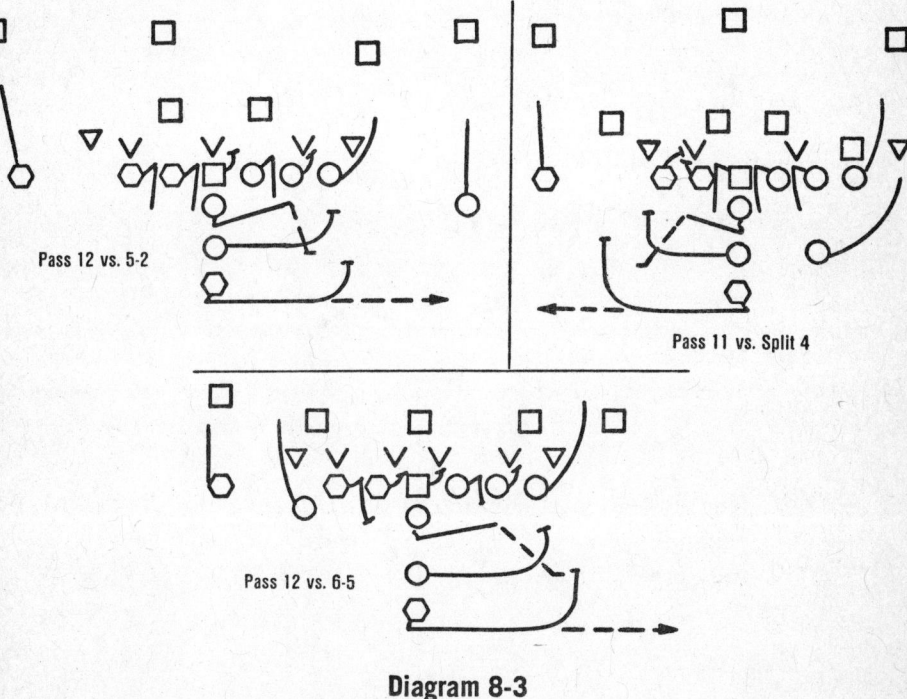

Diagram 8-3

Pass 11/12 Blocking Rules

C: Step playside and block #0 on or off LOS; hinge and block backside if #0 is a linebacker who drops off, versus 6-5 block playside one technique.

Playside Guard: #1 on or off LOS; help center with noseman or one technique or hinge backside if #1 is a linebacker who drops off.

Playside Tackle: In, on, out.

Backside Guard: Gap hinge.

Backside Tackle: Gap hinge.

FB: Lateral channel and chop and roll the number three defender; keep his hands down and do not allow him to get up field.

TB: Run 11/12 option course, blocking playside if needed; otherwise flare playside. (If we are receiving a strong backside rush we ask the tailback to hinge backside and block. (See Diagram 8-4.)

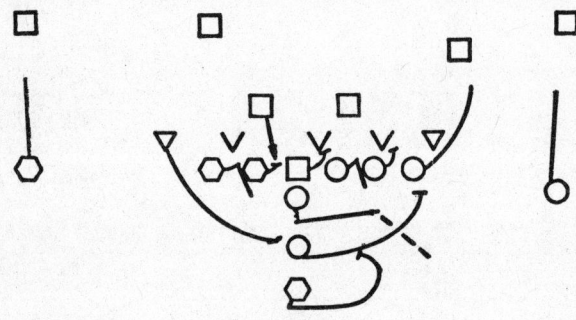

Diagram 8-4

QB: Run 11/12 option, continuing down the line or dropping off, depending on the pattern called; read the defender supporting the corner; accelerate initially to make defenders think option.

PASS 37/38

Pass 37/38 are play action passes off of an inside veer/option fake. After disconnecting, the quarterback accelerates down the line while reading the corner support. He either throws on the run or drops off, depending on the secondary coverage. (See Diagram 8-5.)

Pass 37/38 Blocking Rules

C: Step playside and block #0 on or off LOS; hinge and block backside if #0 is a linebacker who drops off; versus 6-5 block backside one technique.

Play Action Passes, Screens, Draws and Special Plays

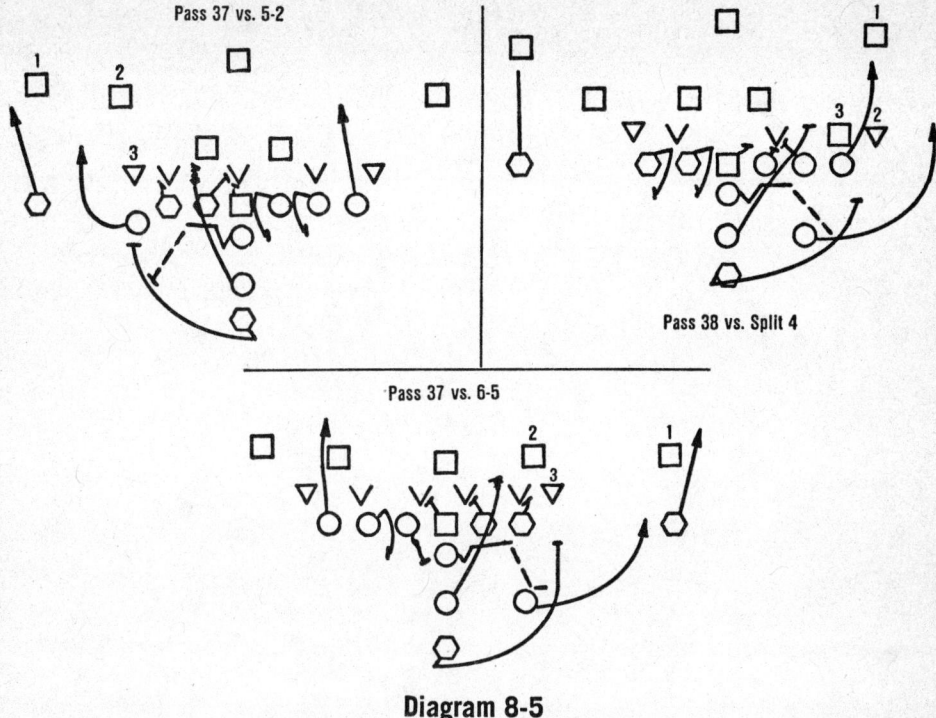

Diagram 8-5

Playside Guard: Block tackle call; you will always block a defender who is on the LOS.

Playside Tackle: In, on, out.

Backside Guard: Gap hinge.

Backside Tackle: Gap hinge.

FB: Run 37/38 veer course and block first linebacker playside; sell the veer first by running hard; no exaggerated faking is needed.

TB: Run 37/38 veer course, cutting your pitch route short and block number three defender; attack him low and keep his hands down. Do not allow him to penetrate upfield.

QB: Execute 37/38 veer, disconnecting while reading corner support; sell the veer first; accelerate off the disconnect and throw on the run or drop off and set up; on short passes, feather the mesh; on longer patterns, stay with the mesh longer to enable receivers to run their legs; read outside linebacker versus three-deep and safety in a four-deep.

To capitalize on defensive reaction to the veer/option play, the playside receivers on pass 37/38 (with no 60 series route called) are to read the secondary coverage as they sprint off the LOS:

1. Four-deep Roll: Depending on the position of the strong safety, the wideout is going to take it up, trying to beat the safety to the deep outside. Inside receiver will run into the seam between the safety and corner. (See Diagram 8-6.)

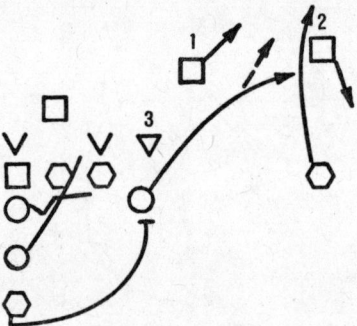

Diagram 8-6

2. Four-deep Invert: Wideout is going to run a quick post or goal route while the inside receiver runs an out route behind the inverting safety. (See Diagram 8-7.)

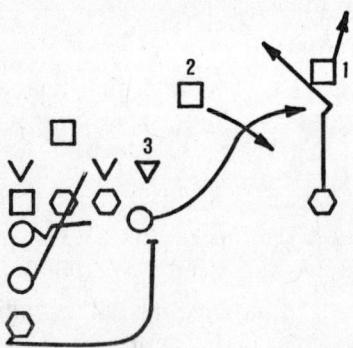

Diagram 8-7

3. Three deep Secondary: Same as four-deep Invert.
4. Three-deep Rotation: Same as four-deep Roll, with receivers trying to expand the two-deep hash coverage. (See Diagram 8-8.)

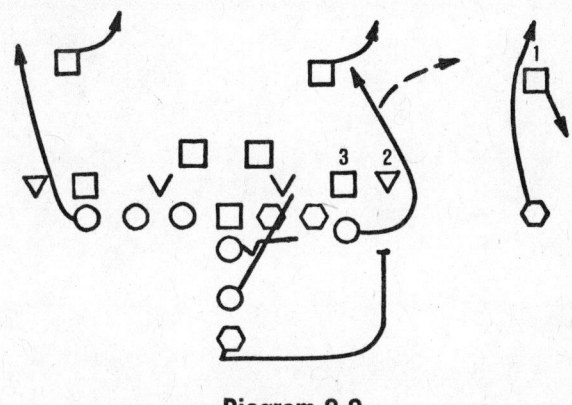

Diagram 8-8

5. Five-under: Same as three-deep Rotation.
6. Man-to-Man Coverage: Crossing patterns between the inside and outside receivers; quick posts or goals; deep patterns. (See Diagram 8-9.)

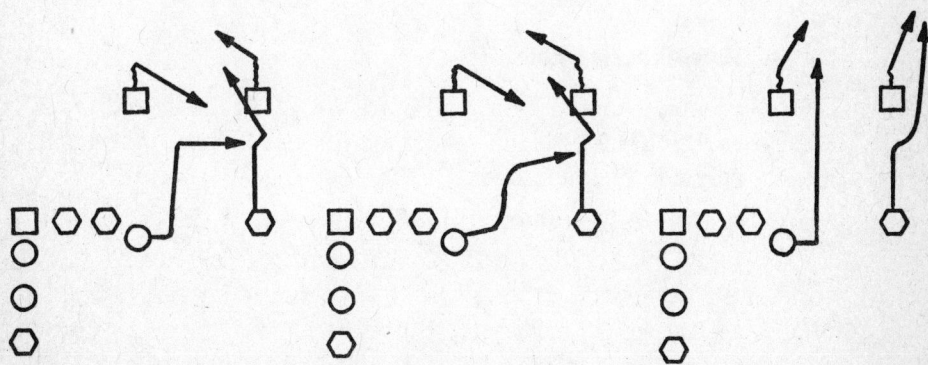

Diagram 8-9

PASS 55/56

A very effective play action pass, pass 55/56 is run off of a power off-tackle fake. The quarterback drops off, sets his feet and throws mostly into the area left open by the linebackers who must honor the play fake. (See Diagram 8-10.)

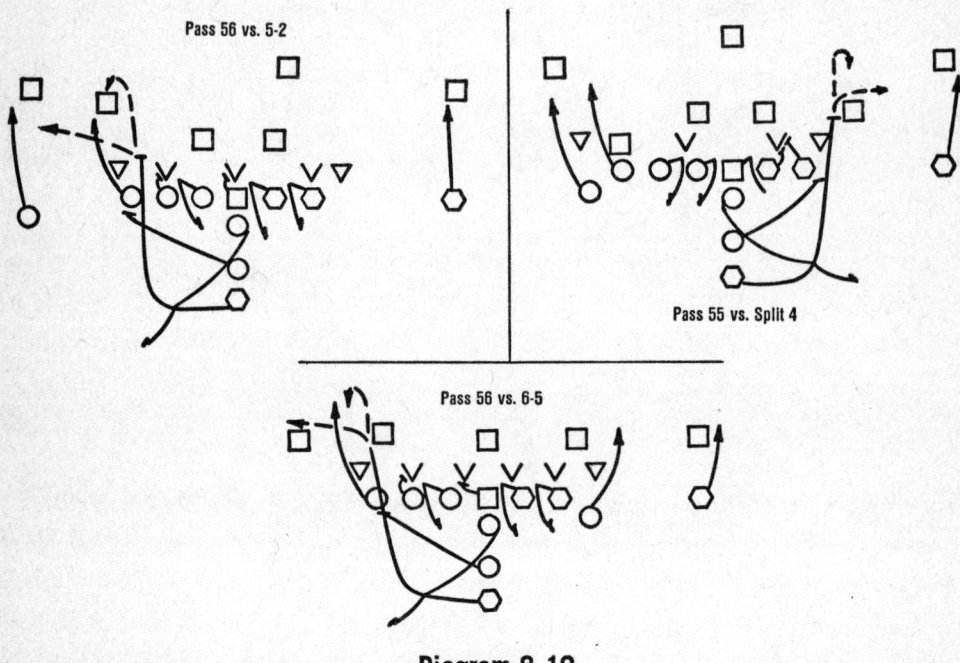

Diagram 8-10

Pass 55/56 Blocking Rules

C: Step playside and block #0 on or off LOS; hinge and block backside if #0 is a linebacker who drops off; versus 6-5 block playside one technique.

Playside Guard: #1 on or off LOS; help center with noseman or one technique or hinge backside if #1 is a linebacker who drops off.

Playside Tackle: In, on, out.

Backside Guard: Gap hinge.

Backside Tackle: Gap hinge.

Play Action Passes, Screens, Draws and Special Plays 211

FB: Drive straight for outside knee of number three defender and chop and roll him; keep his hands down and eliminate him from getting upfield; attack him.

TB: Run 55/56 power as though you are getting the ball; block anyone in the off-tackle hole; if no one to block, run, shoot or curl outside, depending on the outside receiver's pattern.

QB: Reverse pivot, give a good, deep ball fake to the tailback, then drop off three steps, set your feet and throw; don't be afraid to run the ball if the fullback eliminates the number three defender.

PASS 57/58

Pass 57/58 are play action passes off of a blast or isolation fake. This has been one of our most productive play action passes, along with the Boot off the same play fake. (See Diagram 8-11.)

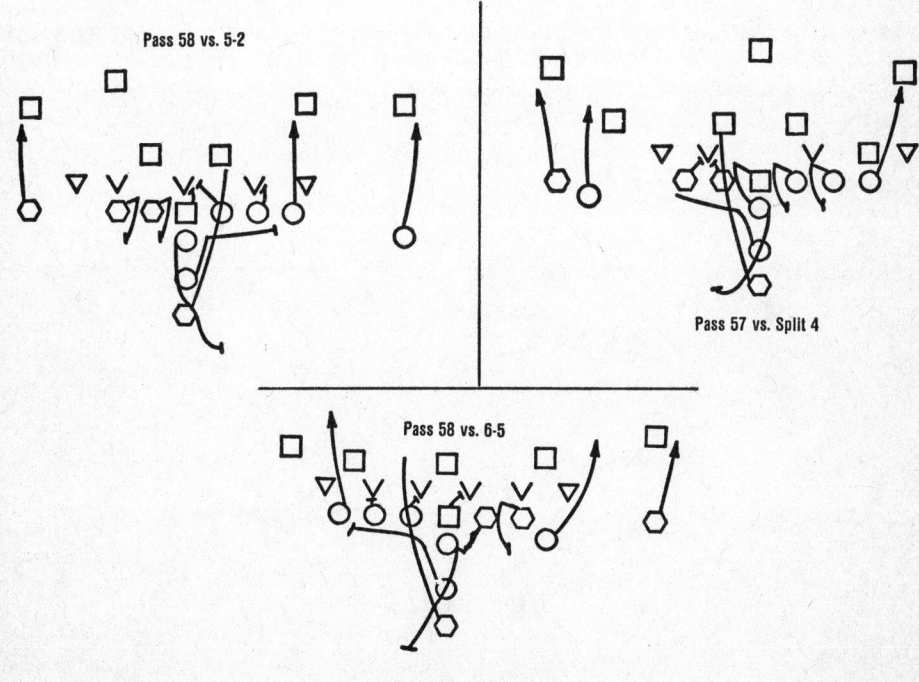

Diagram 8-11

Pass 57/58 Blocking Rules

C: Step playside and block #0 defender on or off LOS; hinge and block backside if #0 is a linebacker who drops off; versus 6-5 block backside one technique.

Playside Guard: Block tackle call; you will always block a defender who is on the LOS.

Playside Tackle: In, on, out.

Backside Guard: Gap hinge.

Backside Tackle: Gap hinge.

FB: Take two steps at playside blast hole, then turn outside and block the number three defender; establish good position on him and do not allow him to get upfield; use digit protection blocking techniques.

TB: Run 57/58 blast, driving into the blast hole as though you have the ball; sell the blast before you block anyone in the blast hole; if no one to block, curl in the middle seam between the linebackers.

QB: Reverse pivot, give a good, deep ball fake to the tailback by dropping your inside shoulder; drop off three steps, set your feet and throw.

BOOT 11/12

Boot 11/12 are play action passes run off of an inside veer/option fake, with the quarterback moving in the opposite direction to throw. It is designed to take advantage of quick defensive pursuit aimed at stopping the inside veer/option (See Diagram 8-12.)

Boot 11/12 Blocking Rules

C: Step playside and block #0 on or off LOS; hinge and block backside if #0 is a linebacker who drops off, versus 6-5 block playside one technique.

Playside Guard: #1 on or off LOS; help center with noseman or one technique or hinge backside if #1 is a linebacker who drops off.

Playside Tackle: In, on, out.

Play Action Passes, Screens, Draws and Special Plays

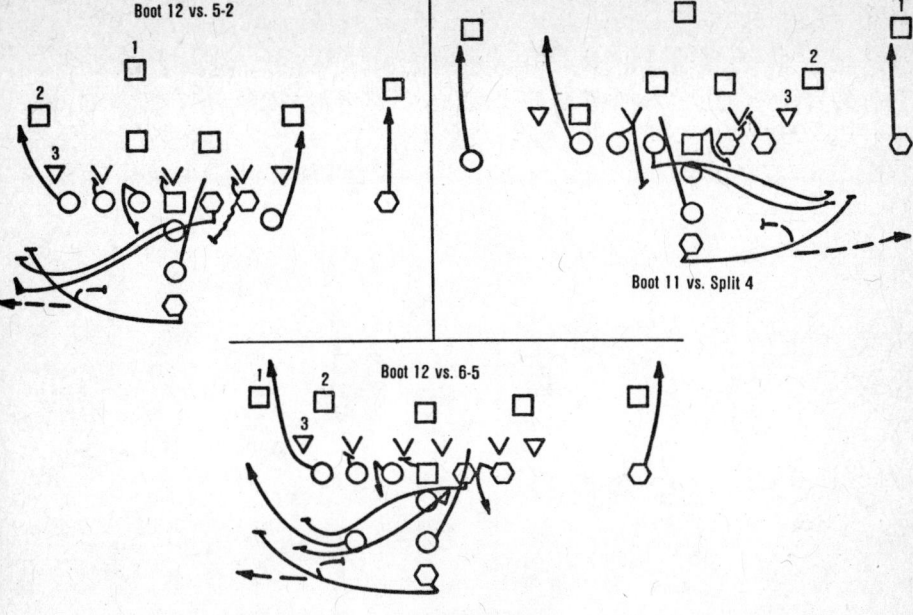

Diagram 8-12

Backside Guard: Pull and deepen while keying the number three defender; establish a head up to outside position while shuffling to remain square to the LOS; use digit protection blocking techniques. If defender is slow-playing, go after him and get his hands down.

Backside Tackle: Gap hinge.

FB: Drive hard for inside leg of the backside guard; sell the veer/option first, then seal the 7/8 hole area from inside/out; meet defenders on their side of the LOS.

TB: Run 11/12 counter option course; help out playside or hinge and block backside; you have the option of flaring playside if we are receiving minimum backside pressure.

QB: Execute 11/12 counter option, stepping deeper on first step to allow pulling guard to get out, continue down the line or dropping off, depending on the pattern called; read the defender supporting the corner; throw on the run if the coverage dictates it.

BOOT 57/58

Possibly the best play action pass in the Swingback-Motion Offense, Boot 57/58 is run off a blast fake with the quarterback pressuring the corner away from the play fake. We used it with good success deep in our own territory when teams anticipated our blasting the ball out. (See Diagram 8-13.)

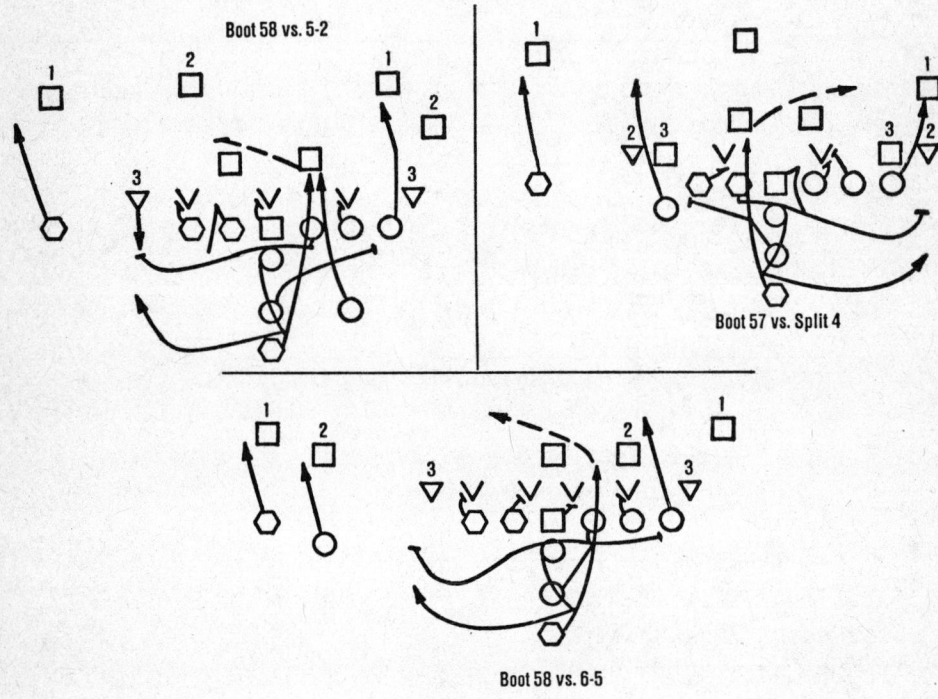

Diagram 8-13

Boot 57/58 Blocking Rules

C: Step playside and block #0 on or off LOS; hinge and block backside if #0 is a linebacker who drops off, versus 6-5 block backside one technique.

Playside Guard: #1 on or off LOS; hinge and help center with noseman or block backside if #1 is a linebacker who drops off.

Playside Tackle: In, on, out.

Backside Guard: Pull and deepen while keying the number three defender; establish a head up to outside position while shuffling to remain square to the LOS; use digit protection blocking techniques (See Chapter 6.); if defender is slow-playing, go after him and get his hands down.

Backside Tackle: In, on, out.

FB: Drive for two steps at blast hole, then turn outside and block the number three defender; establish good position on him and do not allow him inside; use digit protection blocking techniques. (See Chapter 6.)

TB: Run 57/58 blast, driving into blast hole as though you have the ball; if no one to block, drag back to the playside (dotted line in Diagram 8-13.)

QB: Reverse pivot, give a good, deep ball fake to the tailback by dropping your inside shoulder; move or boot away from the fake, initially keying the guard's block and helping set up his block; don't be afraid to run if the guard eliminates the number three defender; yell "Go" and get upfield.

SCREEN PASSES

There are four basic screen passes in the Swingback-Motion Offense. Depending on the type of rush the defense is using, along with the success we are having with the blast and inside veer/option plays, one of the four screens will be used to effectively neutralize a strong defensive rush or to capitalize on a rapidly pursuing defensive unit.

TAILBACK QUICK SCREEN

(See Diagram 8-14.)

Tailback Quick Screen Blocking Rules

C: Digit protection (#0 on or off LOS; first linebacker quickside); Delay three counts before slipping behind your defender (#0 on LOS) to the quick flat area.

SG: Digit protection (#1 on LOS; Delay three counts, then slip behind your defender to the quick flat area.

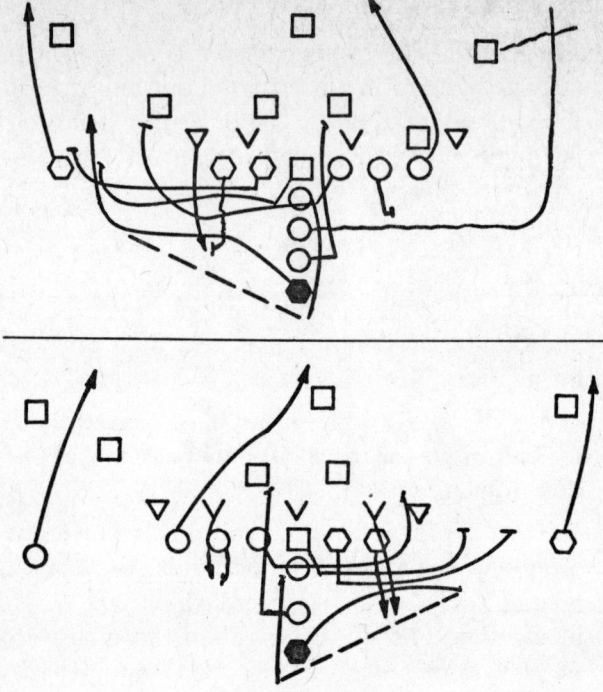

Diagram 8-14

- *ST:* Digit protection (#2 on LOS); Cover pass when it is thrown.
- *QG:* Digit protection (#1 on or off LOS); Delay three counts before slipping behind your defender (if he is on the LOS) to the quick flat area; Attack the first defender to show; You are allowed downfield before the ball is thrown.
- *QT:* Digit protection (Covered on the LOS); Set up and pass block, inviting an outside rush; Sustain block until ball is thrown, then cover.
- *SB/X:* Playside: Runoff technique, then block nearest defender from the outside/in.
  Backside: Gain inside position on nearest defender and impede him from getting to the ball; Use Stalk Block techniques.

Play Action Passes, Screens, Draws and Special Plays 217

Y: Runoff technique, then block safety nearest to the quickside by establishing a position between him and the ball.

FB: Set short to the strongside; Wait for ball fake from quarterback before running a believable fake into the line at your digit protection assignment (1st linebacker strongside excluding Mike linebacker); Hard running in a natural manner is the only fake that is necessary.

TB: Set up quickside in a normal pass blocking posture while keying the offensive guards; When they release to the screen area in the quick flat, you release under the block of your quick tackle and sprint to the screen area. (See Diagram 8-15.)

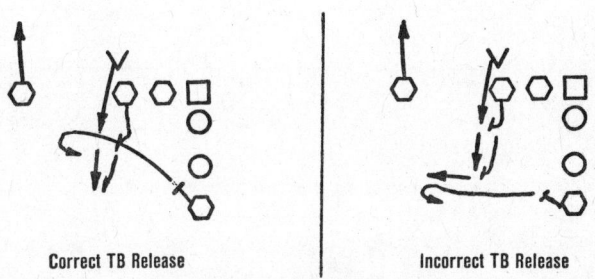

Correct TB Release | Incorrect TB Release

Diagram 8-15

Upon reaching the screen, turn and provide a stationary target for the quarterback.

QB: Drop back, bellying ball and giving the fullback a bare hand fake; Retreat four steps after your fake, look to the strongside while setting your feet; Deliver the ball to the tailback in the quick flat and cover your pass.

The quick guard, center, and strong guard must release behind or under their defender if he is on the LOS. A good rusher will detect the screen and will try to knock down the tailback or will flatten out to the screen area.

Timing between the screening linemen and the tailback and quarterback is the most important ingredient to a well executed screen. The tailback keying the guards helps to establish this timing by insuring that the screen and the tailback arrive at the screen area at the same time.

Everyone must execute on the same "count" speed. This is achieved only through repetition.

58 X SCREEN (See Diagram 8-16.)

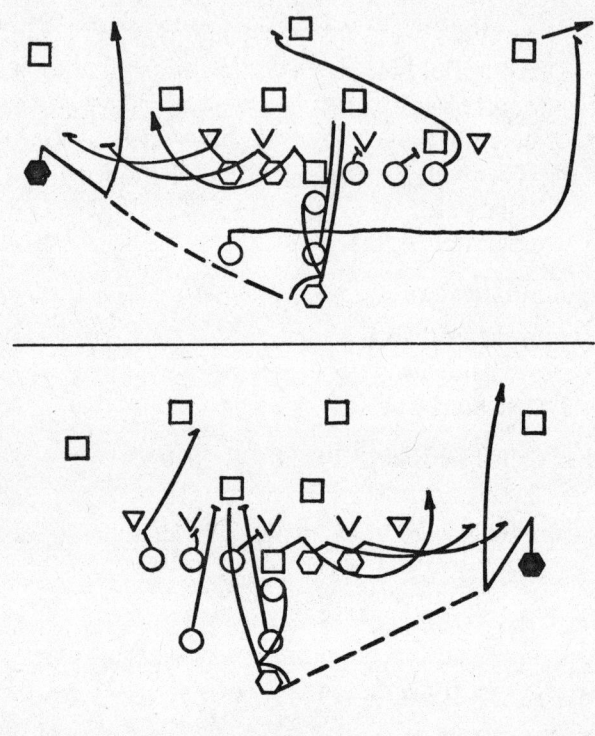

Diagram 8-16

58 X Screen Blocking Rules

C: Step quickside and block #0 defender of the LOS: delay one count, then slip behind defender and sprint to just inside the screen area; turn inside and block from inside to upfield.

SG: Block tackle's call.

ST: Block 58 blast.

QG: Block on or outside for one count. Then slip behind defender and sprint outside to screen area; block upfield.

QT: Block on or outside for one count, then slip behind defender and sprint outside to screen area; block outside to upfield; as you sprint outside, key the outside defender while trying to see the split end in his peripheral vision.

X: Drive upfield for two strides, then retreat on an angle to the quarterback approximately one yard behind the LOS; receive ball and yell "Go." You must be behind the LOS when you receive the ball; if the ball is thrown laterally or backwards, it is a live ball and must be covered if you do not catch it.

Y: Jam on/out to near safety.

SB: Playside/outside: Near safety or walked off linebacker.
Any Inside Position: Lead on isolated linebacker.
Backside: Near safety or corner.

QB: Execute 58 Blast, dropping your inside shoulder and giving a good, deep ball fake to tailback; pivot and throw to split end; throw the ball right at him; if you throw the ball laterally or backwards and it is incomplete, you must cover it because it is a live ball; cover all your passes in the flat.

FB: Run 58 Blast.

TB: Run 58 Blast; you must make the defense believe that you have the ball.

Quarterback Pivots for the 58 X Screen

On a pass to the right the quarterback must take an extra step. After delivering his ball fake he must pivot completely around before he delivers the ball. His pivot should be clockwise. The 58 X Screen to the left requires a simple counterclockwise pivot after the quarterback fakes to tailback.

58 X Screen is a very effective quick screen that has been extremely beneficial in not only sustaining long drives but also in "waste" down (1+5, 2+2, 3+2) situations. It averaged 13.1 yards per attempt and

14.75 yards per completion one season, with those statistics including two receptions for negative yardage.

In order for the defense to think Blast, we often use the power set, positioning the swingback where he can lead the play. Motion is used to force secondary rotation away from the split end, insuring single coverage to the quick side of the formation.

58 Z SCREEN

(See Diagram 8-17.)

C: Same as 58 X Screen.
SG: Block tackle's call.
ST: Block 58 Blast.
QG: Same as 58 X Screen.
QT: Same as 58 X Screen.

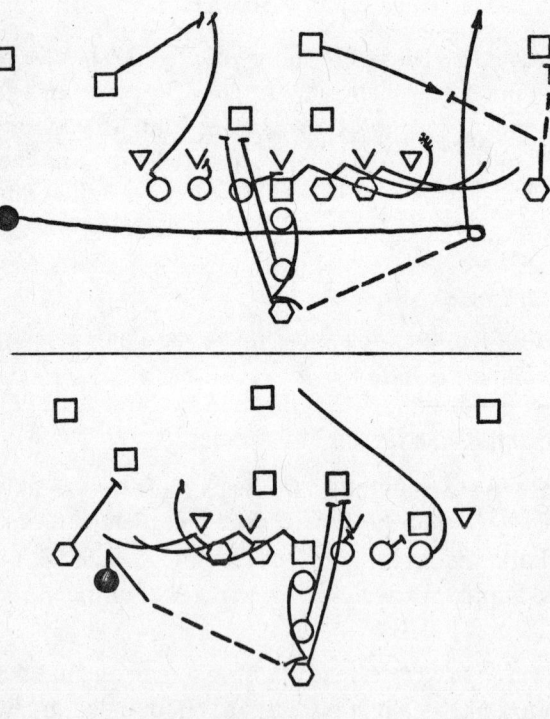

Diagram 8-17

- X: Drive off LOS and block defender responsible for corner support.
- Y: Jam on/out to near safety.
- SB: From outside position: Drive upfield two steps then retreat on an angle toward the quarterback; catch ball and yell "Go," keying the screen blockers.

  From inside position: Fake block and delay one count before releasing to a position equidistant from the split end and quick tackle.

  From fly motion: On snap count plant foot away from LOS and pivot back to quarterback, facing him.
- QB: Execute 58 X Screen, with the receiver being the swingback.
- FB: Run 58 Blast.
- TB: Run 58 Blast.

58 Z Screen with "fly" motion is an excellent play action pass versus defenses that make no adjustment to the swingback. The running fake holds the inside defenders while drawing the perimeter defenders from the outside.

37 Y SCREEN

(See Diagram 8-18.)

37 Y Screen Blocking Rules

- C: #0 to first linebacker quickside; step strongside and block noseman for one count, then slip behind defender and sprint to the screen area; versus a linebacker check the quickside gap, then slip outside to the screen; block inside to upfield.
- SG: #1 on or off LOS; delay for one count, then release behind defender to screen area; block upfield.
- ST: Seal inside for one count, then turn outside behind defender and sprint to an area 4-5 yards outside of the tight end's original position; block outside to upfield.
- QG: Block 37 veer call.
- QT: Block 37 veer call.
- X: Begin stalk on corner, then get up inside the near safety.

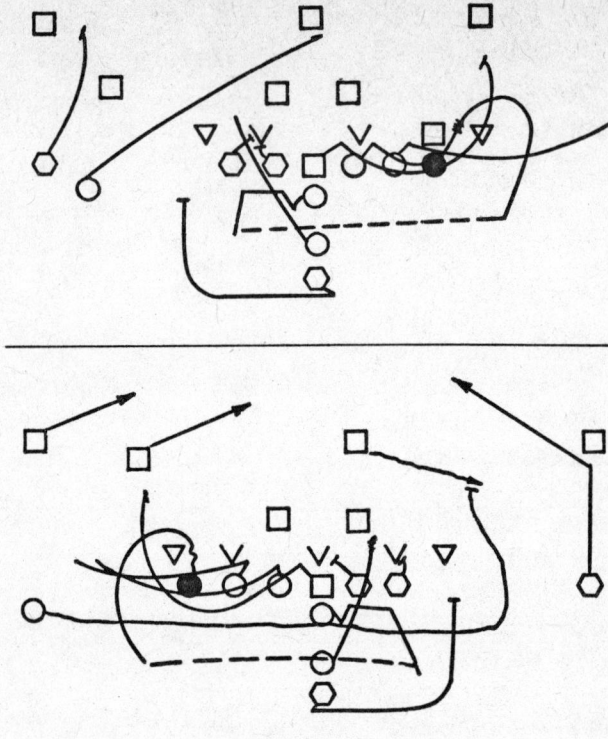

Diagram 8-18

Y: Jam on/out as if play is going quickside; delay while letting defenders react to veer; then turn outside and curl behind LOS approximately 4-5 yards from your original position; receive pass while facing quarterback; yell "Go" and get upfield; you must catch the ball behind the LOS; do not rush the play.

SB: Playside: Block near safety after stalking outside one-third defender.
Backside: Begin 37 veer block, then get up inside of near safety.

QB: Execute 37 veer, disconnecting and accelerating 2-3 steps before dropping off the LOS, pivoting and throwing to the tight end; cover your pass; do not rush your veer execution.

FB: Run 37 veer, blocking first linebacker quickside after you sell the veer.

TB: Run 37 veer, then turn up and block the number three defender.

This screen must be set up. Coaches in the press box must be checking the strongside defenders' reactions when the veer is run away from them. The tight end also must help set the play up, making sure that the outside linebacker (Split 4) or defensive end (5-2) loses sight of him as they pursue the veer. If he releases too soon, those defenders can react to the screen and ruin a potentially positive play.

The center, strong guard, and strong tackle also play a major role in 37 Y Screen. When blocking, they must delay and release under the pursuing defenders, arriving at the screen area just before the ball arrives.

An excellent mesh fake between the quarterback and fullback is another important key to the success of 37 Y Screen. The strongside defenders must believe that the veer is being run away from them. This veer fake, along with the screening linemen, and tight end releasing only after delaying properly, sets up a good football play.

Screen plays in the Swingback-Motion Offense are used to successfully neutralize a strong pass rush (tailback quick screen) or to take advantage of a quick pursuing defensive unit (58 Z Screen, 37 Y Screen).

The entire offensive unit must understand the theory behind each screen. A screen that develops too soon or too late fails to capitalize on the element of surprise, and stands little chance of gaining optimal yardage.

To further insure maximum success, these screen plays must be executed on normal down and distance situations and not solely on the conventional draw/screen downs (2+9, 3+7, etc.).

DRAW PLAYS

In conjunction with the simplified approach theory of the Swingback-Motion Offense, three draw plays using one basic blocking scheme were developed. They utilize a dropback pass fake along with one or two backs as lead blockers, and are excellent football plays that can be used at any time.

TAILBACK LEAD DRAW (See Diagram 8-19.)

Tailback Lead Draw Blocking Rules

C: #0 on or off LOS; first linebacker quickside; you must make the noseman commit himself.

SG: #1 on LOS.

ST: #2 on LOS.

QG: #1 on or off LOS.

QT: Covered on the LOS.

X: Runoff technique, gaining inside position on the corner.

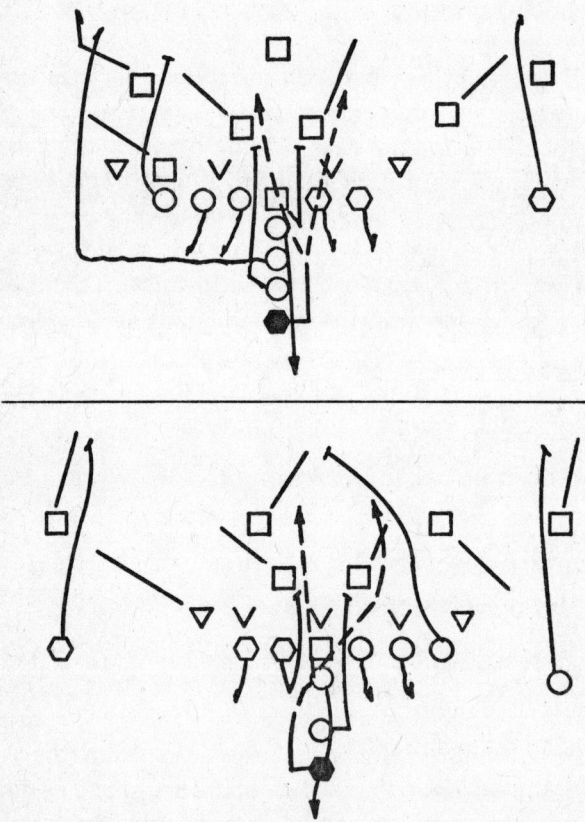

Diagram 8-19

Y: Runoff technique, gaining blocking leverage on the middle safety.

SB: Runoff technique, gaining inside position on the corner or middle safety.

QB: Dropback pass, looking downfield initially, then look ball into tailback's pocket; continue back and setting up to pass at seven-step depth; no exaggerated faking is needed.

FB: Set up strongside, keying your first linebacker strongside (excluding Mike linebacker); on tailback's "Go" attack your key and block him with chop and roll block.

TB: Set up quickside one yard from your original position with your hands up; receive ball from quarterback and yell "Go"; key fullback and center/quick guard's blocks and get into first hole you see; versus a noseman your first move should be off the center's block.

The linemen who are blocking rushing defenders will hinge inside while separating off the LOS, setting up on the defender's inside hip and inviting him to rush to the outside.

To make any draw play effective, the linemen must set up quickly off the line and show pass. The quarterback opens up to the right (right-handed) on both right and left sets, realizing that the tailback will be on different sides. He keeps his eyes downfield as if to pass, and then looks the ball in after his third step is completed.

Because every defender among the linemen and linebackers who can make the tackle is being blocked, we consider the draw a positive running play that can be called at any time.

FULLBACK LEAD DRAW (See Diagram 8-20.)

Fullback Lead Draw Blocking Rules

C: Same as tailback lead draw.
SG: Same as tailback lead draw.
ST: Same as tailback lead draw.
QG: Same as tailback lead draw.
QT: Same as tailback lead draw.
X/Y/SB: Same as tailback lead draw.

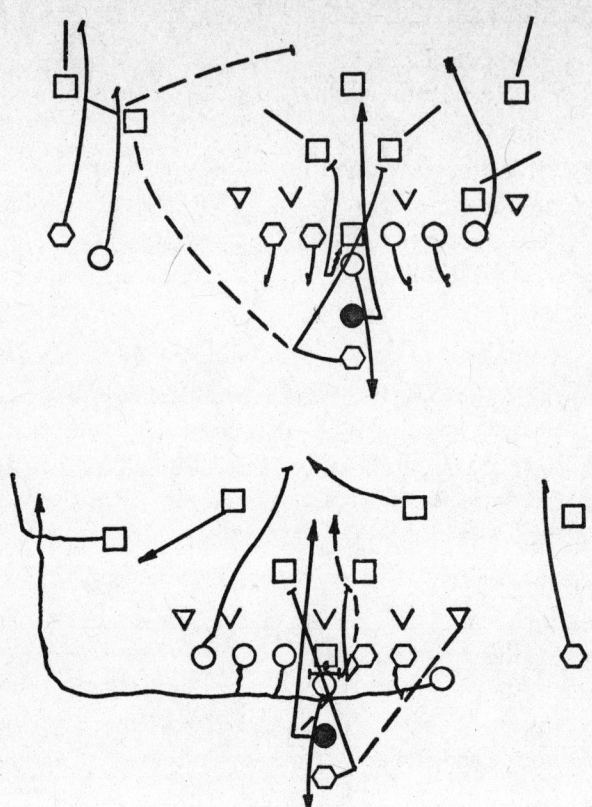

Diagram 8-20

QB: Same as tailback lead draw, only you will give the ball off to fullback, then set up at seven-step depth; because the fullback is closer to the LOS, you will only be able to look downfield as you take away from the center; then look the ball into the fullback's pocket.

TB: Set up quickside, keying the Willie linebacker; if he comes before the fullback yells "Go," block him; if he doesn't come, lead through on the first linebacker strongside; any time the Willie linebacker is inside, lead on him.

FB: Set up strongside one yard from your original position with your inside elbow up; receive ball from quarter-

Play Action Passes, Screens, Draws and Special Plays 227

back and yell "Go"; key tailback and center/quick guard's blocks and get into first hole you see; versus a noseman, your first move should be off the center's block.

If the Willie linebacker is continually pressuring, a "Tony" call can be used versus either a 5-2 or Split 4 defense to the strongside to effectively block the first linebacker strongside.

QUARTERBACK LEAD DRAW (See Diagram 8-21.)

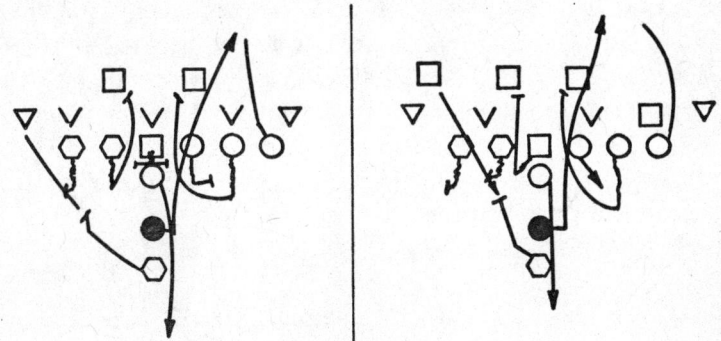

Diagram 8-21

Quarterback Lead Draw Blocking Rules

Linemen: Same as tailback/fullback lead draws.

X/Y/SB: Same as tailback/fullback lead draws.

QB: Five-step drop, keeping eyes downfield while keying the linebacker drops; on fifth step plant right foot (right-hander), yell "Go" and key the fullback/tailback and center/quickguard's blocks and get into the first hold you see; versus noseman, key the center's block initially; carry the ball in your normal passing position as you drop back; do not rush the play.

FB: Same as tailback lead draw.

TB: Same as fullback lead draw.

The quarterback lead draw is an excellent play to complement the tailback and fullback lead draws. Some linebackers will drop cautiously until the quarterback passes both backs. As a result, the quarterback must not shorten his drop. He must pass both backs before he keys the draw by yelling "Go."

SPECIAL PLAYS OF THE SWINGBACK-MOTION OFFENSE

In the Swingback-Motion Offense, special plays are used for the major purpose of exploiting defensive reaction and/or pursuit to anyone of the base running plays. This major premise allows the offensive unit to feel confident in executing each play when the specific situation arises while avoiding the grab bag "gimmick play" stigma.

These special plays afford the offense the opportunity to meet key situations during the course of the game that require something different that will exploit the element of surprise. Through film analysis and alert press box spotters, we are able to determine which special play or plays will be successful. The offensive unit enjoys spending the extra time necessary to polish these plays.

37 (QUARTERBACK) COUNTER (See Diagram 8-22.)

37 (Quarterback) Counter Blocking Rules

C: #0 on LOS; first linebacker strongside; when blocking a linebacker, allow him to react to the veer, then establish body position between him and the quarterback.

SG: In, on, out on or off LOS; when blocking a linebacker, allow him to react to the veer, then establish body position between him and the quarterback.

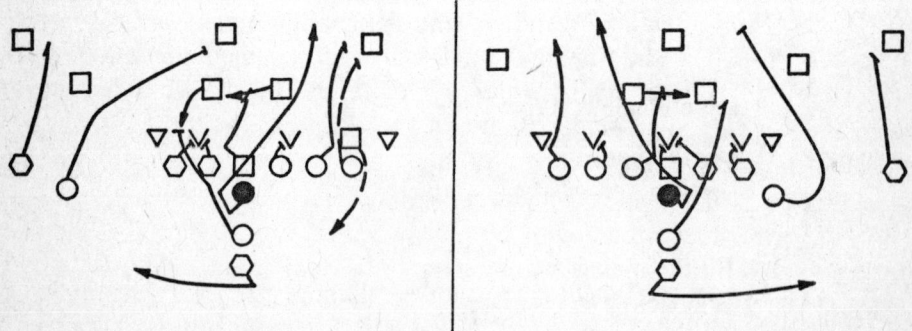

Diagram 8-22

Play Action Passes, Screens, Draws and Special Plays 229

ST: Block "Mike" (out, over, linebacker); versus Split 4 block near corner.

QG: Block 37 veer call.

QT: Block 37 veer call.

X: Run off/stalk technique, getting inside corner defender.

Y: Jam on/out to corner; versus Split 4 block anchor to corner if anchor penetrates.

SB: Middle safety.

QB: Execute 37 veer; shorten your second step and push off to the strongside between the center and strong guard/strong tackle's blocks; selling the veer first achieves the desired linebacker movement; do not rush your execution.

FB: Run 37 veer, blocking the first linebacker quickside.

TB: Run 37 veer, sprinting down the line.

This play will be called as soon as we see the inside linebackers flowing quickly to stop the inside veer/option. The key blocks are made by the center (Split 4) and strong guard (5-2) on the backside linebacker. Once the inside veer is successful and the linebackers begin to fly out of their area, it becomes simply a matter of the center or strong guard shielding or walling off the linebacker once he pursues past their position.

Versus reading down linemen, it may become necessary for the strong guard (Split 4) or strong tackle (5-2) to reach block first. Then, as the defender reacts to the outside, work their hips to the inside and wall them off.

37 X REVERSE (See Diagram 8-23.)

37 X Reverse Blocking Rules

C: Block 37 veer call.

SG: "Mike" block (out, over, linebacker); when rule calls for a block on a down lineman (Split 4), post him until strong tackle makes contact, then slide off to outside for the linebacker or corner.

ST: Block or influence inside; if influencing, release inside and delay, slipping behind defender to the corner defender.

Play Action Passes, Screens, Draws and Special Plays

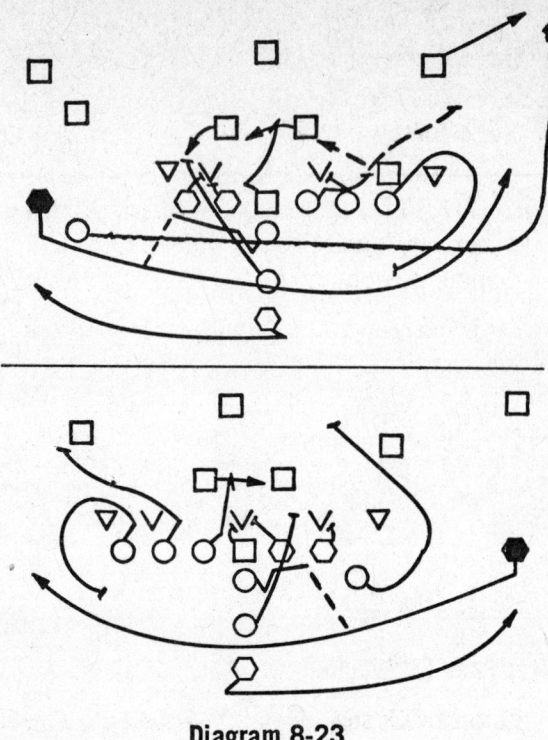

Diagram 8-23

QG: Block 37 veer call.

QT: Block 37 veer call.

X: Cut your split down to 10-12 yards, depending on your speed; drop step and sprint between the tailback and quarterback, receiving the pitch while keying the tight end's block; be ready to deepen your course if the trail defender has his back to the tight end; deepening should make him open up toward the outside where he can then be legally blocked by the tight end.

Y: Inside (5-2) or outside (Split 4) release off the LOS, trying to make the defender over or outside of you lose sight of you; delay one count, then peel outside and adjust your position to the trail defender; keep your block above the waist and don't clip; if the trail man has eliminated himself from the play, turn upfield and become a lead blocker.

SB: Playside: Stalk outside one-third defender.
    Backside: Near safety.
QB: Execute 37 Veer, pitching the ball to the split end once you are forced by the number three defender; make the play look like 37 Veer; look the pitch into the split end's hands.
FB: Run 37 Veer, sprinting outside and faking receiving pitch from the quarterback; make sure that the split end has enough room between you and the quarterback.

This play is designed to take advantage of quick defensive pursuit to the inside veer/option and poor trail technique by the backside number three defender. As with 37 (Quarterback) Counter, 37 X Reverse will be only as successful as 37 Veer.

The tight end must be an actor, releasing off the LOS and delaying or "loafing" to insure that no one remains outside of him as he starts to peel back behind the LOS.

37 VEER PASS (Z) (See Diagram 8-24.)

37 Veer Pass (Z) Blocking Rules

C: #0 on LOS; step playside then extend backside gap hinge.
SG: Gap hinge.
ST: Gap hinge.
QG: Block 37 Veer call; you will always block a defender who is on the LOS.
QT: Block 37 Veer call; you will always block a defender who is on the LOS.
X: Stalk 78.
Y: Deep drag.
SB: Playside: Stalk 73/74.
    Backside: 99/Seam.
    37 Veer Pass Z: Sprint quickside through the tailback's alignment; receive pitch from quarterback and look from number 1 (x) to number 2 (y); sell the veer first and don't hesitate to run with the ball.
QB: Execute 37 Veer, pitching the ball to the tailback (37 Veer

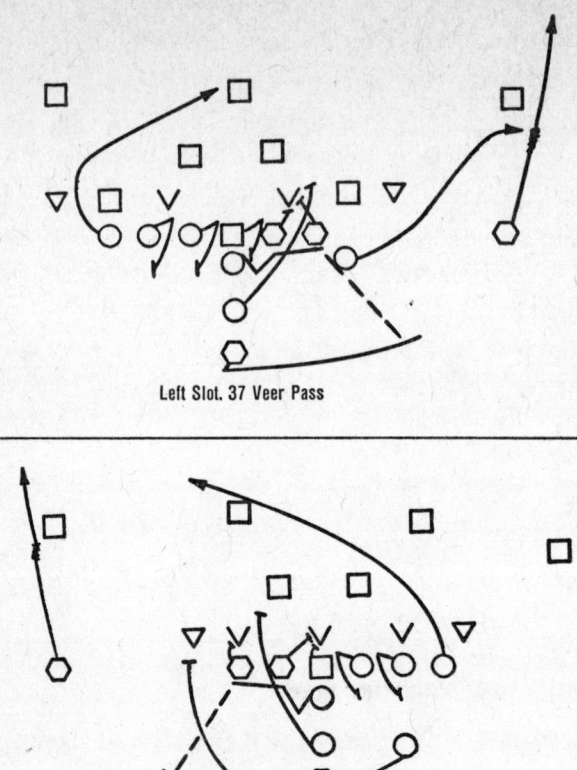

Left Slot. 37 Veer Pass

Right Power. 37 Veer Pass Z

Diagram 8-24

Pass) or swingback (37 Veer Pass Z) only when the number 3 defender forces the pitch; block number 3.

FB: Run 37 Veer, block first linebacker quickside; sell the inside veer by running hard.

TB: 37 Veer Pass: Run 37 Veer, receive pitch from quarterback while sprinting on your pitch relationship course; pull up after selling veer and throw from deepest (1) to shortest (3) receiver.

37 Veer Pass Z: Execute Pass 37 block on number 2 or 3 defender.

The key to 37 Veer Pass (Z) lies in the wideouts stalking their defender until he reacts up to support the veer. As soon as the defender makes his first move toward the LOS, the receiver breaks upfield into his pattern. He is coached to avoid any collision attempt by the defender.

If the defender does not react up, the receivers will read the support and break into an open area. (See Pass 37 Secondary Reads.)

Depending on which back can throw better, and on the defensive front, either 37 Veer Pass or 37 Veer Pass Z will be used. The latter is a better play when the number 2 defender quickly supports the pitch. The tailback is used as a personal protector for the swingback.

The premium on this special pass play is not on accuracy. The tailback and swingback must realize that the deep receiver, if he is open, will be wide open. They must hang the ball up and let the receiver run under it, and must never underthrow the pass.

Index

A

Auburn, 100

B

Backfield blocking, 173-176
Backfield pass blocking, 176-179 (see also Blocking)
Backs:
    alignment, 47-49
    numbering and lettering, 46-47
Bell, Ricky, 116
Blast Block, 173
Blocking:
    backfield, 173-176
        Blast, 173
        Chop and Roll, 175
        Fill, 174-175
        Influence/Turnout, 175-176
        Kickout, 173-174
        Lead, 176
        Log, 174
    backfield pass, 176-179
        aggressive Mike, 176-177
        Digit Protection, 177-178
        Sprint/Jet Protection, 178-179
    basic position, 151-152
    Chop and Roll, 163
    Criss, 155-156
    Double-Team, 154-155
    downfield, 163
    individual techniques, 152-153
    Influence, 162-163
    pass, 164-170
        Gap Hinge, 168-169
        digit protection, 164
        Mike, 164
        Screen, 169-170

Blocking (cont'd.)
    Pass 37/38, 179-180
    pulling, 159-162
    "Railroad" or Wedge, 158-159
    Reach, 153-154
    receiver, 170-172
        crack/stalk, 170-171
        jam on/out block, 172
        near safety/corner, 171-172
        stalk, 170
    Seal, 157-158
    Separation or "Touchdown," 163-164
    tackle calls, 148-149
        quickside, 148
        strongside, 149
    theory, 151
    Tony, 157
    Turnout, 156-157
    worksheets, 150
Boots:
    11/12, 212-213
    57/58, 214-215
Bryant, Paul, 121
Bulldogs of Georgia, 101

C

Cadence mechanics, 41
Center, 26
Chop and Roll Block, 175
"Chuck," 73, 76, 78, 118
College 4-3, 67
Combination blocking, 108
Counting defenses, 66
Crack/stalk block, 170-171
Criss call, 108, 118
Criss Block, 155-156

D

"Dave," 95, 108, 118
Davis, Anthony, 116
Digit Protection, 164-168, 177-178
Disconnect phase, 62-63
Double-Team Block, 154-155
Downfield blocking, 163
Draw plays:
    Fullback Lead, 225-227
    Quarterback Lead, 227-228
    Tailback Lead, 224-225,

E

Eight-man fronts, veer versus, 100-115 (*see also* Veer versus eight-man fronts)
80 Series, 197-202 (*see also* Pass offense)
11/12 counter option, 130-133
11/12 option, 129-130

F

Feathering, 104
50 Defense, 100
58 X screen:
    blocking rules, 218-219
    diagram, 218
    quarterback pivots, 219-220
58 Z screen, 220-221
55/56 Power, 126-129
51/52 Toss, 141-143
57/58 Blast, 121-123
50 Trap, 138-139
Fill Block, 174-175
5-3 Stack, 67
Flare control:
    80 Series, 201-202
    numbering, 191
Fly motion, 50-52
40 Defense, 100
"Fred," 77-78, 80, 119
Fullback:
    blocking ability, 22
    catching ability, 22
    competitor, 21
    durability/size, 22
    respected running ability, 21
    speed/quickness/acceleration, 22

Fullback (*cont'd.*)
    toughness, 21
    Veer/option, 94-95
    veer versus eight-man fronts, 106-108
Fullback lead draw, 225-228
Full I, 34

G

Gap Hinge Block, 168-169
Garret, Mike, 116
"George," 80-81, 119
Georgia Split 60, 67
Give phase, 61-62
"Give" play versus eight-man fronts, 113

H

"Hi-Peel," 52
Hole numbering and line splits, 43-46
Hot curl middle, 186-187
Houston Oilers, 121
Houston Veer Offenses, 100
Huddle:
    mechanics, 37-38
    quarterback, 38-40
Huddle calls, 80 Series, 198-199

I

I-back plays:
    Chuck, 118
    coaching philosophy of running game, 144-145
    Criss, 118
    Dave, 118
    11/12 counter option, 130-133
    11/12 option, 129-130
    55/56 Power, 126-129
    51/52 Flip, 143-144
    51/52 Toss, 141-143
    57/58 Blast, 121-123
    Fred, 119
    George, 119
    Mike, 117
    Technique Numbering System, 121
    Ted, 120

Index

I-back plays *(cont'd.)*
    37/38 Give, 123-124
    37/38 Keep, 124-126
    Tom, 119
    Tony, 119
    traps, 135-139
        special influence rule, 136-138
        specific assignments, 138-139
        specific rule for linemen, 136
        50, 138-139
        30, 138
        20, 138
    20/29 Scissors, 139-140
    21/22 option, 133-135
        blocking calls, 134
        offensive sets, 135
        special assignments, 133-134
    Willie, 119-120
Influence Blocking, 162-163
Influence/Turnout Block, 175-176
Inside receiver technique, 85-88

J

Jake, 136
Jam on/out Block, 172
Jet protection, 80 Series, 201
Junction play, 111-113
"Junkyard" Defense, 101

K

Keep phase, 64-65
Kickout Block, 173-174

L

Lead Block, 176
Lettering of backs and receivers, 46-47
Line of scrimmage:
    explanation, 41-43
    pre-set position, 40
    set position, 40-41
Line splits, hole numbering and, 43-46
Log Block, 174

M

McKay, John, 173
Maryland 6, 67, 69, 101
Mechanics:
    alignment of backs, 47-49
    cadence mechanics, 41
    changing offensive sets, 31-33
    fly motion, 50-52
    full I, 34
    hole numbering and line splits, 43-46
    huddle, 37-38
    "line of scrimmage," 41-43
    motion, 49-56
    numbering and lettering, 46-47
    "open" set, 34
    "over" set, 34
    peel motion, 52-55
    "power," 34
    pre-set position at line of scrimmage, 40
    "pro" set, 34
    quarterback, huddle, 38-40
    set descriptions, 34-37
    set position at line of scrimmage, 40-41
    "slot," 34
    "twin" set, 34
Mesh, term, 59-61
"Mike," 72, 81, 117
Mike Blocking, 164, 176-177
Motion:
    analyzing effect, 49
    considerations, 55-56
    disrupting pass coverages, 49
    "fly," 50-52
    mechanics, 50-55
    "peel," 52-55
    use, 49

N

Near safety/corner block, 171-172
90/70 Series, 182-190 (*see also* Pass offense)
Numbering:
    backs and receivers, 46-47
    flare control, 191
    hole, 43
    Technique Numbering System, 121

O

Offset Eagle, 67
Oklahoma 5-2, 67
Oklahoma front, 100
1/3 Gap Stack, 67
"Open" set, 34
Outside receiver, 82-85, 95
Outside veer/option, 91-93, 96-99
Outside veer quarterback, 93-94
"Over" set, 34

P

Pass blocking, 164-170 (*see also* Blocking)
Passes:
   Boot 11/12, 212-213
   Boot 57/58, 214-215
   11/12, 205
   55/56, 210-211
   57/58, 211-212
   play action, 203-215
   screen, 215-223
   37/38, 206-209
Pass Offense
   80 Series, 197-202
      flare control, 201-202
      huddle, 198-199
      introduction, 197
      jet protection, 201
      mechanics, 197-198
      quarterback thought processes, 199-200
      routes, 199
      sprint protection, 200
   90/70 Series, 182-190
      introduction, 182
      mechanics, 183
      passing tree, 183
      protection, 187-189
      quarterback, 187
      quarterback reads, 189-190
      route descriptions, 184-186
      tight end/hot curl middle, 186-187
   quarterback drops, 182
   receiver legs, 181
   60 Series, 190-197
      introduction, 190-191
      numbering, 191
      passing tree, 195

Passes (cont'd.)
   60 Series (cont'd.)
      pass routes, 192-193
      protection, 196
      quarterback reads, 196-197
      quickside routes, 193-194
      strongside routes, 194-195
      tailback/fullback routes, 191-192
Pass 37/38 tailback blocking, 179-180
Peel motion, 52-55
Penn State, 100
Personnel:
   center, 26
   fullback, 21-22
   quarterback, 19-21
   quickside linemen, 28-30
      guard, 28-29
      tackle, 29-30
   split end, 24-25
   strongside linemen, 27-28
      guard, 27
      tackle, 28
   swingback, 18-19
   tailback, 22-23
   tight end, 23-24
Phillips, A.B., 121
Pin Block, 174
Pitchmen, veer/option play, 89-91
Pitch phase, 65-66
Play Action Passes:
   Boot 11/12, 212-213
   Boot 57-58, 214-215
   11/12, 205-206
   55/56, 210-211
   57/58, 211-212
   mechanics, 204-205
   37/38, 206-209
"Power," 34
Power position, 151
Pre-set position at line of scrimmage, 40
"Pro" set, 34
Pulling techniques, 159-162

Q

Quarterback:
   ability to move offense, 20
   ability to run veer option, 19
   drops, pass offense, 182

Index

Quarterback *(cont'd.)*
   80 Series, 199-200
   getting along with teammates, 21
   huddle, 38-40
   leadership qualities, 20
   mechanics of veer/option, 58-59
   mental alertness/intelligence, 20
   90/70 Series, 187, 189-190
   outside veer, 93-94
   passing ability, 19-20
   poise/attention to details, 20
   reads for outside veer, 96-99
   running ability, 21
   60 Series, 196-197
   speed/quickness/acceleration, 19
   toughness, 20
   veer versus eight-man fronts, 104-106
Quickside linemen:
   guard, 28-29
   tackle, 29-30

R

Railroad Block, 137, 158-159
Randy, 135
Reach Block, 153-154
Read play versus eight-man fronts, 113-115
"Ready," 42
Receiver:
   blocking, 81-82, 170-172 (*see also* Blocking)
   inside, 85-88
   numbering and lettering, 46-47
   offside, 88-89
   outside, 82-85, 95
Rodgers, Pepper, 60, 71

S

"Scraping," 96
Screen Blocking, 169-170
Screen passes:
   58 X, 218-220
   58 Z, 220-221
   Tailback Quick, 215-218
   37 Y, 221-223
Seal Block, 157-158
Separation Block, 163-164

Set descriptions, 34-37
Set position at line of scrimmage, 40-41
7 Diamond, 67
70 Series, 182-190 (*see also* Pass offense)
Simpson, O.J., 116
6-5 Goal line, 67
60 Series, 190-197 (*see also* Pass offense)
"Slot," 34
Smith, Homer, 71
Special plays:
   37 (Quarterback) Counter, 228-229
   37 Veer Pass (Z), 231-233
   37 X Reverse, 229-231
Split end:
   attitude toward blocking, 25
   blocking ability, 25
   catching ability, 25
   running ability, 25
   running disciplined legs, 24-25
   size, 25
   speed/quickness/acceleration, 25
Split 4, 67, 69, 100
Split 6 Defense, 100
Sprint/Jet protection blocking, 178-179
Sprint protection, 80 Series, 200-201
Stalk blocking, 170
Strongside linemen:
   guard, 27
   tackle, 28
Swingback:
   blocking ability, 18
   body control/balance, 18
   catching ability, 19
   discipline, 18
   mental alertness/intelligence, 19
   running ability, 19
   size, 18
   speed/quickness/acceleration, 18
   toughness, 19
   Veer/option, 89-91
   veer versus eight-man fronts, 109-111

T

Tackle calls, 148, 149
Tailback:
   blocking ability, 23
   body balance/agility, 23
   catching ability, 23
   durability/toughness, 23

Tailback *(cont'd.)*
  running ability, 22-23
  speed/quickness/acceleration, 22
  Veer/option, 89-91, 95
Tailback/fullback routes, 191-192
Tailback lead draw, 224-225
Tailback quick screen, 215-218
Technique Numbering System, 121
"Ted," 80, 120
Texas, 100
37 (Quarterback) Counter, 228-229
37/38 Give, 123-124
37/38 Keep, 124-126
37/38 Veer, 75-76
37 Veer Pass (Z), 231-233
37 X Reverse, 229-231
37 Y screen, 221-223
30 Trap, 138
Tight end:
  blocking ability, 23
  catching ability, 24
  mental alertness/intelligence, 24
  running ability, 24
  running disciplined legs, 24
  size, 24
  speed/quickness/acceleration, 23
  toughness/durability, 23-24
"Tom," 80, 119
Tony, 119
Tony Block, 157
Touchdown Block, 163-164
Traps, 135-139 *(see also* I-back plays)
Triple option *(see* Veer/option)
Turnout Block, 156-157
12 Counter Option, 131
29 scissors, 140
20 Trap, 138
20/29 Scissors, 139-140
21/22 option, 133-135
22 option, 134
"Twin" set, 34

V

Veer/option:
  blocking calls/for inside, 76-77
  counting defenses, 66-67

Veer/option *(cont'd.)*
  disconnect phase, 62-63
  fullback, 94-95
  "Fred" call, 77-78
  "George" call, 80-81
  give phase, 61-62
  inside receiver techniques, 85-88
  keep phase, 64-65
  mechanics of outside veer quarterback, 93-94
  mechanics of read, 71-75
  mesh, 59
  "Mike" call, 81
  offside receiver(s), 88-89
  outside, 91-93
  outside receiver, 82-85
  phase one, 69-71
  pitch phase, 65-66
  quarterback mechanics, 58-59
  quarterback reads for outside veer, 96-99
  reading, 68-69
  receiver blocking techniques for inside, 81
  receivers, 95-96
  tailback, 95
  tailback/swingback techniques as pitchmen, 89-91
  "Ted" call, 80
  37/38, 75-76
  "Tom" call, 80
  "Willie" call, 78-80
Veer versus eight-man fronts:
  fullback mechanics, 106-108
  "give" play, 113
  junction play, 111-113
  quarterback mechanics, 104-106
  read play, 113-115
  swingback mechanics, 109-111

W

Wedge Block, 158-159
Wide Tackle, 101
"Willie," 78-80, 119
Wishbone, 100
Worksheets, 150